THE OLD TESTAMENT AND CHRISTIAN FAITH

THE OLD TESTAMENT

AND CHRISTIAN FAITH

A Theological Discussion

EDITED BY   BERNHARD W. ANDERSON

HARPER & ROW, PUBLISHERS

NEW YORK

EVANSTON

AND LONDON

Unless otherwise indicated, scriptural quotations are from the
Revised Standard Version of the Bible.

Contents

Contributors

Bernhard W. Anderson, Professor of Biblical Theology, The Theological School, Drew University, Madison, New Jersey.

Emil Brunner, Professor Emeritus of Systematic Theology, University of Zurich, Switzerland.

Rudolf Bultmann, Professor Emeritus of New Testament and Early Christian History, University of Marburg, Germany.

Oscar Cullmann, Professor of New Testament and Patristic Studies at the Universities of Paris (Sorbonne) and Basel, Switzerland.

John Dillenberger, Professor of Historical Theology, San Francisco Theological Seminary, San Anselmo, California.

John L. McKenzie, S.J., Professor of Biblical History, Loyola University, Chicago, Illinois.

Carl Michalson, Professor of Systematic Theology, The Theological School, Drew University, Madison, New Jersey.

Alan Richardson, Professor of Christian Theology, The University of Nottingham, England.

James M. Robinson, Professor of Theology and New Testament, Southern California School of Theology, Claremont, California.

Wilhelm Vischer, Professor of Old Testament, University of Montpelier, France.

Eric Voegelin, Professor of Political Science, University of Munich, Germany.

Claus Westermann, Professor of Old Testament Theology, University of Heidelberg, Germany.

G. Ernest Wright, Parkham Professor of Divinity, The Harvard Divinity School, Harvard University, Cambridge, Massachusetts.

Abbreviations

ATD	Das Alte Testament Deutsch
BO	Bibliotheca Orientalis
BZNW	Beiheft zur Zeitschrift für die neutestamentliche Wissenschaft
BZAW	Beiheft zur Zeitschrift für die altestamentliche Wissenschaft
BZTK	Beiheft zur Zeitschrift für Theologie und Kirche
EVT	Evangelische Theologie
HTR	Harvard Theological Review
HUCA	Hebrew Union College Annual
IB	The Interpreter's Bible
INT	Interpretation
JBL	Journal of Biblical Literature
JPh	Journal of Philosophy
KuD	Kirche und Dogma
KlT	Kleine Texte für Vorlesungen und Übungen, H. Lietzmann
LXX	Septuagint
NET	New English Translation
NT	New Testament
NTD	Neue Testament Deutsch
OT	Old Testament
1 QH	Psalms of Thanksgiving from Qumran Cave 1
RAC	Reallexikon für Antike und Christentum, ed. T. Klauser
RB	Revue Biblique
RGG	Die Religion in Geschichte und Gegenwart
RSV	Revised Standard Version

ST	Studia Theologica
TD	Theology Digest
TL	Theology and Life
TLZ	Theologische Literaturzeitung
TR	Theologische Rundschau
TWNT	Theologisches Wörterbuch zum Neuen Testament
TZ	Theologische Zeitschrift
ZAW	Zeitschrift für die alttestamentliche Wissenschaft
ZNW	Zeitschrift für die neutestamentliche Wissenschaft
ZTK	Zeitschrift für Theologie und Kirche
ZZ	Zwischen den Zeiten

Foreword

The idea for this "panel discussion" arose during a conversation in a *Gasthaus* in Marburg, Germany, on which occasion Dr. Rudolf Bultmann was the genial host. When asked casually whether he would be willing for one of his essays to lead off a scholarly discussion about the relevance of the Old Testament for the Christian Faith, he not only immediately welcomed the suggestion but took a lively interest in helping to shape a roster of participants. With his characteristic passion for truth he was particularly eager to include scholars who disagreed with his own point of view, so that by means of debate the Church could face with theological seriousness the problem of the Old Testament itself.

I should like to express appreciation to the distinguished members of this international panel who have taken the time, in the midst of their many responsibilities, to contribute to this discussion. Also I owe a debt of thanks to others who have helped to make the project possible: to those who have undertaken the labor of translation; to my colleagues, Dr. Franz Hildebrandt and Dr. Karlfried Fröhlich, who have assisted me with my own translations and at other points; and to my graduate assistant, Mrs. Elise B. Wilson, for her editorial work. And last but not least, a special word of appreciation should be expressed to Melvin Arnold of Harper & Row, who has taken a keen interest in this project since the time we first talked about it in the *gemütlich* Marburg setting.

BERNHARD W. ANDERSON

March 25, 1963
Drew University
Madison, New Jersey

THE OLD TESTAMENT AND CHRISTIAN FAITH

Introduction: The Old Testament as a Christian Problem

No problem more urgently needs to be brought to a focus than the one to which the following essays are addressed: the relation of the Old Testament to the New. This is not just a concern of Old Testament specialists who might be accused of special pleading, or of New Testament experts who cannot escape dealing with the matter in their exegesis of the text. Rather, it is a question which confronts every Christian in the Church, whether he be a professional theologian, a pastor of a congregation, or a layman. It is no exaggeration to say that on this question hangs the meaning of the Christian faith.

Even the language in which the question is formulated indicates that this is primarily and characteristically an issue for Christian faith. The Christian Bible is composed of two parts, the Old Testament and the New Testament. For members of the Jewish community this distinction does not apply. The Jewish Bible is composed of the Law, the Prophets, and the Writings, a tripartite canon which is basically coextensive with the Christian Old Testament. Although the Roman Catholic Church includes additional books and passages found in the Greek translation of Scripture (the Septuagint),[1] there is general Christian agreement

---

[1] For a discussion of this see Bernard Orchard, ed., *A Catholic Commentary on Holy Scripture* (1953), pp. 15–18.

on a bipartite canon which distinguishes between the "old" and the "new." Yet even the terminology for describing the two parts of this canon is not uniquely Christian but is derived from Jeremiah's prophecy concerning the new covenant (Jer. 31:31–34). This passage from Jewish Scripture came to have great significance for the early Church's sacramental liturgy (I Cor. 11:23–26) and soteriology (II Cor. 3; Heb. 8:8–12; 10:16–17). Accordingly when the canon of Christian writings was finally established, it included the books of the Old Covenant (Testament) and the apostolic writings of the New Covenant.

The marriage of the two parts of the Christian canon is not one that easily holds together, and it might seem that divorce would be the best solution of the problem. Christian uneasiness about the Old Testament has had a long history, extending back to the early period of the Church. At first the Gospel of the Cross and Resurrection was proclaimed by appealing to "Scripture" (i.e., the sacred writings of Israel, chiefly the Law and the Prophets) and even difficult problems regarding the inclusion of Gentiles, such as the issue of circumcision, could be dealt with on this basis. But as Christianity moved out into the Hellenistic world, it tended to become detached from this historical mooring. In the early second century there were probably many churches in which reading from "Old Testament" Scripture was not practiced and belief in "the God of Israel" faded imperceptibly into pagan conceptions. As time went along there were various attempts to sever the bond uniting the Christian Gospel and the Scripture of the Jewish people.

The best-known challenge was laid down by Marcion, an influential Christian leader who was expelled from the church at Rome about 144 A.D. Since the essays in this volume refer to him frequently, it may be well to say a few words about him to the general reader.[2] We know about Marcion only through his ad-

---

[2] See further Edwin C. Blackman, *Marcion and His Influence* (1948), and John Knox, *Marcion and the New Testament* (1942).

versaries, who quoted him to attack him—admittedly a very slender reed upon which to lean for historical knowledge. In his no longer extant work, the *Antitheses,* he seems to have construed Paul's contrast between Law and Gospel, the flesh and the spirit, the old age and the new, to mean that Jewish Scripture is antithetical to the revelation in Christ. Hence he proposed a list of "genuine" Christian writings which excluded the Old Testament.

Before we hastily pick up stones to cast at this "heretic," let it be said that the questions raised by many Christians today about the Old Testament betray a sympathy for Marcion, whose attractive teachings gained a considerable popular following in the second century and even later. The God of the Old Testament, we still hear today, is a God of wrath, the stern, severe Judge whose judgments fill men with terror; on the other hand, the God of the New Testament is a God of love, the kind and merciful Father who treats his children with patience and forgiveness. Or, it is said, the God of the Old Testament is understood anthropomorphically as a kind of glorified human being; the New Testament, however, abandons such theological naïveté and affirms that "God is a Spirit." The God of the Old Testament is a warlike Being who satisfies Israel's nationalistic pride by slaughtering his enemies; the God of the New Testament, by contrast, is not bound by nationalistic limitations but is concerned for the universal brotherhood of man. Not many years ago it was fashionable to account for the "difference" between these Old and New Testament conceptions of God by a philosophy of growth or development.[3] According to this view, inferior ideas of God were gradually refined away in the crucible of Israel's history. The line of development ascended through the "ethical monotheism" of the great prophets and finally to Jesus' high conception of the fatherhood of God and the brotherhood of man.

Marcion was undoubtedly a much better theologian than many

---

[3] One of the best expositions of this evolutionary understanding is *A Guide to Understanding the Bible* (1938) by Harry Emerson Fosdick.

modern Christians who have unconsciously become his disciples. He did insist, in his own way, that the Old Testament is revelation, not the story of human discovery. It represented a *true* revelation, he believed, but not the *saving* revelation of the God of Jesus Christ. To be fair to Marcion it must be kept in mind that he was trying to take Paul's teaching seriously. After all, Paul had said that the Jewish Law was holy, that it was given by God; but the Law was weak in that it could not rescue man from sin and bring him into right relation with God. Deliverance from sin had come, not by the Law, but by God's gracious action in Jesus Christ. In the heat of controversy, however, Marcion went much further, owing to the influence of Hellenistic dualism upon his thinking. The God of the Old Testament, he said, is another God, inferior to the God of Jesus Christ. These are actually two different Gods! The Old Testament God is the Creator of this transient world; the God of Christ is the God who redeems men from the world. The God of this world is the God of justice; the High God is the loving Father who is apprehended only through faith in Christ. Following this line of thinking, the discontinuity between the two revelations is absolute. The Gospel "fulfills" Jewish Scripture only in the sense that it supersedes and abrogates it.

Marcion's expulsion from the Roman community was only a prelude to the serious struggles within the Church which lay ahead. Since he had proposed a normative list of Christian writings (ten Pauline epistles and an abbreviated version of Luke), the Church had to begin to face the question as to which Christian writings belong in the "New Testament." But more important for our purpose was the verdict, which perhaps became clearer in the years after Marcion's expulsion, that the Marcionite view of the Old Testament was heretical. Once the Church decided that the Old Testament must be retained in the Christian canon it committed itself to a major hermeneutical problem: what is the nature of the relationship between the Testaments? To pursue this subject from Marcion to the present would require a whole book on the history of biblical interpretation.[4]

In the course of Church history few men have had Marcion's courage to demand that the Old Testament be discarded from the Christian canon. One such person was the famous Church historian, Adolph Harnack (1851–1930), an influential exponent of so-called "liberalism" in the period after World War I. During his whole career he occupied himself with the problem of the relation between Christianity and the Old Testament. In his famous work on Marcion[5] he states that in the second century the Church rightly refused to reject the Old Testament, that in the sixteenth century the retention of the Old Testament was a fateful necessity which the Reformation was not yet able to escape, but that in the period since the nineteenth century the attempt to perpetuate the Old Testament in the Christian canon is the sign of "a religious and ecclesiastical paralysis." Whether this is a valid judgment for the contemporary Church remains to be seen, if not from these essays then from the discussion which one may hope they will stimulate. In any case, it seems highly unlikely that the Old Testament, in view of the weight of tradition and devotional usage, will be officially discarded by the Church. Meanwhile the ghost of Marcion lingers on, appearing more in indifference to or ignorance about the Old Testament than in vehement theological debate. For our time the question of the relevance of the Old Testament for Christian faith is unanswered—and often unasked.

In his reference to the situation in the Church since the nineteenth century, Harnack has drawn attention to a dimension of the problem which is entirely new. It was in that century that the historical criticism of the Bible gained full momentum and reached a peak in the so-called Wellhausen reconstruction of the history of biblical religion along developmental lines. This re-

---

[4] For a brief treatment, see Robert M. Grant, *The Bible in the Church* (1948); also Robert M. Grant, John T. McNeill, and Samuel Terrien, "History of the Interpretation of the Bible," *IB,* Vol. 1 (1952), pp. 106–41.

[5] *Marcion: Das Evangelium vom fremden Gott* (2d ed., 1924).

construction was aided, in the first instance, by idealistic (Hegelian) philosophy and subsequently, especially in America, by evolutionary (naturalistic) philosophy. It is ironical that at the very time Harnack threw down his challenge to Christians to admit the canonical irrelevance of the Old Testament, the whole "nineteenth-century" theological scene was beginning to shift. The prophetic voice of Karl Barth was heard in Europe and that of Reinhold Niebuhr in America. Biblical critics increasingly abandoned the attempt to interpret the Bible along evolutionary lines and began to work at the exegetical tasks of biblical theology.[6] And, above all, there emerged a new interest in the long-neglected subject of hermeneutics which, stated simply, deals with the method of interpreting the Bible biblically. Clearly biblical studies have entered upon a new phase within the past twenty-five years or so. But despite the theological shifts and the changing pattern of biblical studies, there is no denying that historical criticism is here to stay. The Church stands in a new theological situation, one that is unlike the situation at the time of the Protestant Reformation or that of Marcion's time or that of the first-century Church. In our time we must raise in a new way the perennial question of the relevance of the Old Testament for Christian faith.

Rudolf Bultmann's essay stands first in this volume because he has asked the question incisively. The essay, which appeared in 1933 in the first volume of his *Glauben und Verstehen* ("Faith and Understanding") has largely escaped attention in the English-speaking world. Since it first appeared Bultmann has been the center of a debate about "demythologizing" the New Testament kerygma, that is, the interpretation of the Christian message

---

[6] See Walther Eichrodt's review of Fosdick's *A Guide to the Understanding of the Bible* in *JBL,* Vol. 65 (1946), pp. 205–17. Eichrodt uncovers the "widely assumed premises of modern thought" upon which the book is based and, while admitting that it excellently typifies the older, but passing, school of interpretation, says that Fosdick "has, to speak candidly, written the obituary of a whole scholarly approach and method of investigation, making both their inherent merits and their limitations clear to the thoughtful student" (W. F. Albright's English summary, p. 205).

in categories meaningful to a postmythological (i.e., scientific) age. The intensity of this debate, which has been waged largely on the ground of the New Testament, has tended to detract attention from the related hermeneutical problem of the relevance of the Old Testament. This problem Bultmann has also approached in terms of what he regards as a valid historical hermeneutic.[7]

Although Bultmann understands the relation between the Testaments in terms of Law and Gospel, it should be said from the outset that he is not a true Marcionite. Unlike Marcion, who believed that Jewish Scripture and the Christian revelation had absolutely no connection, Bultmann attempts to show that there is an intrinsic relation between the Testaments. Many of the contributors to this volume question whether Bultmann's existentialist interpretation is adequate for opening up a "genuinely historical" understanding of the Bible. Moreover, within the Bultmann school there are signs of a shifting of position which provides a greater possibility for treating the whole Bible positively as a witness to the revelation of God. But taken as a whole the essays show, even when disagreeing vigorously, that Bultmann has provocatively called the Church to face a basic theological question which it cannot and dare not disregard.

---

[7] See his essay, "The Problem of Hermeneutics," *Essays Philosophical and Theological,* James C. G. Greig, trans. (1955), pp. 234–61; also "Is Exegesis without Presuppositions Possible?" in *Existence and Faith* (1960), Schubert M. Ogden, ed. and trans., pp. 289–96.

1   The Significance of the Old
Testament for the Christian Faith

RUDOLF BULTMANN*

I

The question about the relation of the New Testament to the Old can be asked in such a manner that the Old and New Testaments are considered as *sources* for reconstructing *the religion of Israel and the religion of primitive Christianity* and for inquiring into the relation between the two religions. In this case, the general concept of *religion* as an historical phenomenon determines both the question and the comparison of the two religions, and their relationship is understood in terms of historical *development*.[1] The idea of development does not necessarily have to be combined with the idea of progress. The result of the developmental process may be regarded, to some degree or other, as a manifestation of decadence. From a Jewish standpoint, for instance, primitive Christianity, and particularly Pauline religion

---

* Translated by Bernhard W. Anderson.

[1] It is a simple development in so far as both religions stand in historical continuity. To the degree that this is not the case, that is to say, in so far as the phenomenon of primitive Christianity cannot be understood as a stage in the unfolding development of Old Testament religion, extraneous influences from the Orient and from Greek tradition are invoked. The complex phenomenon of primitive Christianity then appears as the result of the whole ancient history of religion in which the Old Testament is only one, albeit an essential, factor.

with its Christology and sacramental faith, can be viewed as a corruption of Old Testament monotheism. On the other hand, Paulinism, with its doctrine of justification and its juristic concepts, may appear as a retrogression from Jesus' Gospel, because it revives Jewish ideas which were overcome in the latter.

Very different views of the phenomenon of *religion* can be associated with such a reconstruction in terms of development. Religion can be conceived as an illusory ideology which will disappear with the development of socioeconomic conditions and scientific knowledge, or as an interesting psychical phenomenon inherent in the nature of man's inner life. Or it can be understood as the highest phenomenon of human spirituality altogether: as awareness of the world's and life's meaning and of the oneness of the human spirit with the divine Spirit who ordains and supports all that is, and consequently awareness of the law to which the individual has to submit with moral intent. For each of these views primitive Christianity may be an important stage of development, but none of them is relevant for Christian theology.

Such relevance is often claimed, however, by those who view *the stage of religious development attained in primitive Christianity as the culmination of the religious life—"piety"—integral to full manhood.* This culmination of spiritual development, they say, provides the critical standard for all time and is an inalienable inheritance. Here monotheism is clearly understood as the idea of the God who is Spirit and is worshiped in a purely spiritual manner; the God whose will is holy and loving, and whom one serves by receiving the commandment of love into his own will; the God who is grace and who, like a father, receives the sinner who penitently beats upon his breast. A universal, ethical faith in God as Father—that is the Christian religion, and it has found its highest representation in the person of Jesus, who was sustained by such a faith and proclaimed it in his preaching.

The relation to the Old Testament, then, appears as follows: in Old Testament religion this monotheism struggles to gain the upper hand over cultic piety and nationalism and comes to fruition in the preaching of the prophets. For it is here that the fight is waged against the cultus and against nationalistic pride; here the insight breaks forth clearly that God is the God of the whole world and of all nations; here God's holiness is perceived to be that of his moral will, to which man is required to surrender himself; here is proclaimed God's forgiving grace for those who are of a broken heart. After it had been covered up by Jewish legalism, Jesus brought this ethical monotheism into full light again by liberating it from legalism just as the prophets had liberated it from cultic piety. There is nothing new in Jesus' religion; it is the same thing as in the Old Testament prophets. Hence he is the end, perhaps the crown, of a development starting in the Old Testament. Whatever goes beyond this in the New Testament—the eschatology and Christology of the Church, Paul's doctrine of justification, etc.—dangerously veils what is essential. It is, at best, a mythologizing disguise of Jesus' pure faith in God, perhaps necessary at the time in order to preserve, in this wrapping, at least the basic ideas. A more mature understanding has to strip off this disguise so that what is essential may stand forth in pure form.

When confronted with the statements of the New Testament, this view runs into peculiar difficulty. Statements about the deity of Christ, the Pauline teaching of justification through the Cross of Christ, the dawn of the new age, and the like, have to be interpreted as mythology which in reality obscures ethical monotheism. All New Testament teachings have to be reduced by critical analysis to the preaching of Jesus, in which case most of what Paul and John say is eliminated and one is left with the puzzle that Paul and John repeat hardly anything of Jesus' preaching.

Now admittedly every interpretation has to be critical, since the statements of the New Testament surely cannot be simply reproduced. If we are to enter into their meaning, they must indeed be freed from the mythological conceptuality (*Begrifflich-keit*) in which, corresponding to the fashion of their time, they are formulated, so that their proper intention may receive due justice. But the question is: what is the standard and the limit established thereby for criticism? The standard can only be the intention of the New Testament itself, little as the interpreter can ever be sure of having grasped it definitively.

In any case, characteristic of the New Testament, in distinction from the Old, is the idea that *man's relation to God is bound to the person of Jesus*. Is this idea mythology? Doubtless concepts of divine sonship in a metaphysical sense, the Virgin Birth, pre-existence, and the return on the clouds of heaven at the sound of the last trumpet may be mythological. But can the idea that God has wrought forgiveness for the world through the Cross of Christ be eliminated as mythology? Can the idea be eliminated that God is accessible only in Jesus Christ? Or does the Christian faith stand or fall with this assertion? And furthermore, while asserting this the New Testament declares at the same time that with Jesus Christ the new age has dawned; that is, it divides the whole of history into two fundamentally different halves: prophecy and fulfillment. To what degree is this mythology that has to be eliminated? To what degree is it essential for the Christian faith?

Is it not true, however, that *Jesus' preaching itself* claims nothing of the kind? Is not his preaching about God as Father and his demand for a new spirit, that of love, independent of all this? Does this not provide the critical standard for eliminating mythology? In answer: first, Jesus' preaching is eschatological preaching as well; that is, it points to the dawn of the new age, and it is in the certainty that God will usher in this age at once that Jesus proclaims God's fatherly disposition and his demand. Thus, if one were to apply the above critical standard, it would even be necessary to eliminate part of Jesus' preaching. Moreover, as we all know, we have to reconstruct Jesus' preaching from the Synoptic Gospels, which is to say, *the New Testament itself presents this preaching only in conjunction with the Church's proclamation concerning Christ*. There can be no doubt: the New Testament does not simply repeat the proclamation of Jesus, but along with it, and indeed first and foremost, it proclaims *him,* that is, it binds the God-man relationship to his person. And there can be no doubt: this is the specifically Christian element of the New Testament and has been regarded as such throughout the centuries of the Church. Thus Luther has already rightly perceived that Jesus, in so far as he engaged in teaching, is not different from the Old Testament prophets; rather, like them, he proclaimed the Law and consequently belongs within the Old Testament.

Hence, if the above-mentioned critical reduction is necessary, then what is specifically Christian is thereby eliminated. Of course, this is not to pass judgment upon the legitimacy of this reduction, but one must realize that in such a case he gives up the very thing that the New Testament and the Christian Church hold to be specifically Christian. The religion which remains is a refined Judaism or a humanism. The relation to the Old Testament is then no longer a problem, of course, nor is the relation to heathenism either. For almost all religions can come together in the recognition of this ethical monotheism.

Whether this approach is right or wrong in itself is not to be discussed here. Rather, we shall deal with the theological problem of the relation of the New Testament to the Old as it emerges only within the faith that is specifically Christian. We are concerned with the question as to whether the Old Testament still has a meaning for the faith which perceives in Jesus Christ the revelation of God.

If, however, this is the specifically theological way to formulate the question, then *the above-mentioned inquiry into the relation of New Testament religion to Old Testament religion is not theologically relevant at all.* It raises the question from the outside by viewing the two—Old Testament and New Testament religion—as historical phenomena and by determining their relationship from a higher vantage point. It does not inquire from within the faith: what does the Old Testament mean for me, for the Church? It does not ask whether the Word of the Old Testament must be proclaimed by the Church and must be heard faithfully as the Word directed to me so that it is a constituent of my faith. It seeks behind the Old Testament a bygone epoch of the history of religion and reconstructs that past. It does not take the Old Testament as a Word which speaks now, calling for response and dialogue. And therefore when one inquires in this manner he makes his own religion into an objectified phenomenon which can be incorporated into a historical development and, whether realized or not, it issues in a relativism. It is as though a man, reflecting upon his development, considers sayings of his deceased father which rise up from his memory or are found in old letters and inquires what bearing those words had on his own development into the person he now is, instead of hearing them as words spoken directly to him in address, demand, or blessing.

II

The problem presents itself quite differently when another question, *genuinely historical* in character, is raised. According to this view, the Old Testament is not seen as the document of a bygone time to be reconstructed from its pages, but rather it is interpreted in terms of the question of *what basic possibility it presents for an understanding of human existence (Daseinsverständnis)*. I label such an interpretation of the Old Testament as genuinely historical because it is based upon the elemental and naïve impulse of turning back to history with a question—not for the purpose of assigning past phenomena to their place within the great context of world history, but in order to learn immediately from the past about those things that concern us, that are problematical for us, and that disturb us.[2] Genuinely historical is that inquiry of the

---

[2] Investigation and reproduction of the context of world history only has meaning—though, to be sure, a very important meaning—to the degree that it serves the kind of interpretation which is genuinely historical. It does that in so far as it aids in reactualizing the past (*Vergegenwärtigung*), i.e., in so far as it renders possible *translation* from a past conceptuality into that of the present. Therefore it plays a critical role so far as it critically calls into question the present conceptuality, since through the medium of the latter we would understand a document of the past wrongly or even not at all.

past which asks the question, Whither? Whence? A genuinely historical inquiry of Plato, for instance, is not one that seeks to understand Plato in the context of a history of problems, but rather one that intends to learn in dialogue with him what man is and how he is to exist. A genuinely historical inquiry of the Old Testament is one which, prompted by one's own question concerning existence, seeks to reactualize (*vergegenwärtigen*) the understanding of human existence expressed in the Old Testament, in order to gain an understanding of his own existence. To enter into such a dialogue with the Old Testament is all the more necessary since the Christian understanding of existence, on the basis of faith, claims for itself to be the only possibility granted by God's revelation and as such can remain genuine and vital only in constant dialogue with other views.

In periods which still had a genuine historical relation to the Old Testament, the understanding of existence expressed in the Old Testament was contrasted to the Christian view under the antithesis: *Law and Gospel.* Thus for Luther, as for Paul, the Old Testament as a whole appears under the concept of Law, that is, as an expression of the demanding will of God. While Old Testament man stands under the divine demand, New Testament man stands under the divine grace which accepts him as a sinner.

In this case, *existence under the Law,* under the divine demand, is understood as *the presupposition for existence under grace.* Only he who knows himself to be limited by God's demand, who is awake to the fact that he never does and never can satisfy this demand, only this man can understand the preaching of the Gospel. In so far as the Old Testament is the Law and embodies the demand of God, it forces sinful man into an existence in which the word of God's grace becomes understandable to him. Therefore God's demand, as embodied in the Old Testament, is also held continually over man in order to assure the understanding of the Gospel, and it is not abrogated with the proclamation of the Gospel.

Thus the Old Testament is the presupposition of the New. Not in the sense of a *historical (historisch)* view, as though the historical phenomenon of the Christian religion had become possible only on the basis of the evolving history of religion attested by the Old Testament; but rather in the *material (sachlich)* sense that man must stand under the Old Testament if he wants to understand the New. *The material connection between Law and Gospel* means that the Gospel can be preached only when man stands under the Law. Certainly, Christ is the end of the Law; but precisely so that he can be understood as the end of the Law (otherwise Christ is not understood at all), everyone who hears of him must also have heard of the Law. More than that: he must hear the Law again and again. True, the believer is once and for all free from the Law and is under the Spirit. But faith, as the possibility of Christian existence ever to be grasped anew, is a reality only by constantly overcoming the old existence under the Law. And going a step further: freedom from the Law does not mean that man is dismissed from the divine demand, that he no longer stands under the 'thou shalt," but rather that this "thou shalt" is validated by a "thou canst," "thou art." Man is freed from the Law in so far as it is supposed to assure him of grace only if he fulfills its demands, but not in so far as it is established anew by grace.

But then the question arises: if the Old Testament stands as the ever valid presupposition of the New—that is, as the demand of God which ever encompasses man—*does it then retain its specifically Old Testament character?* This question surely is to be negated.

The concrete demands of the Old Testament, in so far as they are cultic and ritual in character, are either bound to a primitive stage of man's social life, economics, government, and so on, or to the history of a particular people. By the time of Jesus, in fact by the time of the prophets, these demands had come into conflict with others which are inescapably binding upon man as man. They are obsolete. Invariably they are analogous to the demands that arise out of the concrete cultural, national, and social conditions of a particular period and which more or less painfully bind the individual as law, morals, and custom. We need not look around only in the Old Testament for such demands to limit and fence in our lives. And what about the truly moral demands of the Old Testament? They have by no means lost their authority. The moral demands of the prophets, like those of Jesus, that spring out of human relationship as such and not out of its concrete historical form, are valid as long as there is such relationship on earth. But for this very reason they are not specifically Old Testament demands. Even supposing that they were first clearly apprehended in Israel, they would not be validated for us just by the Old Testament. They are grounded in human relationship itself, and every period finds them simply by serious reflection upon this relationship. It is not just the historical origin of their formulation that validates their claim. And as a matter of fact, they have not been apprehended first or exclusively in the Old Testament.

This also holds true for *Paul*. On the one hand it is true that Paul, in order to proclaim Christ to the Gentiles, must address them as sinners who can understand that they have transgressed God's commandment and have fallen under his wrath, and thus he presupposes that they stand under the Law in a general sense. But, on the other, he cannot presuppose that they stand under the Law in the concrete sense of the Old Testament, nor does he make any effort to place them first under its concrete commandments. He knows that the heathen, too, are acquainted with God's lawful demand (Rom. 1:32). He does not need to direct them to the Old Testament, but only to remind them: "Whatever is true, whatever is honorable, whatever is just, whatever is pure, whatever is lovely, whatever is gracious, if there is any excellence, if there is anything worthy of praise, think about these things" (Phil. 4:8). He knows that the heathen who do not have the Law nevertheless know by nature what the Law demands; their conscience bears witness that the word of the Law is written in their hearts (Rom. 2:14 f.).

Thus the New Testament presupposes the Old, the Gospel presupposes the Law. But *this Law, which is embodied in the Old Testament, by no means needs to be the concrete Old Testament.* The pre-understanding (*Vorverständnis*) of the Gospel which emerges under the Old Testament can emerge just as well within other historical embodiments of the divine Law. Indeed, it is found wherever a man knows himself to be bound and limited by the concrete or general moral demands arising out of the relation to his fellow man which he must acknowledge in his conscience. Everywhere the possibility is present for man to become aware of his nothingness and to come to humility or despair; and everywhere the temptation is present for him to make the moral demand into the means of his self-justification and to suppose that through struggle and achievement, through self-discipline and the leading of a moral life, he will attain his authentic selfhood as a mature, moral personality—or anyway to believe that he ought to and can. Everywhere zeal for God is possible, the zeal which Paul calls "unenlightened" (Rom. 10:2) and which is challenged by the Word of the Cross.

Hence, it can be only for *pedagogical reasons* that the Christian Church uses the Old Testament to make man conscious of standing under God's demand; that the Decalogue continues to be the classical formulation of these demands which direct man into his involvement and responsibility within the Church as well as within the social matrix of his world; and that in the Christian proclamation the demands of the prophets live on because in them, as elsewhere only in Jesus' preaching, the imperative of the divine command rings out with incomparable force and clarity.

There is something else to be added, however. True, the Old Testament, in so far as it is Law, *need* not address us as direct Word of God and as a matter of fact *does* not do it. It speaks to *a particular people who stand in a particular ethnic history (Volksgeschichte) which is not ours.* In so far as we understand it as Law, we do so from that viewpoint which we have designated as the genuinely historical one. That is, in the Old Testament we are confronted with a particular understanding of human existence, vigorously and consistently expressed, according to which man stands under the unconditional "thou shalt." This "thou shalt" does not resound first out of the Old Testament; on the contrary, it is possible for us to understand the Old Testament because from the outset the hearing of this imperative, and the understanding of existence which it implies, is a possibility of our own existence. Nevertheless, this understanding, as a matter of fact, comes to clarity in dialogue with the history out of which we come and by our consciously appropriating it. But the Old Testament, too, has been given to us as a part of this history, and historical dialogue with it only clarifies for us the possibility of that particular understanding of existence with all its consequences.

For in the Old Testament this knowledge that man stands under the "thou shalt" is developed so radically that it pervades the whole understanding of existence. As for ourselves, we are subject to the most diverse influences, owing to the traditions operative in our history. Not only within modern mankind as a whole but also within the individual himself different possibilities of self-understanding are intertwined. Whoever feels the obligation to find clarity is compelled to turn to historical reflection. *And historical inquiry of the Old Testament* may clarify the understanding of human existence embodied in it in such a way that for us also *the question of the either-or of our self-understanding* becomes radically clear. How this is so can be shown here only in a sketchy fashion, of course.

In the Old Testament every idealistic or utilitarian interpretation of the moral demand as it constantly suggests itself is rejected. Whoever reads the Old Testament faces the question of whether he has to understand the awareness of the "thou shalt" as awareness of his dignity or of his creatureliness; whether he is to understand the demand under which he stands as a legal claim, as the road to the achievement of his dignity and the fulfillment of his personality, or as the demand which constrains him to serve his neighbor in obedience to God and which constantly convicts him of his imperfection and guilt. The Old Testament understanding of man comes to expression first of all in the *Creation faith*. For this faith means that man cannot, even by thought, exercise control over the world, but rather in his creatureliness is completely dependent upon the Lord of the world. And *history*, being the sphere in which man's destiny is realized, is not understood in the Old Testament as the mechanical process of human action and thought—as the process of mankind, of culture, of spirit— but rather as God's action, which gives man his destiny and assigns him his tasks. And what is more, man in history does not lay hold upon God in the rational contemplation of eternal order, but in the claim that arises out of concrete events. In the Old Testament—in distinction from Greek thought—a peculiar historical consciousness developed, the consciousness that the concrete answer to man's question concerning the future always springs out of his concrete history. Precisely in time, in the concrete moment, man gains his authentic selfhood (*Eigentlichkeit*) —not in a flight into timelessness where concrete history becomes an illusion. Therefore in Israel the ideal image of the human personality does not arise—the *kalos kagathos,* which confronts the individual as the timeless Idea after which he is to pattern himself. The abstract concept of *arete* and *dikaiosune* does not arise; rather, man is seen in his concrete position before God and the neighbor. As the image of the ideal personality does not develop in Israel, so also no notion of heroes and saints in the Greek sense is found. The significance of the prophets does not consist in the fact that they embody an acme of noble humanity or that they represent *homines religiosi,* but rather in the fact that they speak to the people of their day, calling them to a concrete behavior required by God in which they prove faithful to their God-given history.

Thus in the Old Testament *man is seen in his temporality and historicity (Geschichtlichkeit)*.[3] To understand himself, he is not referred to the universal, the cosmos, so that he may see himself as a part of this realm, nor is he referred to the Logos so that he may find true being in the timeless. Rather, he is direceted into his concrete history with its past and future, with its present that lays before him the demand of the moment in concrete relation with the "neighbor." He does not find himself within a cosmic rhythm which moves according to eternal laws and in which all struggle, all strife, is at eternal rest in God the Lord—here man's highest possibility would be to become aware of this God in *theōria*. But rather he finds himself put by the divine will in a particular place in the stream of temporal occurrence which for him holds the possibility of either judgment or grace depending on whether he acts in obedience to what God requires of him. Thus the relation to God is not one of seeing but of hearing, a fearing and obeying of God, an act of faith. That is, instead of being an optimistic world view, it is an appropriation of the past in faithfulness, a trustful waiting for God in the face of the future, a steadfast obedience in the present.

This understanding of existence, however, is the same as that of the New Testament. It is the same as the Christian view vis-à-vis the Greek, the humanistic, or the idealistic understanding of existence. Our own historical situation is characterized by our encounter with the twofold tradition in which we stand: the Greek and the biblical. Therefore, for us the Old Testament does not just take on the character of an isolated case, historical and contingent, in which a particular understanding of existence is exemplified. Rather, for us the Old Testament stands as a part of our own past, our history out of which we come—for we come out of the history of the Middle Ages in which classical and biblical tradition are bound up in a peculiar unity. The Old Testa-

---

[3] On "historicity" see Bultmann's "The Historicity of Man and Faith," in *Existence and Faith*, Schubert M. Ogden, ed. and trans. (1960), pp. 92–110. —ED.

ment continues to be a living, historical power. And it is *only in critical dialogue with the Old Testament,* whether it turns out positively or negatively, *that we can gain an understanding of existence with such clarity that it directs our own historical will and action.* Moreover, only in such dialogue is it possible to clarify the question, clouded over with confusion today, as to what meaning Christianity has for the present; indeed, as to whether it can claim to have any meaning at all.[4] If a person holds that historical reflection is necessary for gaining a clear view of himself and his contemporary world, and if he has done even a minimum of such reflection, it would be senseless for him to hold on to Christianity and at the same time discard the Old Testament. He can be sure that the Christianity he would like to retain is no longer Christianity. It is either-or: keep either both or neither. Hence it must be said, then, that *our history is the basis for a demand of the Old Testament upon us*—the demand that we hear it and, in dialogue with it, understand our own historical situation.

III

This demand, however, is completely different from what the New Testament and the Christian Church attribute to the Old Testament when they designate it as *revelation,* as *God's Word.* Critical, historical reflection and response to the demand of our own history is not hearing the Word of God and is not faith. But the further question is: what is meant by saying that the Old Testament is revelation, and to what extent, if any, can the Christian proclamation really be related to the Old Testament understood as God's revelation? The question is sharpened when we consider that, out of what has already been said, a new problem arises concerning the relationship of the New Testament to the

---

4 Whoever examines the Old Testament for the extent to which it expresses the mentality of a particular people (the Israelite-Jewish) is stuck in the procedure of a romantic historical view, which is worthless for the present. He has not yet seen that in the Old Testament there is present a particular understanding of human existence which, by virtue of our own history, always poses an immediate question to our own self-understanding.

Old. For if the New Testament understanding of existence is the same as that of the Old, if in the New Testament faith has the same meaning, if—so I can go on—righteousness and grace, sin and forgiveness, mean the same in the New Testament as in the Old, then is there any difference at all? *What, then, is the new element in the New Testament over against the Old?* Does the problem of the relationship of the Testaments prove to be only an apparent one?

Or does not the difference become evident in the above-mentioned opposition of *Law and Gospel?* Does not the New Testament stand over against the Old as Gospel to Law? If so, what was said earlier about the Gospel and the Law has not yet made the real difference clear. So far, it has become clear that the abiding, material (*sachlich*) relation between Law and Gospel is such that the Gospel is not to be understood apart from the law. Furthermore, we have seen that, while Christian existence is indeed existence under grace rather than under Law, this existence under grace is never arrived at once and for all but is vital only as it is ever grasped anew, only as it realizes itself in genuine acceptance of grace and in constant obedience. However, just as existence under grace is always related back to existence under the Law, so also it holds true for the Old Testament that there is no existence under the Law which is not at the same time existence under grace.

Hence is it right to place the Old Testament exclusively under the concept of Law? Or to what extent is it right?

First of all, in the Old Testament existence under the Law is already thought of as existence under grace. For it is by his grace that God has called his people and has given the Law by which they may live. The Law, as such, is a demonstration of the grace of God. And therefore the Old Testament already senses the problem that existence under the Law as grace constantly has to triumph over existence under the Law as law, that is, as mere demand. But there is still more to be said. For in the Old Testament God's grace does not simply consist in the fact that he has given the Law, that he makes demands, as though existence under the Law were identical with existence under grace. The Law has been given to a particular people in a particular history. And God's grace is operative primarily in the fact that he chose this people and concluded a covenant with them, that he called the patriarchs, and that he continues to raise up leaders of the people and prophets—in short, that he has given this people its history as a history of salvation. *The Law is grace only in connection with this history.* The people are not constituted as a people by first obeying the Law but, rather, God's grace precedes, so that obedience is always to occur through faith in God's prevenient and electing grace. God's grace constitutes man's relationship to God and provides the basis of his obedience.[5] Hence existence under the demand of God always is understood as existence under the grace of God.

And what is more, while the Law is understood as the demand of the God who gives the people their history, God's grace is at the same time understood as *the grace of forgiveness*. For the unity of Israel's history is found not only in the fact that God continually holds the people under his demand, but above all in the fact that he maintains his unwavering faithfulness in spite of all the unfaithfulness of the people. God is both at once: the wrathful God who punishes transgressions and the gracious God who abundantly forgives—and to whose forgiving grace man can always turn for refuge. The New Testament is not the first to know the God who "is merciful and gracious, slow to anger and abounding in steadfast love, who does not deal with us according to our sins, nor requite us according to our iniquity," the God who "pities those who fear him, as a father pities his children" (Ps. 103:8–13).[6]

In so far as "gospel" means the proclamation of God's grace

---

[5] Cf. my debate with K. Holl, *TR,* N.F., Vol. 4 (1932), pp. 12 f.

[6] Therefore the Christian Church, without any hesitation, can appropriate the words of the Old Testament, especially those of the Psalms and the prophets, which petition for forgiveness and which promise God's grace. In these words she finds her own faith expressed.

for the sinner, it cannot be said that the Gospel is lacking in the Old Testament and that God's grace is incongruous with the Law. To be sure, it can be pointed out that this Gospel does not ring out everywhere in a pure and unrestrained fashion. It can be said that the idea of sin and forgiveness is not always conceived radically. That is evident, for instance, in the fact that occasionally the petition for God's grace is motivated by the appeal to the creatureliness of man, as in Psalm 103:14–16:

> For he knows our frame;
> He remembers that we are dust.

For as long as man continues to display some quality of his own as the basis for hope in God's grace—though it were even his weakness and nothingness that deserve God's mercy—he has not bowed himself radically as a sinner before God and has not radically understood God's grace.

Alongside such reference to man's creatureliness, however, stands also an utterance in which this creaturely nothingness is traced back to the wrath of God.

> For we are consumed by thy anger;
> by thy wrath we are overwhelmed.
> Thou has set our iniquities before thee,
> our secret sins in the light of thy countenance.
> Ps. 90:7–8

It is God "who heals the brokenhearted, and binds up their wounds" (Ps. 147:3; cf. Isa. 55:15). And in utter humility the supplicant bows before Him:

> Have mercy on me, O God,
> according to thy steadfast love;
> according to thy abundant mercy
> blot out my transgressions.
> Wash me thoroughly from my iniquity,
> and cleanse me from my sin!

For I know my transgressions,
　　and my sin is ever before me.
Against thee, thee only, have I sinned,
　　and done that which is evil in thy sight,
so that thou art justified in thy sentence
　　and blameless in thy judgment. . . .

Create in me a clean heart, O God,
　　and put a new and right spirit within me.
Cast me not away from thy presence,
　　and take not thy holy Spirit from me. . . .

For thou hast no delight in sacrifice:
　　were I to give a burnt offering,
　　　　thou wouldst not be pleased.
The sacrifice acceptable to God is a broken spirit;
　　a broken and contrite heart, O God,
　　　　thou wilt not despise.
Ps. 51:1–4, 10–11, 16–17

Out of the depths I cry to thee, O Lord!
　　Lord, hear my voice!
Let thy ears be attentive
　　to the voice of my supplication!

If thou, O Lord, shouldst mark iniquities,
　　Lord, who could stand?
But there is forgiveness with thee,
　　that thou mayest be feared.

I wait for the Lord, my soul waits,
　　and in his word I hope;
my soul waits for the Lord
　　more than watchmen for the morning, . . .

For with the Lord there is steadfast love,
　　and with him is plenteous redemption.
And he will redeem Israel
　　from all his iniquities.
Ps. 130

This conception of the *grace* of God corresponds to the Old Testament conception of *sin* and the demand of *faith*. For sin is primarily understood not as man's moral offense but as the violation of God's honor, as distrust of God's grace, as murmuring and doubt, as the rebellion of self-sufficient man—in short as unbelief (*Unglaube*). What is required of man is that he renounce self-sufficiency and self-glorification and that he be still and wait for God—in short, faith.

> His delight is not in the strength of the horse,
>   nor his pleasure in the legs of a man;
> but the Lord takes pleasure in those who fear him,
>   in those who hope in his steadfast love.
>
> Ps. 147:10–11

To him shall every knee bow and every tongue swear: "Only in the Lord do I have success and strength" (Isa. 45:23–25). And what Paul proclaims—"Let him who boasts, boast of the Lord" (I Cor. 1:31)—is anticipated in Jeremiah 9:23–24:

> Thus says the Lord:
>   Let not the wise man glory in his wisdom,
>   let not the mighty man glory in his might,
>   let not the rich man glory in his riches;
>   but let him who glories glory in this,
>   that he understands and knows me,
>   that I am the Lord who practices kindness,
>   justice, and righteousness in the earth; . . .

> In returning and rest you shall be saved;
>   in quietness and in trust shall be your strength.
>
> Isa. 30:15

> If you will not believe,
>   surely you shall not be established.
>
> Isa. 7:9

> He who believes will not be in haste.
>
> Isa. 28:16

In such faith the supplicant submits himself utterly to the grace of God. He hopes for this grace and experiences it in the fact that God graciously accepts him and turns away his affliction, that God destroys the enemy hosts before Jerusalem, that he builds again the broken walls of Zion and restores the people to their homeland. And in all this he experiences the forgiveness of God. But if he experiences forgiveness when God confers such gracious favors in his personal life and in the history of his people, does he then always experience it? Can he in faith be certain of God's forgiveness? Even if he does not experience it, he at least hopes for it. And this hope comes to be eschatological hope.

The eschatological hope, as found in the prophetic message, arose out of the radical perception of the sin of the people, who deserved nothing but God's annihilating judgment and who could display nothing before God as the basis for a claim on his grace. If beyond the judgment there unfolds the prospect of a future of salvation, then this future is one of pure forgiveness and grace.

> For my own sake, for my own sake, I do it,
>   for how should my name be profaned?
> My glory I will not give to another.
>   Isa. 48:11; cf. Ezek. 36:22–23

Seen from the standpoint of man, from the standpoint of the people, there is no continuity between present and past. Israel is dead, annihilated by God's judgment. But God's Spirit can, and will, make the dead bones come to life again (Ezek. 37:1–14). God's grace will renew the people.

> A new heart I will give you,
>   and a new spirit I will put within you;
> and I will take out of your flesh the heart of stone
>   and give you a heart of flesh.
> And I will put my spirit within you,
>   and cause you to walk in my statutes
> and be careful to observe my ordinances.
>   Ezek. 36:26–27

Then will God make a new covenant with the people:

> I will put my law within them,
>   and I will write it upon their hearts;
> and I will be their God,
>   and they shall be my people.
> And no longer shall each man teach his neighbor
>   and each his brother,
> saying, "Know the Lord,"
>   for they shall all know me,
> from the least of them to the greatest,
>   says the Lord;
> for I will forgive their iniquity,
>   and I will remember their sin no more.
>
> Jer. 31:33–34

Then it will be true:

> They shall not hurt or destroy
>   in all my holy mountain;
> for the earth shall be full of the knowledge of the Lord
>   as the waters cover the sea.
>
> Isa. 11:9

So far as Israel conceived the idea of God radically by grasping the ideas of sin and grace radically, the faith of the Old Testament is hope; and *the faith of the New Testament stands over against it as the faith which has fulfillment.* For the decisive element of the New Testament and of the Christian faith is that in Jesus Christ God has performed the eschatological deed hoped for, that in Christ he has forgiven sin, has called the New Israel, has bestowed his Spirit. This is what is meant when in Christianity man's relation to God is bound to the person of Jesus: The Christian faith in God is grounded in the fact that God through Christ has reconciled the world to himself (II Cor. 5:19). There is not alongside of God another divine person, as though the Jewish faith in the one God were made complete by faith in a second divine person; nor does the Christian faith give assent to metaphysical speculations about the deity of Christ and his natures. Rather, faith in Christ is nothing else but faith in God's deed in Christ.

However, what bearing does this have on the problem of the relation of the New Testament to the Old? If Christ is understood as God's deed of forgiveness and if just this is God's eschatological deed, then *the concept of God's grace is radically grasped,* that is, forgiveness is not just granted to man in the changing fortunes of the life of the individual or of the people. God's grace is forgiveness pure and simple and it makes man new and strong. "My grace is sufficient for you, for my power is made perfect in weakness" (II Cor. 12:9). The judgment has taken place, the new age has dawned, and mythological speculation about future eschatological events is ruled out in principle.[7] God's forgiving grace is found in nothing else than in *the proclaimed Word,* which God through Jesus Christ has given to the world (II Cor. 5:18–19). The Word is the Light which has come into the world and has given it a new luster; Jesus is the "Word."

So understood, *Jesus is God's demonstration of grace in a manner which is fundamentally different from the demonstrations of divine grace attested in the Old Testament.* For in the latter case, God's forgiveness is inextricably tied up with the destiny of the people (within which the individual also has his destiny), that is, in the Old Testament God's revelation is bound to the history of a particular people. So far as man belongs to this people, he can take comfort in the grace of God. What God has done in this history he has done unto each individual in so far as this individual has an integral place within his people and his people's

---

[7] Here, in the basic thought of New Testament faith, we find the critical criterion for the elimination of primitive Christian mythology, and this elimination must be carried out as already in the Gospel of John and as done indirectly even by Karl Barth when, in a forced manner, he reinterprets the mythological eschatology of I Cor. 15. See R. Bultmann, "Karl Barth, 'Die Auferstehung der Toten,'" *Glauben und Verstehen,* Vol. 1 (1933), pp. 38 ff., especially p. 57.

history. What God has done unto the patriarchs, what he has done unto the people when he summoned Moses, led the people out of Egypt, guided them through the wilderness, and brought them into the Holy Land, he has done even now unto each person, since this history is not past history but present, ever reactualized in the present generation of the people.[8]

In the New Testament, God's deed in Jesus Christ is not understood in the same way; it is not a historical event that is decisive for the history of Israel, so that by virtue of historical solidarity every later generation receives the benefit of what Jesus meant to his generation. Jesus cannot be remembered like Abraham or Moses, nor can his Cross be remembered like the crossing of the Red Sea or the giving of the Law at Sinai. For *he is the eschatological deed of God* which makes an end of all ethnic history (*Volksgeschichte*) as the sphere of God's dealing with man. The contemporaneity of the saving event accomplished in him is not mediated through the continuous *Volksgeschichte* and through the tradition which both accompanies and forms a constituent element of that history. The message of the forgiving grace of God in Jesus Christ is not a historical account about a past event, but rather it is *the Word which the Church proclaims,* which now addresses each person immediately as God's Word and in which Jesus Christ is present as the "Word." For in this Word the individual is confronted immediately by God, God's forgiving grace. He is not to look to demonstrations of God's grace found in historical events of the past, deducing from them that God is gracious and accordingly may also be gracious to him; rather, God's grace confronts him directly in the proclaimed Word.

The Congregation, *the Church,* is not a sociological entity, an ethnic (*Volks-*) or cultural community bound together by the continuity of history; but is constituted by the proclaimed Word of

[8] This comes to expression clearly, for instance, in the Jewish Passover liturgy; cf. Herrmann L. Strack and Paul Billerbeck, *Kommentar zum Neuen Testament aus Talmud und Midrash* (1928), Vol. 4, excursus 4: "Das Passahmahl," p. 68.

God's forgiveness in Christ and is the community of this proclamation, the community of preaching and of faith. It has no history as ethnic (*völkische*), national, and cultural communities have their history. In the Church it is not possible to speak of the "Fathers," say Augustine or Luther, in the way we speak of Christ, since he is the eschatological deed of God. Thus it is not possible to speak of the Fathers of the Church in the way Israel spoke of its "Fathers." In Israel God's gracious activity was continued in the individual leaders and prophets whom God raised up from time to time. This history has come to an end. The old has passed away; the new has come.

But this also means: *to the Christian faith the Old Testament is no longer revelation* as it has been, and still is, for the Jews. For the person who stands within the Church the history of Israel is a closed chapter. The Christian proclamation cannot and may not remind hearers that God led their fathers out of Egypt, that he once led the people into captivity and brought them back again into the land of the Promise, that he restored Jerusalem and the Temple, and so on. Israel's history is not our history, and in so far as God has shown his grace in that history, such grace is not meant for us. For this very reason it is quite possible, from the Christian viewpoint, to call the Old Testament Law; seen from its own point of view, the Old Testament is both: Law and Gospel.

This means, however, that *to us the history of Israel is not history of revelation.* The events which meant something for Israel, which were God's Word, mean nothing more to us. To be sure, when we engage in historical reflection, when we enter into a critical dialogue with the historical past out of which we have come, even the history of Israel may say something essential. The exodus from Egypt, the giving of the Law at Sinai, the building of Solomon's Temple, the work of the prophets, all redound to our benefit in so far as these are historical episodes which form a part of our Occidental history. In the same sense, however, it can be said that the Spartans fell at Thermopylae for us and that Socrates drank the hemlock for us. And in this sense Jerusalem is not a holier city for us than Athens or Rome. But that is something completely different from speaking of God's revelation in Christ as the Word of forgiveness. Dialogue with our own history in a spirit of critical reflection is fruitful for us; but only when we already believe are we justified in tracing this fact back to God's activity in history! For what we discern in that dialogue with history, so far as it reveals and presents to us the possibilities of human self-understanding, is also discerned by unbelief. Faith must have another basis.

For the Christian faith Israel's history is not history of revelation. To be sure, this statement is to be differentiated from the further question of *whether and to what extent the Old Testament could signify revelation for the Christian faith,* that is, the Old Testament itself, freed from its history, as God's Word which speaks to us directly, rather than in the way it spoke to, and must be understood by, Israel and Judaism. One thing is clear: the Old Testament cannot, out of its own pages, give itself this validation. If it is not validated by the fact that in it the tradition of our own history speaks to us, then it can receive its validation *only from Christ.* This means: the Christian faith seizes the Old Testament, so to speak, maintaining that what it says could not be understood formerly except in a provisional and limited sense and can only now be said and heard properly. But this just means: to the Christian faith the Old Testament is not in the true sense God's Word. So far as the Church proclaims the Old Testament as God's Word, it just finds in it again what is already known from the revelation in Jesus Christ.

In any case, *the New Testament and primitive Christianity itself go about it this way.* What is written in the Old Testament, it is held, is written for our sakes upon whom the end of the ages has come (I Cor. 10:11; cf. Rom. 15:14). Thus *the Old Testament is interpreted out of the eschatological consciousness* that all preceding things were provisional and only now receive their true meaning.

Is this view sensible and possible, and to what extent is this so? In the New Testament and elsewhere in primitive Christianity an obvious way to use the Old Testament is that of *scriptural proof.* The truth of the Christian faith, the necessity and soteriological significance of Jesus' fate, are validated on the ground that this faith, these events were already foretold in the Old Testament. Such a proof from Scripture is, as a matter of fact, impossible. The alleged prophecies of the Old Testament, taken in their own meaning, are in some instances not prophecies at all; in other instances they are not directed toward Jesus or the Christian Church but simply portray the Israelite-Jewish hope for the future. Most of the passages must be understood—e.g., with the aid of the allegorical method—contrary to their original sense in order to yield a suitable prediction. This only shows, however, that the faith stood firm without predictive proof; such proof was only discovered subsequently. In fact, scriptural proof cannot really convince anyone, especially today; but what is more, it must not convince anyone. Faith which would believe on the basis of such proofs is not genuine faith at all. The scriptural proofs of the New Testament must be abolished not just on the basis of rational, historical criticism but for the very reason that they only obscure the character of faith.

However, can the Old Testament be understood by faith as the Word of God in another sense? One thing is clear: in this case *the Old Testament ought not to be understood contrary to its original sense,* as this sense is to be established by historical research alone. For if this sense were changed, then it would no longer be the Old Testament that speaks. And that is precisely our question: whether the Old Testament still speaks as God's Word to those who have heard, and now hear, the Word of the New Testament. Every form of allegory is idle play or nonsense.

If Jesus Christ alone, as God's eschatological deed of forgiveness, is God's Word to man, then all words which help to make this Word understandable, by bringing man into the situation in which he can understand it and by unfolding its implicit under-standing of existence, are *God's Word in an indirect (vermittelt) way*. In this sense the Old Testament can be God's Word. It con-tains that understanding of the correlation of Law and Gospel which is normative for the Christian understanding of existence. In it is clearly expressed that existential understanding of man as the creature who, in his historicity, stands under God's claim. In it is articulated the consciousness of sin and the hope for God's grace which rest on the basis of the Christian assurance of sin and hope which have been overcome and fulfilled, yet which are ever to be overcome and fulfilled again. We who have been called to faith are those who—so to speak—see their image mirrored in the Old Testament. Hence the Christian proclamation can hold the Old Testament before us as our reflected image, just as Paul in I Corinthians 10 holds the wilderness generation before his con-gregation—not as a scriptural proof but *pros nouthesian* (10:11). Thus faith seizes the Old Testament and, in the power and au-thority of faith, dares to direct to us the words of the Old Testa-ment which once were not spoken for us, in order that we may obtain understanding for our situation and for the Word of Christ which is spoken into this situation. In this sense, the Old Testament can be called *prophecy,* the New Testament *fulfill-ment.*

It *can* be so, and perhaps it will be normally; of course, it does not *have* to be so. Even within the New Testament itself there is, in this regard, a great difference. Some writings of the New Testament—a few of Paul's letters, the Gospel of John, the First Epistle of John—make little or no reference to the Old Testa-ment. It all depends upon the situation of the proclaimer and of the hearer. If, however, the Old Testament is taken up into the Church's proclamation as God's word, then the inviolable condi-tions are: (1) that the Old Testament is used in its original sense, although without its original reference to the Israelite people and their history, and thus that every form of allegory is discontinued;

(2) that the Old Testament is adopted only in so far as it is actually promise—that is, preparation for the Christian understanding of existence. To this extent one may say that Christ already speaks in the Old Testament.

2 Is the Old Testament the Propaedeutic to Christian Faith?

ALAN RICHARDSON

The rise of scientific biblical criticism in the latter half of the eighteenth century rendered untenable the traditional Christian conception of divine revelation. No longer was it possible to conceive of revelation as consisting in infallible oracles of truth written down in the inspired text of Holy Scripture. In Germany the main stream of Protestant theology in the nineteenth century took its direction from Schleiermacher, who attempted to formulate an alternative view of divine revelation, now that it could no longer be identified with the divinely given propositional truths of the Bible. The dominant Continental nineteenth-century view, nowadays often called Liberal Protestantism, sought to ground theological truth upon the deliverances of the religious consciousness, the stream of awareness of God, which came into the world as a positive historical religion with Jesus and his Church. The significance of Jesus was generally held to reside in the fact that historically it was he who introduced into the world that new kind of God-consciousness, that new relationship between man and God, which is the distinguishing characteristic of the Christian religion.

36

This type of view, of course, denies to the Old Testament any unique role which it had played, in the traditional conception, in the communication of revelation. True, Jesus was a Jew, and therefore in order to understand him it is necessary to study the development of Jewish religious ideas and institutions, since they would obviously throw valuable light upon his "psychology." But at best thé Old Testament was only the propaedeutic to Christian faith. The prophets at their highest and best might indeed have enjoyed some remarkable anticipations of that experience of God which later was actualized in Jesus and his Church, but much the greater part of the Old Testament moved on an altogether lower plane. The Old Testament merely recorded man's evolution toward the true God-consciousness; its realization of human spiritual potentiality, however, was only partial, and when that which is perfect is come, that which is in part is done away. Besides, other religions also had their own remarkable spiritual achievements, and they also anticipated the new God-awareness that was perfected in Christ. The proper theological understanding of non-Christian religions, whether Jewish or Gentile, was by means of the scientific comparative study of religions (*Religionsgeschichte*).

Thus, on the Liberal view, it can be only for pedagogical reasons that the Christian Church uses the Old Testament to make men conscious of the truth of the Gospel of Christ. Other teachings concerning human existence—such as Plato's, for instance—might also thus be used pedagogically. The Old Testament revelation of God is bound to the history of a particular people, whose history is not our history. Our history is just as closely bound up with that of the Greeks as with that of the Hebrews; Jerusalem is not a holier city for us than is Athens or Rome. On this Liberal Protestant view Israel's history is not for Christian faith the history of revelation; for the Christian faith the Old Testament is not in the true sense God's Word. The religion of the Old Testament is not intrinsically more closely related to Christ's revelation of God than is the religion of Confucius or of Mohammed, even though extrinsically the historical connection is closer. Christ was a Jew, and the God-consciousness which was his gift to his followers naturally expressed itself in Jewish forms. But it could also, and actually did, express itself in forms drawn from the higher paganism of the Hellenistic world. The Jewish envelope of New Testament faith is only an external; the pure "religion of Jesus" must be divested of its first-century garments. In orthodox Liberal Protestant terminology, the kernel must be separated from the husk; in more up-to-date terms, the eschatological kerygma must be demythologized.

The antecedents of this tradition of thought are to be sought in eighteenth-century positivist notions of history. As Lessing declared, the universal truths of reason could not be founded upon particular truths of history, and therefore the truth of religion, or the locus of revelation (for those who still believed in a divine revelation), was to be grounded in reason, not in history. The nineteenth century, though it searched diligently for the Jesus of history, found it expedient to ground the truth of religion, or the locus of revelation, upon religious experience rather than upon the relativities of history. In the twentieth century the futility of the search for the Jesus of history was at last acknowledged, but the Liberal tradition adapted itself to the new situation. A virtue was made of historical skepticism and the kerygma of Christianity, or the locus of revelation, was affirmed to be existential encounter.

No new discovery is claimed for the observation that Bultmann's theology is a logical development from nineteenth-century Liberal Protestant ways of thinking. The point has often been made hitherto. For instance, Karl Barth speaks of Bultmann's inheritance from W. Herrmann and ultimately from Ritschl and Schleiermacher.[1] And Paul Althaus says that in Bultmann Ritschl's value judgments have come back in a new form: whereas

---

[1] Karl Barth, *Die kirchliche Dogmatik,* Vol. 3, 2 (1948), p. 535.

Ritschl speaks of value for salvation, Bultmann speaks of significance for man—"the kinship is unmistakable."[2] According to this mode of thinking, dominant in Germany in the nineteenth century and in the first two decades of the twentieth, the truth of the Gospel is known to us through our awareness of Christ's saving influence upon us. Bultmann represents this experience-theology in the more fashionable twentieth-century existentialist mode. The Reformers' *pro me* has been exalted into the supreme methodological principle of dogmatics.[3] This type of theology provides a convenient escape route from the morass of historical skepticism into which the false positivistic notions of eighteenth-century historicism have lured us. What the historical Jesus actually said and did cannot be known, but fortunately it does not matter; revelation is not something which happened centuries ago; it is what takes place here and now in the individual's existential encounter with the kerygma. Not history but "experience" is the locus of revelation.

Whatever may be this kerygma which we existentially encounter, it is not the kerygma which the apostles proclaimed, since they proclaimed an historical fact, namely, that Jesus had been raised from the dead. Bultmann's kerygma is in truth "another gospel." Before we adopt such a desperate expedient might it not be wiser to retrace our steps and look again at the principles of the positivistic historicism of the unhistorically minded eighteenth century?

Historians of nineteenth-century theology have often called attention to the Ritschlian disparagement of the Old Testament as revelation. Ritschl regarded the Old Testament as an indispensable auxiliary to the understanding of the New Testament

---

2 Paul Althaus, *The So-called Kerygma and the Historical Jesus,* David Cairns, trans. (1959), p. 83.

3 H. Diem, *Dogmatics,* Harold Knight, trans. (1959), pp. 13 f., quotes H. J. Iwand: "At least from A. Ritschl through the line of W. Herrmann up to R. Bultmann and F. Gogarten this methodological use of the *pro me* is practised as something typically Protestant . . ."

and even used agreement with the religious ideas of the Old Testament as a test of the canonicity of the New Testament writings; but at best the Old Testament was for him no more than propaedeutic and was hardly a source of revelation as such. In the later editions of his work even

the comparison of the Christian kingdom of God with the preparatory stages of ethical society in history is omitted, and the love of God is exclusively confined to the historical Christian Church, which, by acknowledging Christ as its Lord, itself comes to stand in the same relation as he to God . . . "All love of man originates according to Christian ideas in the revelation of God in Christ." From such statements it would directly follow that before Christ there was neither a revelation of God nor an ethical association of men . . . It is evident that the limitation of the divine revelation solely to the person of Jesus, whose historical connection with the religion of Israel is undeniable, verges close upon the denial of revelation altogether.[4]

Ritschl's disciple, Herrmann, is even more emphatic in denying that the Old Testament is to be regarded as revelation in the same sense as the New Testament. We may, if we wish, call Hebrew prophetism or even Plato's *Gorgias* revelation, but Herrmann insists that we must guard against giving it the same significance or value as the supreme and unique revelation in Christ, and thereby dimming the glory of the latter.

The Church [Hermann holds] has erred in putting the Old Testament alongside of Christ, instead of keeping him apart and above all; for in him alone all that is true meets, and finds perfect expression. Yet revelation at a lower stage, and so of lesser worth, there has been, not only in Israel before Christ but even outside of Israel. "We by no means wish," says Hermann, "to deny altogether that the savages of New Holland have a knowledge of God and the stirrings of real religion, accordingly a communion with God. But how that is brought about for them we do not know. We cannot even transplant ourselves into the religious life of a pious Israelite with a complete understand-

---

[4] O. Pfleiderer, *The Development of Theology in Germany*, J. F. Smith, trans. (1890), p. 189.

ing. For the facts which acted on him as the revelation of God have for us this power no longer."[5]

This is a crucial point in the discussion of whether the Old Testament is for us revelation, or Holy Scripture, in the same sense as is the New Testament. The Ritschlian school, though with certain qualifications and misgivings, clearly thought not. The divine revelation was concentrated almost entirely within the person of Christ. Herrmann especially represents Christ as standing in historical isolation, having relations only to the individual believer, whereas Ritschl allows a more important place to the Church which by its evangelistic testimony has communicated to us the knowledge of Christ. But Ritschl and his school completed the process begun by Schleiermacher: "The distinct separation of theology from philosophy, which was already desiderated by Schleiermacher, becomes an accomplished fact in Ritschl. The only proper religious authority is the person, the word, and the work of Christ, as the testimony of the first Christian community has made us to know them."[6] It is this making Christ known to us that constitutes the New Testament as the uniquely Christian Scripture; but even here it is not the New Testament as such which is the vehicle of revelation, but only so much of it as is relevant to our awareness of salvation in Christ.

The Christian believer, starting from his experience of salvation through Christ, gradually comes to understand and make his own the facts and truths offered for his intelligence and appropriation in the New Testament; but not the whole New Testament as such is a revelation to him, only what his faith can make its own nourishment.[7]

It is not Christ as he is in himself, in his "substance" and "natures," that is revealed in the Christian revelation, but only the

---

[5] A. E. Garvie, *The Ritschlian Theology* (1899), p. 211. The quotation is from Herrmann's *Verkehr des Christen mit Gott* (1886), p. 49; Eng. trans. by J. Sandys Stanyon, *The Communion of the Christian with God* (1906), p. 53.

[6] F. Lichtenberger, *History of German Theology in the Nineteenth Century* (1889), p. 580.

[7] Garvie, *op. cit.*, p. 209.

Christus pro me. Christ is known through our experience of salvation, not through the communication of metaphysical truths about his essential being or of dogmas concerning his relation to the First and Third Persons of the Trinity.

The kinship of Bultmann's thought with that of the Ritschlian school is unmistakable as regards both the Old Testament and the New. Bultmann would retain the Old Testament, because in dialogue with it we can grasp our own historical situation. Moreover, it teaches us valuable lessons about our situation, such as that our existence under law is also an existence under grace. Furthermore, its radical grasp of the ideas of sin and grace gave rise to the eschatological hope of the prophets that God would save his people; this eschatological hope of the prophets is fulfilled in the New Testament proclamation of faith in Jesus Christ. But this fulfillment, he maintains, is fundamentally different from the Old Testament's claim that God's saving action was present in the historical events of Israel's life as a people. The New Testament faith is not (like Israel's) a testimony to God's action in the historical life of a particular people. We cannot rest upon an historical tradition about Jesus as Israel rested upon the tradition of God's deliverance at the Red Sea. Positivistic historicism has destroyed the notion that there is any reliable historical tradition of Jesus upon which we can build; about the actual life and historical person of Jesus we can know "practically nothing." The Christ of Christian faith, according to this view, is not the Jesus who healed the sick, raised the dead, taught in parables, preached to the poor, challenged the religious leaders, was handed over to the Gentiles, was crucified, dead, and buried, and on the third day rose again from the dead. The "history" of Jesus, like that of Israel, is over and done with; in any case, like Israel's history, it is not our history. The Christ of Christian faith is the eschatological deed of God, which makes an end of all *Volksgeschichte,* that is, of all history, since all history is the history of peoples. Henceforth all that matters is the individual's decision in the crisis which occurs when he hears the preaching in which Christ is present in the Word. The *Christus pro me,* the Christ of existential encounter, is the revelation of God; Christ is known in the individual's experience (even if it is "existential" experience, and this is what Herrmann would have said if he had known the term) of salvation. It follows that not all the New Testament is revelation; indeed, much of it is a fantastic mythology begotten of Jewish apocalyptic fanaticism and gnostic cosmological speculation; much of the rest of it is pseudohistory, mere folk tradition and legend. Even the apostolic kerygma, that Christ died for our sins according to the Scriptures and that he has been raised on the third day according to the Scriptures, is not the kerygma which is to be proclaimed today and which "becomes" the Word of God, the contemporary, saving eschatological event. This "other Gospel," the kerygma of Bultmann, has been freed altogether from history: Israel's history is not the history of revelation—the history of that people of whom Jesus was born, amongst whom he lived and taught; that people which handed him over to the hated foreigners for execution, but from whom also arose the witnesses of his resurrection; *this* history is not the history of revelation. This is surely another way of saying that the Christian revelation is not a historical revelation. And, of course, the reduction of Christ to a theological formula, "the eschatological saving event," without historical (and therefore human) content, is a new docetism.

But all this is, after all, only the logical working out of the Ritschlian denial that the Old Testament is revelation in the full and unqualified sense. The Ritschlians had regarded the Old Testament as revelation only in so far as it had here and there made explicit the valid ideas about God that had arisen out of the religious experience of the prophets, or in so far as it could communicate the God-consciousness of the prophets to us. Bultmann, having identified revelation with the eschatological event of the preaching of Christ, is unable to find a parallel to such an event in the Old Testament and is driven to the Marcionite conclusion that "for the Christian faith the Old Testament is not in the true sense God's Word." The Ritschlian era, in which Bultmann's formative years were spent, never succeeded in solving the problem of the Old Testament and therefore the problem of biblical revelation. It realized that the traditional view of the biblical revelation as truths written down in divinely inspired Scriptures was no longer tenable in the light of the new historical and critical methods, but it never conceived that any other solution was possible than that the truth of the Old Testament resided in those progressively higher ideas about God which were developed from the religious experience of the prophets. It never understood that the essential and differentiating factor in the Old Testament, as in the New, was a kerygma concerning God's saving action in the history of his people.

The biblical proclamation in both Testaments concerns the mighty acts of God in history; men's ideas and experiences are only secondary and are not the heart of the Bible. The latter-day Ritschlianism of Bultmann and his followers no more understands the kerygma which differentiates the whole Bible from all other "religion" than did the Ritschlianism of the Liberal classical period. Since that period, however, there has arisen a new understanding of the biblical revelation as based upon God's action in the history of the old and the new Israel.[8] This new understanding is, of course, not new in any absolute sense; it is the recovery of the ancient Catholic faith of the Church, which to Bultmann appears only as a farrago of gnostic speculation and Jewish apocalyptic fanaticism, but which in our days shows vigorous signs of triumphing at last over the fateful error of eighteenth-century historicism. The latter was one of the roots of the Ritschlian theology, and it led in the declining years of the Ritschlian influence to extreme historical skepticism. Because the kerygma of God's action in the Old Testament was not understood, the kerygma of God's action in the New Testament had to be reduced to the bare proclamation that the "eschatological event" has hap-

---

[8] E.g., G. Ernest Wright, *God Who Acts* (1952).

pened. The fatal defect of all forms of Ritschlianism lay in the failure to understand the Old Testament and therefore the entire biblical revelation. Here lay the source of the misconception of the Christian faith as a matter of religious experience (or existential encounter) and the failure to recognize that God is revealed in the history of his people, whose "God-consciousness" is only a distillation from their historical experience of his saving action. The Easter faith of the Church is not the result of a number of individual "existential" encounters with the preached "eschatological event" (whatever this may be), but is the outcome of a people's continuing experience of an historical salvation. The Church will sing next Easter, and every Easter after that:

> Come ye faithful, raise the strain
> Of triumphant gladness;
> God hath brought his Israel
> Into joy from sadness;
> Loosed from Pharaoh's bitter yoke
> Jacob's sons and daughters;
> Led them with unmoistened foot
> Through the Red Sea waters.[9]

We may agree that "every form of allegory is idle play or nonsense," but something much more important than this remains to be said:

God's saving action in Israel's history is the pattern and type of his action in Jesus Christ, who is the eschatological event only because he is supremely the historical event. Allegorical interpretation, we may agree, is outmoded and outgrown; but typological interpretation is the center of the New Testament's own understanding of history.[10]

If one supposes that God's action in history is mere mythology, the New Testament view of history will have been set aside in

---

[9] St. John of Damascus, *c.* A.D. 750; J. M. Neale, trans.
[10] Cf. G. W. H. Lampe and K. J. Woollcombe, *Essays on Typology* (1957), pp. 29–35.

favor of a view of the nature of the historical which took its origin in the rationalism of the Enlightenment. And it will have to be admitted that typology must be discarded along with allegorical interpretation, since there are no knowable historical correspondences upon which it can be founded.

It is not possible here to enter into a discussion of why today the eighteenth-century conception of history and historical methodology, after dominating much biblical exegesis for so long, is now at last being abandoned by many biblical scholars and theologians. If a reason may be stated without elaboration, we may say that the new attitude arises from the fact that their study of the Bible has involved them in an engagement with the past, with the history of the Israel of God, which has challenged them to decision at a deeply personal level and has forced them to assert that there is a more solidly historical basis for belief in those mighty acts of God in history than rationalist historicism allows to be possible. How near at times Bultmann himself has come to perceiving the truth of this post-Ritschlian insight! His own account of biblical hermeneutics, with its understanding of the exegete's involvement in the history which he investigates, points clearly in the direction by which biblical exegesis may escape from the toils of rationalist historicism.[11] If he has not liberated himself from the assumptions of eighteenth-century historical methodology, at least he has indicated the door his followers may pass through; and there is happily evidence before our eyes that some of those who have been brought up in Bultmann's school are willing to see what awaits them on the other side of the door.[12]

One further point may be added. It is an occupational idiosyncrasy of professional biblical scholars to imagine that Christian faith rests upon their ability or inability to solve the historical problems that are raised by it. It does not. It rests upon the testi-

---

[11] See especially his essay, "The Problem of Hermeneutics" (1950), in *Essays Philosophical and Theological,* James C. G. Greig, trans. (1955), pp. 234 ff., Eng. trans. of *Glauben und Verstehen,* Vol. 2.

[12] See, for instance, James M. Robinson, *A New Quest of the Historical Jesus* (1959), and Günther Bornkamm, *Jesus of Nazareth* (1960).

mony of a people, amongst whom contemporary Christians are numbered, to the great things that God has done for them and through them in their own history—not the history of another people, not a history long since over and done with, but a living history which is not something alien from them, but part of themselves, of their innermost being, making them what they are, constitutive of their very existence.[13] Biblical history is not at all what eighteenth-century rationalism meant by history. It is kerygmatic history, the history of ourselves, which, when we acknowledge our membership in the believing community, is known to be the true history of the people to which we belong. All Christian history is Church history; all biblical history, Old Testament history as well as New, is Church history. Outside the Church the biblical history is merely *Religionsgeschichte,* as it is for post-Enlightenment historicism. The history of Israel, including the history of Jesus, is our history, and it cannot mean to outsiders what it means to us. It can be understood only from within. What the "professional" biblical scholar will make of it depends upon whether he looks at it from the inside or the outside, but in either case our awareness of the truth of our history does not rest upon his investigations. The Christian faith rests upon the apostolic testimony to God's action in history, and the Church is an apostolic Church because it is the community that receives and bears the apostolic testimony. The biblical exegete can elucidate this testimony, but he can neither verify nor refute it *qua* historian, since the acts of God are not accessible to the techniques of scientific investigation.

The Old Testament is not adequately described as the propaedeutic to Christian faith. Temporally, of course, the faith and history of the Old Testament come before the faith and history of the New Testament. But the Old Testament is not propaedeutic in the sense that it can be laid aside when the New Testament is written. The Old Testament is the kerygmatic record of God's saving action in that history which is completed in the New Testa-

---

13 This theme is treated at greater length in my book, *The Bible in the Age of Science* (1961), chap. 8.

ment. God's saving activity in history is the theme of both Testaments, and neither Testament alone contains the complete record of it. Each Testament, however, testifies to the whole of God's saving activity, not merely to a part of it. The Old Testament bears witness to the saving action of God which will be completed in Christ; the New Testament testifies that the events it records are the fulfillment of those saving acts of God about which we learn from the Old Testament. Thus the Old Testament is not merely propaedeutic to Christian faith, since Christian faith itself is faith in God's salvation of the world through his action in the history of his chosen people, which culminated in the historical death and resurrection of Jesus Christ and the coming of his Church.

3 Bultmann against Marcion

CARL MICHALSON

"The most important of the problems Christians had to face in the early centuries"[1] was the question of the significance of the Old Testament. Yet the rise of the modern historical method still has not contributed substantially to a solution of those early problems. One sign of that fact is the continual oscillation between claims to the continuity of the Testaments and claims to their discontinuity. Indecisiveness about the significance of the Old Testament relative to the New is as evident today as it was in the days which antedated historical science.

Rudolf Bultmann calls for an end to that vacillation by refusing to regard the Old Testament as revelation for the Christian. The New Testament and not the Old expresses the form in which God is now calling his people into existence. Therefore, for a Christian to take the Old Testament as revelation would require either exegetical anachronism or exegetical guile. What Bultmann means by the Old Testament as *Vorverständnis*, however, separates his decision from Marcionism. For while he keeps the discussion strictly within the historical discipline, he finds a way of

[1] Jean Daniélou, *Origen*, Walter Mitchell, trans. (1955), p. 140.

maintaining the Christian relevance of the Old Testament. Of course, historians have always been able to abandon their academic tools while ascending to the pulpit; but they have not found it easy to live with the dualism in that procedure. For example, is it theologically defensible to select one's Easter text from a Psalm? If it is, ought one to claim of this text, as Wilhelm Vischer once did, that "we do not understand a single word in the whole Bible if we do not find Jesus Christ in this word?"[2] This may be called an extreme example. Yet is it any more acceptable for an Old Testament scholar, Martin Noth, to announce that the exegesis in the commentaries he is editing (*Biblischer Kommentar*) will bear in mind, above all else, that "the New Testament preaches Christ as the end of the Old Testament acts of God?"[3]

Canonicity makes one book of the Bible. Not having supplied a rationale for that decision, the Church has accustomed itself to finding Christianity in these pre-Christian texts. Historical method up to this time has not seriously challenged that primitive procedure. Bultmann, however, proposes a revision which makes historical method more fully historical, yet without violating the interests of Christian piety. The clue to his proposal is in the understanding of the Old Testament as *Vorverständnis* or pre-understanding to the New Testament. The force of his suggestion is in the way it transcends the subject-object structure which up to now has prevailed in the historical sciences, even among theologians.

An historical method which does not deliberately employ a pre-understanding tends to handle its data from the outside. The past is reconstructed from the point of view of a spectator. Battles are reported by those who have never fought in one; love and

---

[2] The reference is to his Easter sermon in Basel in 1943, cited by H. W. Hertzberg, "Zur neueren Auslegung des Alten Testaments," in *TLZ*, No. 4 (1949), p. 221.

[3] Cited by Hans-Joachim Kraus, *Geschichte der historisch-kritischen Erforschung des Alten Testaments von der Reformation bis zur Gegenwart* (1956), p. 440.

death by those with no personal empathy for either. An historian in this tradition is "the great eyepiece," as Count von Yorck identified Leopold von Ranke. He examines his data at a distance. But as Samuel Beckett once observed, the eye is hard of hearing. The historian whose materials will speak is the one who adopts a procedure beyond the limits of mere voyeurism. *Vorverständnis* is Bultmann's alternative to hermeneutical voyeurism.

The examination of the Old Testament as a body of knowledge which can be held in separation from one's commitments has contributed enormously, of course, to the understanding of the subject matter. Has it resolved, however, the traditional problems of the significance of the Old Testament for the Christian faith? Within the subject-object framework, where questions are raised from the outside, historical method has found no consistent way of determining the relation between the Old Testament and the New. That is the implicit force of much of what Bultmann says in his essay included in this volume. For instance, history like nature proceeds developmentally, so that what is old always bears some genetic relation to what is new. In that sense there is undisputed continuity between the Testaments. By the same rubric, however, movements in other parts of the East and in Greece are also in continuity with the New Testament. Moreover, when the doctrinal content of the two Testaments is considered, there are grounds for continuity as well as for discontinuity. The New Testament retains the historical consciousness of the Old Testament and its accent on the transcendence of God. Yet, judged by content, the Old Testament is a book of prophecy simply, while the New Testament is a book of fulfillment. As Bultmann points out in his essay on "Prophecy and Fulfillment," the concepts of covenant, kingdom of God, and people of God, whatever their verbal similarities to New Testament concepts, are so fundamentally different as to illustrate discontinuity between the Testaments.[4]

---

[4] *Essays Philosophical and Theological*, James C. G. Greig, trans. (1955), pp. 191 ff. Reprinted in *Essays on Old Testament Hermeneutics* (1963), Claus Westermann, ed., pp. 50–75.

Pre-understanding, however, is the key to overcoming the material considerations of this subject-object framework. In so doing, it provides a consistent pattern for discerning the relation between the Testaments. In respect of its being a pre-understanding to the Gospel, the Old Testament is always in continuity with the New. If one knew what that claim means for Bultmann, one would readily understand why it is wrong to classify Bultmann with Marcion and Harnack, who proposed the elimination of the Old Testament from the canon on the grounds of its discontinuity with the New.

What, then, is a *Vorverständnis*, a pre-understanding, and in what sense can it be said that the Old Testament plays that role in relation to the New? Pre-understanding is the historical procedure which overcomes the external approach to historical data by a method of appropriating history inwardly. It does not function as an elite form of historical understanding. It claims rather to be the method but for which much of history remains dumb. Pre-understanding is a method of putting questions to a body of historical material where the questions originate in one's own concern for living. Where that occurs, the material cannot be an indifferent object of investigation. It involves the question of the very meaning of one's life. According to this method, there is no understanding of history which is not also an understanding of one's own life.

What occurs in this way of understanding history is often referred to as "existential hermeneutic." The truth is that it was developed by Bultmann long before existentialism became articulate in Martin Heidegger. His Marburg professor, Wilhelm Herrmann, had taught Bultmann that the Christian faith always expresses itself in relation to "what concerns us, what is problematical for us." As Karl Barth, another pupil of Hermann has said, "We learned theology from Herrmann through our pores." But Bultmann learned this particular lesson better than Barth, and therefore has never deviated from the claim that the understanding of God always involves an understanding of man. A man who speaks about God always does so on the basis of some particular understanding he has of himself.

Wilhelm Dilthey helped Bultmann to turn Herrmann's intuition into historical method. Dilthey had learned from Schleiermacher that exegesis and understanding are not two stages in a process of interpretation. They are identical. One does not first examine the text and then understand it. Understanding is immediate to a proper method of examining a text. The crucial presupposition for understanding historical materials is, according to Dilthey, "the interpreter's relationship in his life to the subject which is directly or indirectly expressed in the text."[5] Therefore no interpretation can be said to be presuppositionless. Proper interpretation presupposes prior understanding, *Vorverständnis*— the putting of a question important to the interpreter. One cannot understand political history without some appreciation of the state and of law, or economic history without some concept of economics and society, or religion and philosophy without some understanding of what they are. One cannot assimilate Luther's Wittenberg theses without an actual sense of the protest prevailing in his time against Catholicism.[6] Joy is not understood in history by one who has had no personal anticipation of it. Discussions of gratitude and responsibility, love and hate, are abstract apart from some inkling that these are in some sense "my own possibilities." Similarly, "I must have a *Vorverständnis* for sin and forgiveness if I am ever to understand when I am spoken to about them."[7] "The fact that when Christian preaching strikes a man it can be understood by him indicates that he has a *Vorverständnis* of it."[8]

A specific understanding of the subject matter of the text, on the basis of a "life-relation" to it, is always presupposed by exegesis; and

---

5 *Ibid.*, p. 241.

6 See Bultmann's "Ist voraussetzunglose Exegese möglich?" *TZ*, Vol. 13, No. 6 (1957), p. 413. Eng. trans. by Schubert M. Ogden in *Existence and Faith* (1960).

7 Bultmann, *Glauben und Verstehen,* Vol. 1 (1933), p. 161.

8 *Ibid.*, p. 295.

in so far as this is so no exegesis is without presuppositions. I speak of this understanding as a "preunderstanding." . . . If we approach history alive with our own problems, then it really begins to speak to us. Through discussion the past becomes alive, and in learning to know history we learn to know our own present; historical knowledge is at the same time knowledge of ourselves. To understand history is possible only for one who does not stand over against it as a neutral, nonparticipating spectator, but himself stands in history and shares in responsibility for it. We speak of this encounter with history that grows out of one's own historicity as the *existentiell* encounter. . . . It means that, for historical understanding, the schema of subject and object that has validity for natural science is invalid.[9]

The significance of the Old Testament for Bultmann is precisely in this role as pre-understanding to the Gospel. As his treatise contained in this volume expresses it, the Old Testament helps us "grasp our own historical situation." The Old Testament's consciousness of the historicity of man supplies the prior understanding which makes it possible for the New Testament message to be heard. The historicity of man is the consciousness that "the concrete answer to man's question about the future springs from his own concrete history" (p. 19). On this ground, Bultmann can appropriate the traditional Lutheran model of the relation between the Testaments as the relation of Law to Gospel. The prophecy-fulfillment model he cannot accept because it encourages the comparison of bodies of doctrine which one may consider without involving himself. On the prophecy-fulfillment model, as we have seen, one is more impressed with the discontinuity between the Testaments than with the continuity, unless from a stance within the New Testament he typologizes or allegorizes the Old Testament faith after the historiographically loose manner of the early Church. But when one enters into the Old Testament as a condition of existence under the Law, the existential groundwork is laid for hearing the message of justification by

---

[9] Bultmann, "Is Exegesis without Presuppositions Possible?" in Ogden, *op. cit.*, p. 294.

faith communicated through the New Testament Gospel. When one enters into the Old Testament effort to realize the covenant of God within history and appropriates as one's own the "inner contradiction" and "miscarriage" of that method, he is prepared to receive the news that God has brought this method to an end through Jesus of Nazareth.[10]

Are there concrete illustrations of how this method is put to use in an exegetical situation? There are, and they illustrate the claim that the Old Testament is a pre-Christian text in which one must not find what was not there for those who wrote it. Historical method is honored. What then is the Christian significance of these pre-Christian texts? Their Christian significance is in their ability to evoke the *Vorverständnis* to which the Christian faith can speak. In Bultmann's Marburg sermons there are only two sermons based upon Old Testament texts.[11] But then Luther, who devoted twenty-eight of his thirty-two Bible-teaching years to the Old Testament, preached five times as many sermons from New Testament texts as he did from Old. In fact Luther is even on record as asserting that "the Old Testament is not to be preached."[12]

One of Bultmann's sermons draws on the promise to Noah following the flood: "While the earth remains, seedtime and harvest, cold and heat, summer and winter, day and night, shall not cease" (Gen. 8:22). It takes no great access of inventiveness to calculate the response when it is known the sermon was preached in Germany on May 9, 1937. The question of the revelation of God in nature is raised at a time of year when nature is most suggestive of God's beneficence and in a political climate which is eager to endorse what comes naturally. "In the susceptibility of man for the fullness and splendor of nature is hidden a susceptibility for God." Yet nature is full of riddle and ambiguity. Therefore, de-

---

[10] Cf. Bultmann, "Prophecy and Fulfillment" in *Essays*, pp. 205–208; in Westermann, *op. cit.*, pp. 72–75.

[11] *This World and the Beyond: Marburg Sermons by Rudolf Bultmann,* Harold Knight, trans. (1960).

[12] *Weimar Ausgabe* 20; 579, 11.

votion to the powers of nature is a risk. A sinister power is at work there which cannot reveal itself to our hearts. In fact, faith in nature fails to understand the properly *human* nature. For man is not simply nature but spirit, image of God. "If he forgets that he has his life to live in responsibility to God, his life is a riddle and his death is hideous." God is present in nature, therefore, chiefly in the sense that nature "compels man to ask about God."

The other sermon was preached under even more dramatic circumstances, on June 23, 1946. The text is from Lamentations: "The goodness of the Lord is that we are not cut off. His mercy has no end." Bultmann raises this question with his congregation: "Is the world of the Lamenter different from the one in which we live?" The consolation he offers to the depressed people of Germany is in the conclusion that "God is our portion." That means "we stand before a choice—God or the world. I choose God— he is my portion, even though I build only on faith and hope and have nothing visible and concrete at hand." We must "wait quietly," "be patient," and "make each decision by confessing the Lord and turning away from the world." "Why should a man complain about the punishment of his sins?" (Lam. 3:39.) The answer? "Only the patient have the inner calm to adjudicate the guilt question. But we stand before God, and before him none of us is pure." Is not the choice for God rather than the world the abandonment of human hope? Yes, but for a hope which is beyond human hope. But is not the Christian preaching concerned with the grace of God? Yes, but "the Gospel of grace says not that we are spared the Cross but that the Cross is itself grace, that God kills in order to make alive." That is the true patience—to be prepared to hear in God's *No* to our wishes his secret *Yes!* The way into the darkness of death is already the beginning of the life of resurrection. Not that we hope only in "the future glory which God shall give." Rather, as the Apostle Paul says, "We rejoice in our sufferings" (Rom. 5:3–5).

In this handling of the Old Testament text is discernible a

continuity with the New Testament based purely on the role of the Old Testament as pre-understanding to the New. In identifying with the structure of the experience of the Old Testament, one is prepared to hear the truth of the New Testament. One of the most widely applauded of the preachers who has specialized in the use of Old Testament texts is the Basel pastor, Walter Lüthi. Prior to the last war he impressed the German people deeply by what has been called "the unerring aim" of his preaching. "Without engaging in politics, he clarified the situation of those days from the Scriptures," especially from Daniel, Habakkuk, and Nehemiah. Consider, for instance, the rule of Habakkuk over a situation in which law was impotent and the Chaldeans stood at the gate. Nowhere does Pastor Lüthi say in his sermons, "These are the Germans!" "That is Hitler!" In fact, the sermons are directed to the Swiss, and particularly to the people of Basel![13]

Gerhard Ebeling reports his own use of an Old Testament text to illustrate how a modern may enter into the Old Testament. Toward the end of the war, when the report of Hitler's death was circulated throughout German army installations, Ebeling asked his "entirely nonchurchly comrades" to let him read something from the Bible. He chose Isaiah 14, which is a song of triumph over the demise of the king of Babylon. As he reports, "the silence that followed the reading impressively testified to how readily it was heard."[14] According to Ebeling, "The immediacy with which the text is heard rests on the actual or intended correspondence of the present situation with the one in which the word had its original locus."[15] I believe Bultmann presses this hermeneutical case a step further, however. The Old Testament does not simply presuppose in its hearer an existential correspondence. It helps to create that correspondence by evoking a pre-understanding which in turn contributes to the hearing of the New Testament.

In the early Church the Old Testament was regarded as the

---

[13] Hertzberg, *op. cit.*, p. 220.
[14] Gerhard Ebeling, *Die Geschichtlichkeit der Kirche* (1954), p. 4.
[15] *Ibid.*, p. 12.

sacred Scriptures to which the New Testament was the exegetical appendix. Bultmann has completely reversed that arrangement. However, he should not for that reason be linked with Schleiermacher's project to make the Old Testament an appendix to the New. The New Testament is the sacred Scriptures for Bultmann; but the Old Testament is its exegetical preface. One might respond that it is consistent with the intention of Christianity for Bultmann to elevate the New Testament to prominence as sacred Scriptures, or even to reduce the Old Testament to exegetical preface. But the plain fact is that the Old Testament for Bultmann is not the *indispensable* preface. Other literature may substitute as pre-understanding to the New Testament. In his incautious way Søren Kierkegaard anticipated Bultmann's position:

This is the reason my soul always turns back to the Old Testament and to Shakespeare. I feel that those who speak there are at least human beings: they hate, they love, they murder their enemies, and curse their descendants throughout all generations, they sin.[16]

A Protestant need not become alarmed about that position, however, for three reasons. First, the biblical canon is not closed, so that one need not concede grudgingly that extracanonical literature is often productive of faith. Second, the Protestant principle of *sola scriptura* refers to a biblical mode of understanding and not to the Bible as a book. Third, for Christians the Old Testament will always be an indispensable preface to the New just because in the New Testament the Gospel has been interpreted through the texts of the Old Testament, however justifiable that procedure may have been historiographically.

A major value in the association of *Vorverständnis* with the Old Testament is the way it clarifies Bultmann's much-debated hermeneutical method. I have in mind several of the most popular objections to his method.

1. Do not historical procedures require the historian to aban-

---

[16] *Either/Or*, David F. Swenson and Lillian Marvin Swenson, trans., Vol. 1 (1944), p. 22.

don all presuppositions? Yet Bultmann standardizes pre-understanding. For Bultmann *Vorverständnis* is indeed an indispensable presupposition for historical understanding. But culturally or psychologically conditioned prejudice is something utterly different. Prejudgments disfigure historical reality; pre-understanding delivers it from latency to life. Objective historical data which have not been brought into correspondence with personal existence often function as prejudice, thwarting historical illumination. In Jesus' time, for instance, some held the dogma regarding the expected Messiah that "no one will know where he comes from" (John 7:27). That was a prejudgment in terms of which Jesus could not have been received as the Messiah, for everyone recognized him as "the son of Joseph, whose father and mother we know" (John 6:42).[17] Pre-understanding, unlike prejudice, does not screen out the future selectively. It holds existence open to the future, receptively.

2. Is not *Vorverständnis* a species of natural theology which compromises the traits of uniqueness and surprise in the Gospel? True, some of the motives in existential hermeneutics correspond to some of the motives in natural theology. New revelation would be incomprehensible to persons living in the age prior to that revelation if there were not some general preparation for it. However, a pre-understanding is not to be confused with a religious a priori which makes religion a universal possibility. Universals, like objective historical data, exist outside the understanding. The realities of faith, on the other hand, exist in and for the understanding. This is the meaning of Bultmann's alleged individualism. Existential individualism is not in conspiracy against community, such as a people or church constitute. It is against communities based on universals which rule like axioms or fates, independently of the decisiveness of the participant.

The customary objection to natural theology is that by contributing positive knowledge to the moment of revelation, it engages in a form of intellectual righteousness-by-works. This

---

[17] Cf. Bultmann, *Das Evangelium des Johannes* (1953), p. 40.

charge cannot hold against the strategy of *Vorverständnis.* Pre-understanding is not a positive knowledge; it is wholly negative and questing. It is composed not of answers at all, but only of questions. When the exegete takes his *Vorverständnis* for final understanding, he falsifies. When the existing man allows his pre-understanding to become "an assured state of affairs"[18] he has fallen into sin. Sin is not a destruction of man's ontological structure, but a perversion in his hermeneutics. Sin is what makes it impossible for man to ask questions about God in any but a perverted way.

The bearing of this analysis upon the significance of the Old Testament is most provocative. Traditionally the Church has tended to regard the Old Testament as a prefiguration of the New, a foreshadowing, an *umbra veritatis,* a shadow of the truth. For Bultmann, as for Luther after 1519 (the year of his break with medieval hermeneutics), the shadow of the Old Testament is not a mysterious twilight from which Christians may derive positive allegorical or even typological meanings. The shadow is a condition of real night.[19] The knowledge of the Old Testament as pre-understanding is not-knowing knowledge, as different from New Testament knowledge as night is different from day. Yet, it is continuous with New Testament knowledge. Continuity here obviously cannot be analogous to the smooth continuity of water and milk. The relation is not so homogeneous. Nor is it, on the other hand, as discontinuous as water and oil. The relation is not so dichotomous. It is a continuity, however, such as exists between thirst and water.

3. What, then, is the significance of the much-vaunted "hermeneutical circle" in which textual answers and interpreters' questions presuppose each other? Does not the very form of the question determine the substance of the answer? Do Old Testament, existential-type questions really deliver the full-bodied

---

18 Bultmann, *Essays,* p. 117.
19 Luther, *Weimar Ausgabe,* 3; 243, 37 f. Cf. Gerhard Ebeling, "Die Anfänge von Luthers Hermeneutik," *ZTK,* Vol. 48 (1951), p. 212.

Christian message from the New Testament womb? Here two things should be observed on Bultmann's behalf. First, the purpose of the hermeneutical question is not to change the text, not even to modernize it, but to understand it. Karl Barth, in his little writing on Bultmann, has complained that he does not see how by Bultmann's method he would go about interpreting the Bible to his children, let alone to modern man. Bultmann replied to Barth in a still unpublished letter that the primary test of hermeneutics for Barth should be whether he can interpret the Bible to himself.

Second, Bultmann candidly admits that the form of the question does tend to pervert the answer of the text. That fact, by itself, would be calamitous, were it not for the additional fact that the text has an integrity of its own which asserts itself over against the interpreter, challenging the form of his questions. Everyone knows that in Bultmann's thinking the interpreter is not a *tabula rasa,* a passive receptacle upon which history writes its answers. It is equally true in Bultmann's thinking, however, that neither is the text a passive object. The interpreter does not simply wrest from the text the answers to his prior questions. Bultmann observes that the new affects one's old understanding, "like a benign or shattering fate," by "putting the old in question, breaking it down, and making it new"; thus "the old can understand the new if the new is its negation."[20] The work of an exegete is a theological work, not by virtue of the hermeneutical method, but by virtue of the text being interpreted.[21] The decisive thing in a biblical hermeneutic, then, is not the possibility of an understanding which is accessible to the interpreter in such a way that he can choose at will or even decline to choose. The decisive thing, rather, is that the interpreter is confronted with possibilities he cannot grasp as his own.[22] Therefore the Old Testament in Bultmann's view is not simply on call to the interpreter's interrogation.

---

[20] Bultmann, *Glauben und Verstehen,* Vol. 1, p. 296.
[21] *Ibid.,* p. 133.
[22] *Ibid.,* p. 161.

That would be to miss the major point in the Old Testament as pre-understanding. Rather, the Old Testament quickens the historical consciousness of man, evoking his questioning spirit. These questions in turn become his threshold to an understanding of the New Testament, but not without the opportunity for the New Testament itself to reshape the question of the Old more closely to the image of its own intention.

The medieval cathedrals of Europe are veritable mirrors reflecting in their portals and windows the stories of the Bible. The Old Testament story preponderates. In the Sainte Chapelle the entire Old Testament seems unfolded in its windows, but the story of Christ is limited to two windows. That ratio does not seem unfair to the New Testament, however, for in these churches and cathedrals every Old Testament story seems to have the New Testament consummation stamped upon it. When Samson rips the gates of Gaza from their hinges or Elisha raises the widow's daughter, the Resurrection of Christ is clearly prefigured. When Isaac carries wood for sacrifice, he prefigures Christ carrying the Cross. The history of Christian art, like the history of the Church, is the history of the exegesis of the Scriptures. But Old Testament themes treated as prefigurations of the New Testament are the exegesis simply of the New Testament. The Church art of the future need not perpetuate that monotestamentalism. That would be Marcionism in a very deceptive form. Marcionism is monotestamentalism which calls for the rejection of the Old Testament. Ironically, the Church from the very beginning has sponsored creeping Marcionism by exegetically absorbing the Old Testament into the New. Historical criticism developed the first effective block against this exegetical deception, but provided no theological rationale for reading the Bible as one book. The importance of Bultmann's analysis of the Old Testament as *Vorverständnis* to the Gospel is in showing one possible way to terminate creeping Marcionism in the Church. The Old Testament has a right to be represented on its own, according to its own intention. What, then, would be its justification in a Christian setting, reminding one as it does of the days before God's covenant in Christ? Samson, Elisha, and Isaac would still be there, but now as figures of real historical life, undergoing real moral crisis, real human pathos, real trust in the faithfulness of God. That figuration is not prefiguration but pre-understanding. If it leads the worshiper to the message of Cross and Resurrection, it will do so free of dogmatic prejudices which distort. It will do so by opening life to Gospel possibilities through the evocation of sheer humanity.

4 History and Gnosis

Eric Voegelin

A debate with Professor Bultmann is an intellectual adventure to be enjoyed. In his essay on the relevance of the Old Testament to Christian faith there is no less at stake than the meaning of theology, philosophy, and history. Moreover, the essay is joined with related studies in a volume to which its author has given the title *Glauben und Verstehen* ("Faith and Understanding"), indicating thereby his conception of theology as the enterprise of *fides quaerens intellectum*. The inquiry, therefore, is linked to the great problem of faith and reason. Philosophically, furthermore, he is not content to leave the conflict of the two truths in the form given to it by the Scholastics, but transfers it into the contemporary medium of existentialism, in particular that of Martin Heidegger, to whom the volume of essays is dedicated. And finally, the inquiry receives its tone from Bultmann's work of demythologizing, a work motivated by the responsibility of making the Gospel in its purity accessible to men of our time to whom its symbolism has become strange. The problems raised by Bultmann thus are presented with the authority of both spiritual concern and intellectual penetration; they cannot be evaded, they must be answered.

A critical examination of the principles which have induced

Bultmann to deny theological relevance to the Old Testament is forced into definite form by certain characteristics of his work, the decisive one being the vein of Gnosticism running through it. Under the aspect that concerns us presently, gnosis is a mode of existence which distorts the order of being by placing negative accents on world and history and correspondingly positive accents on the means of escaping from them. The thinker who interprets human existence in this mode need not necessarily indulge in wrong propositions with regard to reality; his purposes may be served as well by focusing attention on the means of escape into world-transcendent reality to the neglect of large sectors of mundane reality. A gnostic thinker, therefore, can exert a peculiar fascination, especially in troubled times. He deals with the all-absorbing mystery of human existence and, provided he is a competent scholar, his voice will carry conviction because what he has to say positively is true. If, then, he is careful enough not to draw attention to the sectors of reality omitted (sometimes the construction of a system is helpful for the purpose), the inexpert reader will be overpowered by what impresses him as the light of truth. A good deal of the fascination Heidegger's work holds for the unwary is due to the subtle blending of truth presented with conviction and untruth through omission. In Bultmann's work, though it is fundamentally Christian, the gnostic strand is still effective enough to place important areas of reality beyond the horizon of his inquiry. Under the circumstances adumbrated, a critical examination of his essay would run against a blank wall if it were to extend only to the positive propositions, for Bultmann's scholarship, as is well known, is excellent. Hence I shall proceed, first, by presenting Bultmann's positive thesis as well as the modifying corollaries; then I shall submit the thesis to critical analysis until it becomes clear that the argument has a semblance of consistency only because an important sector of reality was omitted from consideration; and when the omitted sector is determined, finally, I shall explore the gnostic motivation of both the omission and the thesis.

I

Bultmann's essay on the theological irrelevance of the Old Testament to Christian faith is written in a discursive and persuasive style which makes it incumbent on the critic to disengage the theoretically relevant passages from their context.

Toward the beginning of the article Bultmann formulates the "theological" question: "Whether to the faith that sees in Jesus Christ the revelation of God, the Old Testament still has relevance"; and toward the end he gives the succinct answer:

"To the Christian faith the Old Testament is no longer revelation as it has been, and still is, for the Jews. For the person who stands within the Church the history of Israel is a closed chapter . . . Israel's history is not our history, and in so far as God has shown his grace in that history, such grace is not meant for us . . . To us the history of Israel is not history of revelation" (p. 31).

Between the beginning and the end, Bultmann engages in a series of reflections which admit the historical and ontological (*sachliche*) relevance of the Old Testament to the Christian believer. We must also present these qualifying reflections disengaged from their circumstantial context.

1. Since the Christian understanding of existence (*Daseinsverständnis*) claims to be the only true one, it is burdened with the duty of justifying its claim against all rival interpretations of existence.

2. While the rule, formulated in a general manner, appears to apply to all other modes of existence, presumably also the Far Eastern ones, Bultmann recognizes a special duty with regard to the modes which, through the continuity of history, are constituent of our own present, i.e., the Hellenic and Israelite. In particular with regard to the Israelite he insists that only in a critical encounter with the Old Testament shall we gain clarity concerning the interpretation of existence that guides our own historical will and action. The Old Testament cannot be simply

abandoned; for our own historical present, in order to be adequately understood, requires justification before its tribunal.

3. The historical dialogue with the Old Testament is compulsory for the Christian, because the Gospel, by its self-interpretation, is the "end of the Law." If the Christian wants to understand precisely the "end" or "fulfillment" that has come with Christ, he must understand what the "Law" means.

4. Up to this point the argument is historical in the same sense that it requires the Christian to have an adequate knowledge of the Old Testament in order to understand the language of the new body of literature that has grown in its *ambiance*. From here onward, however, the argument seems to take an ontological turn. For Bultmann considers that the pagans understood the message of the Gospel quite as well as the Jews. The "Law," though it has achieved in Israel an optimal clarity of meaning, expresses the generally human experience of existing under the divine "thou shalt." The Gospel, it is true, presupposes the Law. "But the Law that embodies itself in the Old Testament needs by no means to be the Old Testament concretely." The pre-apprehension (*Vorverständnis*) required for understanding the Gospel is given wherever man experiences himself in conscience bound by the general moral demands that grow from his existence in society. If the Christian churches prefer the Old Testament for inducing pre-apprehension, their reasons are primarily pedagogical; the Old Testament deserves preference because the Decalogue and the Prophets present the demands with incomparable power and clarity. (Bultmann, as far as I can see, makes no attempt to reconcile the present argument with the preceding one.)

5. In his essay on "The Problem of Natural Theology,"[1] Bultmann has further clarified the concept of *Vorverständnis* which I have rendered as pre-apprehension. The clarifications contained in this essay must be added to the argument. From the position of theology, Bultmann asserts, unbelief (*Unglaube*) is the funda-

---

[1] "Das Problem der 'natürlichen Theologie,'" *Glauben und Verstehen,* Vol. 1 (1933), pp. 294–312, as yet untranslated.—ED.

mental constitution of human existence. Philosophy interprets this constitution of unbelief as the original freedom in which existence constitutes itself. In the very act of interpreting existence as constituted in freedom, however, philosophy knows the questionableness of freedom; for in knowing about the free resolve to take charge of existence as one's own (*das Dasein übernimmt sich selbst*)[2] it knows the alternative of rejecting the decision and also the possibility of faith, though the possibility will appear as "senseless" to the philosophical position in which "sense" is synonymous with existence in freedom. Nevertheless, in spite of the difference of opinion concerning "sense," Bultmann assumes the understanding of faith from the philosophical position to be identical with the self-understanding of faith. "For faith understands itself as the concrete resolve, the concrete decision in a concrete situation constituted by the word of the Gospel and by fellow man." Hence, inasmuch as philosophy elaborates the pre-Christian understanding of existence, it creates the pre-apprehension of faith—with the reservation, however, that the character of *Vorverständnis* accrues to unbelieving existence in retrospect from the position of faith.

6. Through the clarification of *Vorverständnis* the ontological intention of Bultmann's argument has been established beyond a doubt. "Law" and "philosophy" are co-ordinated as two variant expressions of the generally human pre-apprehension. Moreover, Bultmann accepts the philosophical interpretation of existence (or, as we should say more cautiously, what he considers a philosophical interpretation) as true, endows it with the character of "natural theology," and considers it the task of theology to elaborate the meaning of faith "in constant debate (*Auseinander-*

---

[2] *Das Dasein übernimmt sich selbst* is a stock phrase of Heidegger's existentialism. The English reader should not be deprived of the joy of knowing that the phrase in German has a double meaning not intended by its author. It can be rendered either as "existence takes charge of itself" (the meaning intended) or as "existence overreaches itself" (what, indeed, it does when it takes charge of itself). Needless to say, no philosopher would play with the fire of "taking charge" of his existence.

setzung) with the natural understanding of unbelieving existence."
When the argument is presented in this rigorous form, its
gnostic character becomes visible. Above all, we can recognize
the technique of identification, familiar from Hegel's gnosis, by
which historical phenomena are transformed into states of consciousness. We start from the Law, which in historical concrete-
ness is the Torah. Through identification, not formal but in
substance, the Torah changes into the "thou shalt" that is alive
in everyman's conscience. And the "thou shalt" as pre-apprehension of faith becomes identical with unbelieving existence in freedom as interpreted by the philosopher. The historical relation
between the Law and the Gospel, between the Old and the New
Testament, is thus transformed into the ontological tension between the natural existence of man and the Christian existence in
faith. History in the sense of the *progressus* of mankind in time,
shrouded in the mystery of a meaning incompletely revealed—
the history we have in mind as long as we are not existentialists—
has somehow disappeared. Moreover, with the transformation of
history into ontology the relation between Bultmann's theology
and Heidegger's existentialism comes into better view. For Bultmann's identifications, as they reduce history to existence, make
sense as an enterprise of *fides quaerens intellectum* only under the
assumption, first, that Heidegger's existentialism is philosophy
at all (and not, as I have indicated on another occasion, a type of
gnosis) and, second, that it is the true philosophy of existence. In
Bultmann's work Heidegger has moved into the position that in
Scholasticism was held by the *Philosophus*.

II

The oscillation of things between the status of historical phenomena and of moments (in the Hegelian sense) in a gnostic
speculation is possible only if the fundamental concepts of history, philosophy, and theology are sufficiently indeterminate to
allow for such movement. Indeterminacy of terms as a gnostic
symptom is correlative to the device of identifications. By inde-

terminacy is not meant equivocation of terms. It can be characterized rather as a disturbance of contact with the reality to which the terms refer. The terms are neither developed through adequate analysis from reality nor do they, when used, refer to the reality to which the reader would assume them to refer. This brief characterization must be sufficient for the present purpose. I shall now consider Bultmann's thesis—that the Old Testament is historically but not theologically relevant to Christian faith— under the aspect of its indeterminacy.

For this purpose we shall imagine a reader with a liberal education, a man who is conversant with the Western tradition of philosophy and theology, without being attached to a particular school. Such a man, when reading Bultmann's thesis, will be baffled by the intentions of the author. What fundamental opposition should exist between theological and historical relevance, he will ask himself. Is God's revelation not a revelation to man in society and history? Is the revelation from Sinai and the conclusion of the Covenant not an historical event? Is it not even an event that marks an epoch in history? Does not Bultmann himself speak of a history of revelation to Israel? And should not the history of mankind, in which this epochal revelation to the sector of mankind called Israel occurs, be a theologian's concern? And if these revelations reported in the Old Testament are historically but not theologically relevant, should not the same rule apply to Christ? Is the Incarnation of the Logos not an historical event, again marking an epoch? Will the Christian theologian say that the Incarnation is theologically irrelevant to Christian faith, too? The questions are pertinent, especially the last one.

At this point of his questioning it will be time to furnish the reader with the opening sentences of Bultmann's *Theology of the New Testament*.

The message of Jesus belongs to the preconditions [*Voraussetzungen*] of a theology of the New Testament, but it is not part of it. For the theology of the New Testament consists in the unfolding of the thoughts in which Christian faith assures itself of its object, its ground, and its consequences. Christian faith, however, exists only from the time of a Christian kerygma, i.e., a kerygma that proclaims Jesus Christ as God's eschatological deed of salvation, Jesus Christ as the crucified and resurrected. And such proclamation is given only in the kerygma of the *Urgemeinde,* not in the message of the historical Jesus.[3]

The reader's reaction to this information will be a mixture of relief and new bewilderment. He will be relieved to find Bultmann consistent enough to let the message of Jesus fall under the theological ban just as much as the Old Testament, but he will wonder why only part of the New Testament falls under it. He will then be relieved, again, by the definition of "Christian faith" as the formal object of theology in relation to which everything else falls off to the level of mere history, because he may hope that the definition of theology will bring the answers to his questions. But as soon as he starts pondering the rather restrictive definition it will arouse new misgivings because he can find no reason for it. For Bultmann will accept as the unquestioned starting point of the theologian's work neither a body of dogma nor the *litterae sacrae,* embracing both the Old and the New Testament, but wants to let his object emerge from the New Testament itself by applying historical and philological methods to the literary text. If theology, however, is identical with the critical exposition of a literary source by the methods of historical and philological science, for the purpose of making intelligible the message of Christian faith contained in it, there seems to be no reason why the term theology should apply only to the historian's work on the New Testament (or even only a part of it) and not equally to his work on the Old Testament. As a consequence, the thesis that the Old Testament is theologically irrelevant to Christian faith would mean no more than that Judaism is not Christianity—a proposition which the reader can accept, though he does

---

[3] The author's translation from the German original, now available in English: *Theology of the New Testament,* Vol. 1, Kendrick Grobel, trans. (1951), p. 3.—ED.

not know why this truism should be advanced as a notable discovery. Clearly, however, in distinguishing between historical and theological relevance of the Old Testament Bultmann wants to do more than distinguish between the Israelite-Jewish and Christian modes of existence under God for the sole purpose of more carefully elaborating the specific character of the latter (though that is also one of his purposes). He rather wants to break the continuum of revelation between them: the revelation of the Old Testament has to be an event entirely apart from that of the New Testament. It seems to be impossible, however, to achieve this separation on the level of history and historical method in their conventional sense—for who can deny the continuous stream of history in which early Christianity emerges from its Israelite and Jewish antecedents? How can historical method furnish a reason why the work of the Christian theologian should be confined to the *evangelium de Christo* as its formal object, excluding the *evangelium Christi* and the Old Testament? And how can historical method justify the exclusion of history itself from theological exploration? Against such questions there still stands Bultmann's thesis: Though there are both a "history of Israel" and "our history"—a revelation both to Israel and through Christ, a theology of both Old and New Testaments—there can be no theology of the history of revelation that embraces them.

When the imaginary reader has arrived at this point in his reflections, he will conclude that Bultmann, since he cannot have derived his thesis through the use of historical method, must have introduced a selective principle from elsewhere so as to be able to select certain parts of the canonical text as specifically "Christian" while rejecting others as irrelevant to "Christian faith." And furthermore, though the reader may not be sure whence the principle of selection did come, he may wonder about the implications of its use. For if the "history of Israel" is not "our history," perhaps "our history" is not "Israel's"—and if not Israel's, is it anybody else's? If the reader thinks through the implications of the thesis, he may discover that Bultmann has come very close to the position of Jaspers that Christianity is of interest to Christians only, while the rest of mankind should rather be concerned about the vistas opened to human reason by the "axis time" between 800 and 300 B.C. in which the great philosophers and religious founders appeared in the major civilizations, a Confucius and Laotse, a Buddha and Zoroaster, the prophets of Israel and the philosophers of Hellas.

A piece of work in science is not a solipsistic outburst. It is socially bound to the past of predecessors who have once elaborated the problems now under revision, and to the future of readers who will accept the revision as legitimate and build their own work on the new basis. That is what is called co-operation in science. I have introduced the imaginary reader representing the tradition of problems because he has the duty to ask his questions and the right to have them answered. If the answers are not forthcoming, something is wrong. By means of this device we have established, first, indeterminacy of terms as the nature of the trouble and, second, the restrictive definition of theology as the source of the disturbance.

It would be premature, however, to formulate the implications of the result, for Bultmann raises a further issue that must be clarified. His endeavor to break the theological link between the Old and New Testaments is motivated by his opposition to the methods of allegorical interpretation and scriptural proof which intend to supply the link in question. The point needs careful consideration, because in this concern Bultmann is on solid critical ground. It was Nietzsche who in Aphorism 84 of the *Morgenröthe* scoffed at Christianity as the religion

. . . which during the centuries since its foundation performed that unconscionable philological burlesque around the Old Testament; I mean the attempt to pull the Old Testament from under the body of the Jews with the assertion that it contains nothing but Christian doctrine and belongs to the Christians as the true Israel, while the Jews had only usurped it. One indulged in a frenzy of interpretation and supposition which could not possibly have had a good conscience. However much Jewish scholars protested, everywhere the Old Testament was supposed to speak of Christ and nothing but Christ.

Every historian will share Nietzsche's disgust with the abuses of interpretation as well as with doctored translations, even if he does not follow him in his conclusions. Bultmann shares it, too. He forcefully insists that though the Old Testament can be considered the Word of God at a remove (*in vermittelter Weise*) because it conveys an understanding of the relation between Law and Gospel, it must be so understood only on the condition that its original meaning (in the philological sense) be preserved and allegoresis be renounced. This is no more than a demand of intellectual honesty. Nevertheless, the demand, justified though it is, does not touch the issue itself. For however long the catalogue of hermeneutic abuses be made, it remains a negative demonstration; it cannot prove, as Nietzsche assumes, that the link does not exist. Against the assumption stands the fact that the abuses are not a late development in Christianity but go back in continuity to the scriptural proof and allegorical interpretation used by the New Testament writers themselves, who sensed the link to exist even though they used inadequate instruments for expressing their conviction.

Bultmann is, of course, aware of this problem. He disposes of its several aspects by various methods. A first aspect is the strictly philological one of adequate interpretation. In Bultmann's opinion scriptural proof and allegoresis do not become any better if a New Testament writer uses them; a fanciful scriptural proof does not become true if it is to be found in St. Matthew. Nothing can be said against this part of his position. Under a second aspect he recognizes frankly that the authors—in particular he mentions St. Paul—interpret the Old Testament indeed from their new eschatological consciousness, in which the older Scripture only now reveals its true meaning. This interpretation, in his opinion, is justified as long as it brings to fuller understanding the creatureliness of man under the claims of God. "We, as the men called to believe, find ourselves mirrored in the Old Testament." That is to say that we, as natural men, are mirrored in the Old Testament. Bultmann suppresses the decisive point by switching from the historical to the ontological level; only ontologically, not in any theological respect, does the Old Testament become something like a secondary (*vermittelt*) Word of God. If in regard to the second aspect the ontological evasion could be used in order to suppress the issue, there seems to be no possibility of evasion in regard to the third point, that is, the theology of history explicitly contained in the New Testament, as for instance in Romans 9–11. To be sure, these chapters abound with scriptural proof, so that numerous philological exceptions could be taken; and since their interpretation of the Old Testament is inspired by St. Paul's eschatological consciousness, one still could let them slide into the ontological rubric. Nevertheless, on this occasion the issue itself becomes thematic—no philological method or device of identification can dispose of the hard core of St. Paul's theology of history, that is, his profound concern with the structure of history itself. We must consider the issue briefly.

The revelation of God to man occurs in concrete situations to concrete human beings who receive it representatively for all men. History has a structure inasmuch as it has representative centers of reception from which revelation is communicated to the rest of mankind. This structure of history is a "mystery" in the sense of Romans 11:25. The mysterious structure had occupied even the prophets. As early as the eighth century one can notice the intensified experience of the "Word of Yahweh" as the ordering force of history, with its powerful expression in Isaiah 9:8 ff. In the sixth century, in Deutero-Isaiah, the experience of the "mystery" crystallized in the vision of an exodus of Israel from itself to penetrate with its revelation all mankind. The mystery then assumed a very disconcerting aspect in the time of St. Paul when the revelation through Christ that had come to Israel seemed to penetrate pagan mankind but was not accepted at the center of its reception, among the Jews themselves. St. Paul was so profoundly disconcerted by the extraordinary structure he saw in formation that he was driven to assume a special gift of wisdom, given to the *perfecti*, who by its virtue could penetrate the mystery and reveal the future course of history, and to act as a *perfectus* himself by predicting the future course in Romans 11:25 ff.

Even if we discount the special sorrow of St. Paul, the mystery remains as torturing today as it has ever been in the past. It can be summed up in the three questions, often asked in the age of the Enlightenment and since: (1) Why is there a history of revelation at all? Why is revelation not given to mankind from the beginning? (2) Why does revelation operate by the clumsy method of being given to representative men or communities, to be communicated by them to the rest of mankind? Why is revelation not given to all men equally? (3) Why do the centers of reception become only partially effective? Why do men engage in the resistance from which the structure of historical mankind as we know it results? The answer to these questions would define the meaning of history. But no answer can be given. And when we receive one nevertheless, as in the desperate attempt of Romans 11:25 ff., we must agree with Bultmann's judgment, expressed in his *Theology of the New Testament,* that the answer is no more than a flight of speculative fancy. The mystery must remain intact as the core of every theology, or for that matter philosophy, of history. It must not be downgraded to a problem capable of resolution.

We can resume the question of what Bultmann has to say concerning the Pauline theology of history—for the issue is real, even though we have little use for the apocalyptic fancy in which St. Paul manifests his sorrow on the occasion. The information on the answer will not be surprising to those who are familiar with the existentialist technique of debate: Bultmann has nothing to say on the Pauline theology of history; he does not mention the subject. In an essay on the theological relevance of the Old Testament to Christian faith, the New Testament sources of its central theme are treated as if they did not exist. At the critical point, Bultmann uses the existentialist technique of annihilating reality by excluding it from the universe of discourse.

We can only state the negative result—nothing more can be said about an essay that evades every pertinent question. Nevertheless, we cannot leave the matter as it stands, for though we are not overly interested in the thesis itself (it hardly raises a meaningful issue, since empirically we have no knowledge of a Christianity to which the Old Testament is theologically irrelevant), the motivations of the peculiar construction merit our attention.

III

In 1954 Bultmann published an article on history and eschatology in the New Testament ("Geschichte and Eschatologie im Neuen Testament")[4] in which again the theology of history became thematic. Though the article enters into the substantive problem no more than the earlier one, at least the reasons for the peculiar reticence become visible. I shall first draw the main line of the argument, which concerns the changing conceptions of history.

1. The Greeks understood the historical process as part of cosmic movement which, in spite of all surface changes, reproduces always the same constellations.

2. The Israelites understood history as the field of unlimited dominance of the God who had chosen Israel as his people. It is essentially the history of Israel according to the divine plan; and the future of salvation, even when it is painted in supernatural colors, is always understood as intramundane.

3. In the postexilic Jewish conception the expectation of an intramundane future of salvation is retained, but the new apocalyptic elements of a "Son of Man" as the savior, as well as of the two aeons, enter and combine with a world-historic view of the empires in Daniel. While the older Israelite conception makes the

---

[4] Reprinted in *Glauben und Verstehen*, Vol. 3 (1960), pp. 91 ff. See now *New Testament Studies*, Vol. 1, E. Kraft, trans. (1954), pp. 5–16.

process meaningful through insight into the justice of God which guides history toward its end, the later Jewish apocalypse illumines history through knowledge of the secret counsels of God. In the older view the individual as part of the community is responsible for the destiny of his people; in the later view the individual is responsible only for himself. The community of the nation has been replaced by a community of individuals.

4. In the message of Jesus, then, both conceptions are present, though the apocalyptic view distinctly preponderates.

5. In the early Christian community Bultmann observes a tension between the received Israelite conception and eschatological expectation, a tension which is resolved in the "decisive change" that the "secret of history" shifts from divine guidance of Israel's history to the eschatological events, be they the eschatological drama proper (as in I Cor. 15:51 ff.) or the events of Incarnation, Passion, and Resurrection.

6. The same "decisive change," only more marked, is to be noted in the theology of St. Paul. The older Israelite conception is still present, but "history is swallowed up by eschatology." "St. Paul's understanding of history does not originate in his reflections on the history of Israel, but in his anthropology." The course of history from Adam through the Law to Christ consequently can be cast in the form of the autobiographical "I" in Romans 7:7–25a. Salvation has definitely shifted from fulfillment in the people's history to the individual as a member of mankind. With this shift, however, eschatology has lost its meaning as the end of history; it has become the end of individual human existence. The history of the past is transformed from this new position into the history of the individual who is freed from sin and death to life under grace (Rom. 6:14).

While the history of the people and the world loses in interest, another phenomenon is now discovered: the true historicity of human existence. The decisive history is neither world history, nor the history of Israel or other peoples, but the history experienced by every man himself. To this history the encounter with Christ is the decisive event, in fact it is the event by which individual man begins in reality to exist historically, because he begins to exist eschatologically.[5]

To the believer in Christ the old aeon has indeed reached its end; he lives in the aeon of fulfillment under grace.

7. The further development of a theology of history in this direction was, in Bultmann's opinion, impaired by the nonoccurrence of the expected Second Coming. The generations after Paul did not have the force to live in his eschatological tension; and the time of waiting for the Parousia degenerated into a chronological category. The eschatological consciousness changed into sacramental piety, the Church from a community of the saints to an institution of salvation (*Heilsanstalt*). Eschatology became partly a doctrine concerning the end of the world; partly it was replaced by sacramentalism. The interim period of expectation moved back into world history, because Christianity was viewed as a world phenomenon having a history.

8. The development just adumbrated seems to Bultmann to obscure "the understanding of the history of Jesus as an eschatological event." The true understanding is St. Paul's and more particularly that of the Gospel of St. John with its gnostic strand.

It is characteristic that gnosis abandoned the Old Testament and with it the faith in a God who as Creator is also the Lord of history, as well as traditional eschatology. In St. John and the Johannine epistles the abandonment of traditional eschatology is accompanied by the renunciation of any appeal to the testimony of Old Testament history, though the faith in a Creator God is retained.[6]

9. This seems to Bultmann "the true resolution of the problem: the Now receives eschatological character through the encounter with Christ, because in this encounter the world and history come to their end and the believer as a new creature is *entweltlicht*." Nevertheless, some history seems to be left, for Bultmann insists on the reality of the "paradox" that the eschatological event has

---

[5] *Ibid.*, p. 102.
[6] *Ibid.*, p. 98.

occurred in history and still occurs wherever the message of Christ is preached. This remnant of history, however, is no more than "profane history"; it must not be understood as "history of salvation" (*Heilsgeschichte*). What has ultimately come to light is the dialectics of human as historical existence. "The history of man as a person can no longer be understood as a function of world history, it lies beyond world history." In these formulations Bultmann concentrates his own position.

I am not concerned with the correctness of Bultmann's description of the various conceptions of history in every detail. Only *en passant* be it noted that serious exceptions must be taken to his characterization of the Hellenic and older Israelite views. I am interested rather in the elusive premises which allow him to arrive at the odd thesis about the Old Testament. In the earlier article, with its burden of indeterminacy and identifications, the disturbing factor proved to be the restrictive definition of theology. This crucial issue we shall now examine in the light of the second article just presented.

Disregarding all questions that would arise if the postulates of pre-Reformation theology were taken into consideration, and conceding to Bultmann the widest latitude of a Protestant freedom of inquiry, we still must say that he has radically broken the bond of tradition inasmuch as he does not accept the Bible integrally as the source of truth *in rebus divinis*—as the body of materials to be clarified and ordered by the Christian theologian. Moreover, since his definition of theology, which determines the selection as relevant, or rejection as irrelevant, of certain parts of the Bible, is not developed through analysis from the source itself but imposed from the outside, it cannot for its justification plead the methodological principle that every interpretation of a source must be selective. Since, furthermore, the existentialist conception of man to which Bultmann's definition conforms does not even faintly approach the fullness of the Bible's understanding of man, the definition of "Christian faith" as the formal object of theology inevitably becomes both restrictive and destructive. As far as this procedure affects the autonomous status of theology, the debate must be left to the theologians—but I must note as one of the phenomena of the times that a Christian theologian of stature, succumbing to the *Zeitgeist,* surrenders the autonomy of his science to one of the intellectual eruptions of a diseased age. My own remarks will be confined to the philosophical implications of the surrender.

The definition is destructive because it is grafted on an existentialism which ironically takes its name from the denial of existence to everything but the moment of a man's flight from existence toward an eschatological future. In Bultmann's formulations the denial is manifest in the distinctions between a "decisive" or "true" and a presumably "indecisive" or "untrue" history. "Decisive" or "true" is the history experienced "by every man himself." Historicity becomes in fact a category of exclusively human existence; the encounter with Christ is the event by which man begins to exist historically "in reality," because his existence has become "eschatological." In this encounter "world and history come to their end"; the believer in Christ has been *entweltlicht,* i.e., the world has lost to him the index of reality. And by the same token history has lost its index of reality, a modification which Bultmann indicates by applying to history the title "profane." Since Bultmann, as a Christian theologian, has to force existentialism on the recalcitrant word of the Bible—which has a few things to say about such "indecisive" and "untrue" matters as God and man, the world and society, the history of peoples and of mankind—the formulations are inevitably awkward because the same vocabulary has to be applied to the "true" as to the "untrue" reality. The secularists among the existentialist thinkers are strategically better placed because, in elaborating the problems of "true" historical existence, they can ignore the "untrue" reality; they simply do not talk about God and the world, about the nature of things and man, ethics and history. In a sense, therefore, we have to be grateful to Bultmann for his attempt to square the biblical circle with existentialism, because only in such forced confrontation will the philosophical poverty of existentialism be convincingly demonstrated.

This judgment of philosophical poverty, however, must be qualified. To be sure, it is justified with regard to a movement that uses philosophical vocabulary and pretends to give a philosophy of existence; but one must also recognize that the "philosophy" in existentialism is a façade behind which an entirely different, a nonphilosophical intention is at work. Again, we must be grateful to Bultmann's survey of the conceptions of history for having pointed out the nonphilosophical motivation behind the annihilation of world and history. "It is characteristic that gnosis abandoned the Old Testament," he says rightly; and it is the gnostic element in the Johannine writings that leads to "the renunciation of any appeal to the testimony of Old Testament history." The hatred of world and history, the experience of man as a stranger thrown into the prison of the world, the hope of escape from the untrue to a true reality, the understanding of this situation as the means of escape, the consequent negative characterizations of world and history as a magic opus of destruction— this complex of experiences and actions is indeed gnosis. In the New Testament, of course, the complex is no more than a strand; and not even the Gospel of St. John, as Bultmann points out, will go so far as to declare the God of the Old Testament to be the daemonic Creator of the world prison from which man is to be released by a messenger of the true God. But a strand it is without a doubt; and this strand is virulent enough in Bultmann to follow St. John in his removal of Old Testament history from relevance to Christianity.

Gnostic thought must be treated with circumspection. From the fact that gnosis is not philosophy it does not follow that everything a gnostic thinker has to say is wrong. For at the core of gnostic analysis of existence in our time, or of gnostic speculations of antiquity, there is an immediate experience of man's situation in the world. And while the interpretation of reality based on the experience can go wildly astray if it takes a frag-

mentary truth for the whole truth, the immediate experience itself cannot be wrong. We have indeed experiences of alienation;
of being strangers in a world that is not ours; of a true measure of
existence that is not taken from existence in this world; of a true
reality, not of this world, whence this measure comes to us; of a
longing for that other world, for a new heaven and a new earth;
of a diminution of reality attaching to life in this world, the
Pauline tonality of the "as if not"; in brief, of "eschatological
existence." There is an experience of history being swallowed up
by eschatology, as Bultmann formulates it; and again we have to
be grateful to him for having sketched in his survey the process
in which this experience is differentiated from the more compact experiences in which it was formerly embedded. A new phenomenon "is now discovered: the true historicity of human
existence." To this sentence of Bultmann we must take exception
only as long as it arrogates the monopoly of history to human
existence and relegates the history of mankind, especially the
history of Israel, to a limbo of theological irrelevance. But we
can accept it if it is understood to mean that in the encounter with
Incarnation the individual human existence has come into view
as the point of transcendental irruptions which constitute history.
While in compact experiences of the imperial type the area in
which history is divinely constituted was located in the empire
under its ruler, with individual man participating in history only
through his membership in the empire; while in the Israelite experience of the covenant type the ruler and the empire receded
and society existed in immediacy under the kingship of God; in
the encounter with Incarnation, we may say, history has become
articulated down to individual man, who through his faith participates in the constitution of history. If the meaning be restricted
in this manner, as pertaining to a differentiation of experience,
Bultmann's analysis has admirably clarified one of the most
complicated problems that plagues the philosophy of history.
Moreover, it should be stressed that his reliance on contemporary
existentialism has substantially aided the success of his analysis.

The preceding paragraph opened with a warning against a *non sequitur*. From the fact that an interpretation of reality is wrong it does not follow that the experience at its core does not contain a truth. We must now warn against the inverse *non sequitur*. From the fact that a truth has been differentiated through a new experience it does not follow that everything else known as true in the more compact experience has now become untrue. From the fact that an experience of "eschatological existence" has been differentiated it does not follow that a Christian is an existentialist who believes in Christ. Bultmann says, "The history of man as a person can no longer be understood as a function of world history, it lies beyond world history." This verdict seems to me hardly acceptable, either as a whole or in its parts, because throughout it uses unanalyzed concepts. In a debate with a theologian it will not be inapposite to appeal to the Bible, I hope, and to insist that the subject of history is neither the world nor the individual person but mankind as symbolized through Adam and his descendants. Further excluded from the discussion should be certain terms frequently used by Bultmann, such as *Heilsgeschichte* (the invention of a nineteenth-century theologian) and "profane history" (I have not been able to discover its origin). Let us speak simply of the history of mankind, articulated by concrete societies and the human beings who are members of them. This history is partly structured by such events as the Sinai Covenant and the Incarnation, commonly called revelations; partly by other irruptions of transcendent reality, such as the illumination of a Buddha or the opsis of a Plato; and to the largest extent by the compact experiences of divine reality in archaic and primitive societies which do not yet display a clear differentiation of a *theologia supranaturalis* from the *theologia civilis*, to say nothing of the anti-Christian *theologiae civiles* which dominate the contemporary scene. Among these structuring events the encounter with Incarnation holds the dominant position because it has differentiated the "eschatological existence," as Bultmann calls it, of individual man and has correspondingly, with optimum clarity, established the comprehensive society of mankind as the subject of history. The event has affected history in several respects; more immediately pertaining to the present issue are the following:

1. The epiphany of Christ has occurred in history and is part of its structure.

2. In its wake Christian churches and Christian civilizations have developed which, again, have become part of the structure of history.

3. Our knowledge of history has changed through the aforementioned differentiations of "eschatological existence" and the comprehensive society of mankind as the subject of history.

4. Our sense of history has changed through awareness of the tension between all history transacted on the level of human intentions and the mysterious drama of mankind enacted unknowingly by finite actions.

About the importance of these changes there can be no doubt. Nevertheless, none of them has affected the nature of man. As I have formulated it on another occasion: the leap in being is not a leap out of existence—and when I use the term existence I use it as a philosopher, not as an existentialist. Man still exists under God in the world, within the limits set by his nature, within society and history, with all the obligations and responsibilities such existence entails. Hence, the various formulations of Bultmann suggesting an annihilation of history must be considered fallacious. A partial truth newly differentiated has mistakenly been assumed to exhaust the truth contained in the formerly compact experience of history.

The fallacy inspires the style of Bultmann's survey of conceptions of history. The conceptions follow one another as a series of increasingly true propositions concerning history, culminating in the "true solution" formulated by Bultmann himself. This is, on principle, the method used by Auguste Comte when he lets the symbolic forms of theology, metaphysics, and positive science form a series of increasingly true propositions concerning reality, ignoring the fact that theology and metaphysics deal with areas of reality not covered by science. As a consequence of the fallacious assumption that the newly differentiated sciences of the external world are coextensive in scope with theology and metaphysics, the large sectors of being not accessible to the methods of natural science will be either neglected or even denied the status of reality. In contemporary gnostic movements the Comtean fallacy has become one of the most effective instruments for the purpose of annihilating reality. In the same manner as Comte, Bultmann assumes the reality covered by the differentiated truth of "eschatological existence" to be coextensive with the reality covered by earlier conceptions of history. The differentiated truth becomes the "true resolution" of a problem, the earlier conceptions correspondingly the "untrue resolutions" of the same problem. Under this assumption the earlier conceptions must indeed be considered irrelevant, since they are no more than obsolete and inadequate formulations, now to be superseded by a better understanding of history. In one respect, therefore, Bultmann's philosophy of history is a variant of Comte's; and this factor must be recognized as one of the determinants in Bultmann's thesis of the theological irrelevance of the Old Testament, as well as in his omission of the Pauline theology of history.

The relation to Comte has its general significance as an instance of the variegated roots which Bultmann's position has in the movement of modern gnosis. In addition, however, the application of Comte's method to conceptions of history has a specific importance for both the theologian and philosopher inasmuch as it affects the problem of prefiguration. Earlier in this study, I have declared my sympathy with Nietzsche's and Bultmann's revulsion against the misuse of scriptural proof and allegoresis, but at the same time I cautioned that there is more to the issue than meets the philological eye. For prefiguration, as can now be said with more precision, has its solid basis in the historical process of differentiating experiences and symbols. Christ is indeed prefigured in the Old Testament, especially in Isaiah and Deutero-Isaiah, even though in specific cases zealous interpreters have found more in it than there is to be found. This ebullience of scriptural proof, as well as the controversies in its wake, are caused by the inadequacy of a method which does not distinguish between experience and symbolization. Compact experiences will be expressed by compact symbols; and the full meaning of compact symbols cannot be understood without analysis of the motivating experiences —an analysis which obviously can be conducted only from the historically later position of experiences that have differentiated from the compact complex. The symbols created in the process of differentiation, however, will specifically express only the area of reality newly differentiated. Their creators, absorbed by the importance of their new insight, will rarely shoulder the burden of creating additional symbols for the areas of reality left behind in their passionate search for the specific truth. Hence, when reflection turns to the continuity of the historical process and when, in order to demonstrate the continuity, the later position is confronted with the earlier one on the level of symbols (and that is what scriptural proof does), the peculiar problems of prefiguration will arise. Symbolisms like the Isaianic Prince of Peace or the Deutero-Isaianic Suffering Servant can, according to the interpreter's preference, either be locked up in the history of Israel as an autonomous entity, if the reflection is addressed to their compact surface, or be drawn into the continuous history issuing in Christ and Christianity, if the reflection recognizes behind the compact surface the differentiated area of truth which they also embrace in their compactness. Bultmann's philological method, while deprecating scriptural proof and allegoresis, uses their very technique of relating successive positions in a continuum on the level of symbols, but since he recognizes only the compact surface of the earlier symbols and disregards the tensions of experience pointing to future differentiation, the result is a separation of the history of Israel from that of Christianity. This result, however, should not become an occasion for hasty criticism of Bultmann's method. On the contrary, it is the only result at which one can arrive if philological method is used conscientiously. The drastic result, even if we admit that Bultmann would not have arrived at it unless the gnostic factor in his work had supplied the motive power, should rather make us aware that the historical process in which experiences and symbols differentiate requires more than philological methods for an adequate exploration. Even though a spiritually sensitive reader of the Bible may be satisfied with scriptural proof, it is time that prefiguration should emerge from the twilight of benevolent acceptance into the full light of a science of experience and symbolization.

If we come to an end, it is not of problems barely outlined, but of an inquiry which purports to elucidate Bultmann's thesis. Its motivations proved to be rather complex. At their core we found the reliance on a gnostic existentialism that wills the annihilation of nature and history. Over long stretches, this existentialism could be successfully used as an instrument of interpretation because Christianity, in the encounter with Incarnation, has indeed differentiated "eschatological existence"—a mode of existence which, if taken as the integral existence of man, can blend into genuine gnosticism. Moreover, gnostic tendencies of this type are present in the New Testament, especially in its Johannine parts. Nevertheless, setting aside the personal factor of Bultmann's Christianity, which motivates his theological concern with the New Testament, the very text proved an insurmountable obstacle to a radical derailment into gnosis. For the reality of Scripture is much larger than the reality admitted by existentialism, and since in particular it includes history, Bultmann's gnosticism had to assume intermediate forms. Among them we have especially stressed the indeterminacy of terms with its attendant difficulties —difficulties which the existentialist theologian cannot escape, for his text forces him to deal with the problem of history, while the secular existentialist can easily dispose of them by excluding history from his universe of discourse. In spite of paying the debt of indeterminacy, however, Bultmann could not quite avoid resorting to existentialist technique, when at the crucial point he had to suppress the Pauline theology of history. We then had to dwell on his criticism of scriptural proof and allegoresis, as well as on the support it derives from the critical methods of both philology and Comteanism. This issue is, in my opinion, of primary importance for every philosophy of history, quite independent of Bultmann's existentialist theology. Within the limits of the present study I could no more than suggest it, stressing its implications for the problem of prefiguration. Within the context of Bultmann's articles, however, the positivistic arguments have only supporting rank; the center of motivation is the existentialist will to annihilate history.

What has to be critically said against Bultmann's thesis I have made plain. Against the existentialist will no argument is possible. I can only say that I prefer to be troubled, in the company of St. Paul, by the mystery of history.

5 Everywhere the Scripture Is about Christ Alone[1]

WILHELM VISCHER*

In Christianity "man's relation to God is bound to the person of Jesus."[2] The question arises whether this also holds true for the Old Testament. Only in that case can it be God's revelation for the Christian faith. Bultmann denies this.

The proof of a historical development of Israel's religion leading up to the religion of Jesus cannot be adequate for the Christian faith (pp. 8–13). This is correct. But is Bultmann right when he insists that the approach that inquires into the relation of the New Testament religion to that of the Old is "not relevant for Christian theology" (p. 12)? This would mean that 99 per cent of biblical scholarship, including the greater part of Bultmann's lifework, is irrelevant. This is not altogether impossible. It depends entirely on whether or not that approach points to an

---

* Translated by Thomas Wieser.

[1] "Universa scriptura de solo Christo est ubique." *Luthers Vorlesung über den Römerbrief, 1515/1516,* Johannes Fricker, ed. (1908), at Romans 15:15–16.

[2] R. Bultmann, "The Significance of the Old Testament for the Christian Faith," *supra,* p. 11. [Unless otherwise indicated, quotations are from this essay.—ED.]

90

existing reality. In fact there is a relationship between the Old and the New Testament in terms of the history of religion. Therefore, a theological inquiry must reckon with the history-of-religion approach, lest the fact of this relationship be ignored. We may reject this approach, but its rejection is the very indication of its relevance.

A *"genuinely historical" question* is raised when the Old Testament "is not seen as the document of a bygone time which can be reconstructed from its own pages; but rather (when it) is interpreted in terms of the question of what basic possibility it presents for an understanding of human existence" (p. 13). In this definition "not" must be amended to "not yet" unless it is proposed that the genuine historical question can ignore history. Even an historical approach to Plato, which attempts to learn from him who man is and how he ought to live, does not exclude but includes an attempt to understand him in the context of a history of thought.

Bultmann first discusses the classical attempt of contrasting the Old Testament understanding of human existence with the Christian understanding under the antithesis of *Law* and *Gospel*.

In this case, existence under the Law . . . is understood as the presupposition for existence under grace . . . In so far as the Old Testament is the Law . . . [it] is the presupposition of the New. Not in the sense of a historical [*historisch*] view . . . but rather in the material [*sachlich*] sense that man must stand under the Old Testament if he intends to understand the New [pp. 14 f.].

According to Bultmann, however, the Church can recognize the Law of the Old Testament as the embodiment of the divine demand only after having divested it of its specific Old Testament character. Especially the *cultic and ritual demands* are no longer valid. They

. . . are either bound to a primitive stage of man's social life, economics, government, etc., or to the history of a particular people. By the time of Jesus, in fact by the time of the prophets, these demands had come into conflict with others which are inescapably binding upon man as man. They are obsolete [p. 15].

This is the well-known theory created by the most superficial approach to the history of religion. It has just been labeled by Bultmann as "not relevant for Christian theology." Now a general reference to the "concrete . . . conditions of a particular period" is deemed a sufficient explanation for the fact that the cultic and ritual demands of the Old Testament are "obsolete." Bultmann has failed to notice, first of all, that in the Old Testament these demands are an essential part of the understanding of human existence. For they indicate how sinful man can live before God in spite of his awareness "that he never does and never can satisfy this [God's] demand" (p. 14). Second, according to the New Testament these cultic demands are not "obsolete" because of a cultural development, but because Jesus Christ has fulfilled them once for all through the sacrifice of his life for the sake of all mankind. Third, by pondering these cultic demands the Christian believer realizes what it means to live by God's grace in Jesus Christ.

In contrast to the cultic demands *the truly moral demands of the Old Testament* have "by no means lost their authority," according to Bultmann. Why not? "The moral demands of the prophets, like those of Jesus, which spring out of the human relationship as such and not out of its concrete historical form, are valid as long as there is such a relationship on earth. But for this very reason they are also not specifically Old Testament demands." Man can know "by nature what the Law demands"— what the demands are "arising out of the relation to his fellow man which he must acknowledge in his conscience" (pp. 16 f.). This statement calls for the following critical comments. First, the general or concrete moral demands that arise out of human relationship are by no means the same everywhere. The conscience does not give every man the same advice. Second, the moral demands of the Old Testament do not constitute a uniform law; what is required at one point may contradict a demand issued at another point. In order to do the right thing man must ask what is required of him here and now. Third, according to the Old Testament, the moral demands arise neither "out of human relationship as such" nor "out of its concrete historical form." God gives them. Fourth, God gives them to Israel in such a way that through them he reveals himself as the Lord of all men. Therefore they are valid for everyone in principle, and also in practice whenever God, in dealing with Israel, directly or indirectly confronts mankind with them.

We would have to deny the true significance of the moral demands of the Old Testament if, like Bultmann, we were to lift them out of their proper context; if we should think of the "thou shalt" as springing, not out of the "I AM,"[3] but instead out of the human relationship, they would be obsolete after all.

Bultmann himself realizes this when he maintains that *critical dialogue with the Old Testament,* however useful and necessary it may be for us, is "response to the demand of our own history," but it "is not hearing the Word of God and is not faith" (p. 21). This hold true even in the event that we find the Old and New Testament in agreement in their understanding of human existence (pp. 18–20). In fact, we cannot do justice to the Old Testament understanding of existence by exclusively interpreting it as Law and thereby contrasting it to the New Testament under the antithesis of "Law and Gospel." "Seen from its own point of view, the Old Testament is both: Law and Gospel" (p. 31).

In the Old Testament existence under the Law is already thought of as existence under grace . . . The Law, as such, is a demonstration of the grace of God . . . The people are not constituted as a people by first obeying the Law but, rather, God's grace precedes, so that obedience is always to occur through faith in God's prevenient and electing grace . . . And what is more, . . . God's grace is at the same time understood as the grace of forgiveness. For the unity of Israel's history is found not only in the fact that God continually holds

---

[3] Here the author refers to divine asseverations such as "I AM WHO I AM" (Ex. 3:14) or "I am Yahweh your God . . ." (Ex. 20:2).—ED.

the people under his demand, but above all in the fact that he maintains his unwavering faithfulness, in spite of all the unfaithfulness of the people [pp. 22–23].

Finally, the Old Testament does not lack the thought of *eschatological hope.* "The eschatological hope, as found in the prophetic message, arose out of the radical perception of the sin of the people. . . . If beyond the judgment there unfolds the prospect of a future salvation, then this future is one of pure forgiveness and grace" (p. 27). In spite of the basic agreement between the Old and New Testament in their understanding of human existence, Bultmann adheres to the conviction that the Old Testament is not revelation, that it is not God's Word.

To a certain degree Bultmann seems to admit not only a unity in the understanding of existence but also a unity in faith, when he discusses *hope and fulfillment.* "So far as Israel conceived the idea of God radically . . . the faith of the Old Testament is hope; and the faith of the New Testament stands over against it as the faith which has fulfillment" (p. 28). But Bultmann thereby intends to express a contrast rather than a connection. It would be futile to raise the question with Bultmann whether it is not a misrepresentation of the Old Testament in its original sense if it is placed exclusively under the aspect of hope, just as it is misleading to place it exclusively under the aspect of the Law. Bultmann has not the slightest intention "to support the naïve meaning of promise and fulfillment." Only an "eschatological interpretation" can speak in a legitimate sense of promise and fulfillment. For "fulfillment is not an empirical historical reality but an eschatological reality."

In a later essay, "Promise and Fulfillment" Bultmann elaborates on this theme.[4] He discusses three terms under which the New Testament takes up central concepts of the Old and at the

---

[4] "Weissagung und Erfüllung," published in *ST*, Vol. 2, 1 (1948); Eng. trans. in *Essays Philosophical and Theological*, James C. G. Greig, trans. (1955), pp. 182–208; reprinted in *Essays on Old Testament Hermeneutics* (1963), Claus Westermann, ed., pp. 50–75.

same time interprets them in a new, that is, eschatological way: the idea of God's covenant with a people, the idea of the kingdom of God, and the idea of the people of God. All three prove to be "an impossible basis for a historical development and cannot be transformed into reality within history." "The failure demonstrates the impossibility, but as a failure it is a promise . . . Hence it is clear that *the new covenant is a radically eschatological dimension,* that is, a dimension outside the world, and to belong to it takes its members out of the world."

This same distinction and separation obtains in the present essay under discussion: *"In the Old Testament God's revelation is bound to the history of a particular people"* (p. 29). This is why the Old Testament is no longer revelation for the Christian faith (p. 31). For "if Christ is understood as God's deed of forgiveness and if just this is God's eschatological deed, then by this token the concept of God's grace is radically grasped, that is, forgiveness is not just granted to man in the changing fortunes of the life of the individual or of the people. God's grace is forgiveness pure and simple . . . God's forgiving grace is found in nothing else than in the proclaimed Word which God through Jesus Christ has given to the world" (p. 29). "In this Word the individual is confronted immediately by God" (p. 30). Is this a correct understanding of the distinction? How far-reaching is it? Is it true that, according to the New Testament, *"Jesus is God's demonstration of grace in a manner which is fundamentally different from the demonstrations of divine grace attested in the Old Testament"* (p. 29)? There can be no dispute over the fact that God's revelation is bound to the history of a particular people and that Israelites and Jews believe in God only as participants in this history; likewise, only in the context of this history are they sinners as they do not trust his Word. However, Bultmann does not see, and he does not admit, that *in the Old Testament salvation is grasped through obedience in faith.* Membership in the people and participation in its history are not sufficient. In this history God confronts his people with the demand of faith. Bultmann denies this when he says that "so far as man belongs to this people, he can take comfort in the grace of God" (p. 29). This is true, but only in the context of faith.

What God has done unto the patriarchs, what he has done unto the people when he summoned Moses, led the people out of Egypt, guided them through the wilderness, and brought them into the Holy Land, he has done even now unto each person, since this history is not past history but present, ever reactualized in the present generation of the people [p. 30].

This too is true, but in the sense that thereby the present life of the people is then and there confronted with the demand of faith. Each generation is told: "Hear, O Israel: this day you have become the people of the Lord your God. . . . I have set before you life and death, blessing and curse, therefore choose life, . . . loving the Lord your God, obeying his voice, and cleaving to him . . ." (Deut. 27:9; 30:15–20; see also 29:10–15).

Bultmann's contention that ethnic incorporation and historical participation as such secure salvation reveals an error which the Israelites actually committed time and again. But it is revealed as an error throughout the Old Testament, not only in the message of the prophets but through the whole dialectic of Israel's history. God has chosen Israel and he guides its history in order to demonstrate in this example of concrete human history that the relationship between God and man is one of pure and complete trust. God's covenant rests neither in nature nor in history but entirely in faithfulness and trust. This implies from the outset and at any given moment the possibility that the chosen people may fail this trust and, therefore, come to fall on the faithfulness of God. The Old and New Testament are united in their judgment that the possibility of this failure has become a stern reality.

However, neither the New nor the Old Testament finds the sin of the chosen people in their (erroneous) belief that their trust in, and obedience to, God should be "innerworldly and historical."

It is true that in the new covenant the barrier is broken down between Israel and the other nations. This is an important difference. But it is not absolute, and it does not mean under any circumstances that the Old Testament is no longer revelation for the Church. Bultmann himself does not refer to the removal of the national barrier when he says that in the New Testament revelation is no longer bound to the particular history of a nation. Rather, he refers to the radical eschatological difference. In the New Testament *"the people of God is no longer an empirical historical entity."*[5] The Old Testament shows the failure of the attempt to become the people of God within history. This explains for Bultmann the fact that "in the New Testament, God's deed in Jesus Christ is not understood in the same way [as are the demonstrations of divine grace in the Old Testament]; it is not a historical event that is decisive for the history of Israel (p. 30).

In fact, however, the New Testament asserts that *God's deed in Jesus Christ is not merely one but rather THE decisive event for the history of Israel.* First, Jesus' life from his birth under the rule of Augustus up to his execution under Pontius Pilate is a historical event; more precisely, an event of the history of Israel. The acknowledgment of this fact does not require belief in Jesus as the Christ. But neither does the Christian faith imply the denial of this fact, nor the need for declaring it irrelevant.

Moreover, the New Testament speaks of Jesus by constant reference to the Old Testament in order to indicate that God's deed in Jesus Christ is the judgment (*krisis*) and the truth of the Old Testament, and that only in this context can it be understood and believed as God's eschatological deed.

This is also the meaning of the "proof from Scripture." It is a mistake to believe, as Bultmann does (p. 33), that its purpose is to "prove" what can only be grasped by faith, or to approach and criticize its method of quotation from the point of view of modern literary criticism.[6] For these quotations presuppose the unity of tradition and indicate key words in order to recall a larger context within the Old Testament.

---

[5] *Ibid.*, (Eng. trans.), p. 204. (Westermann, *Essays*, p. 71.)
[6] *Ibid.*, pp. 182 ff.

The historical facts are already ignored by Bultmann when he says:

> To be sure, when we engage in historical reflection, when we enter into a critical dialogue with the historical past out of which we have come, even the history of Israel may say something essential . . . In the same sense, however, it can be said that the Spartans fell at Thermopolae for us and that Socrates drank the hemlock for us. And in this sense Jerusalem is not a holier city for us than Athens or Rome (pp. 31 f.).

We are not discussing here what should be recognized as essential in the past out of which we have come. We are concerned with the historical periods that are essential for the events reported in the New Testament. And here the history of Israel is incomparably more important. Jesus was executed neither in Athens nor in Rome but in Jerusalem.

But this is not all. The Christian faith is not "somehow" related to the history of Jesus in the context of the history of Israel, but to the New and the Old Testament. In them Jesus of Nazareth and the developments originating with him are proclaimed as the final and decisive act of a drama which proceeds in the dialogue between God and his people. This final act has been prepared by everything that is said in the Old Testament. Therefore, we must assert against Bultmann that "every later generation receives the benefit of what Jesus meant to his generation" (p. 30). Even more, the benefit extends to each preceding generation; not "by virtue of historical solidarity" but in the power of God for all who in faith allow themselves to be grasped by it.

The New Testament proclaims the good news that Jesus lives his history and his relationship to God not only for himself but for all who believe in him, by demonstrating that all of Jesus' words, acts, and suffering are related to the Old Testament and represent its fulfillment. He is the Amen, the ground and the truth of everything that is written therein about God's presence. All the men and women who are mentioned there and have something to say, live from his life; they are all guilty of his death; he died and rose again for the forgiveness of their sins. *Therefore* we, too, are permitted and commanded to believe that he died because of us and rose for us; therefore we, too, may live before God as those who died and rose together with him.

Jesus, the end of the Old Testament, is also its goal. According to Bultmann, the death of Jesus represents such an exclusive contradiction of the Old Testament that it can no longer be revelation for the Christian faith. In reality, the whole Old Testament centers around the *end of Israel.* The divine covenant is broken as soon as it is concluded. "You cannot serve the Lord, for he is a holy God." This is the verdict of both Moses and Joshua. "The end has come for my people Israel," is what God proclaims through the prophets.

This end which marks every hour of God's encounter with his people is proclaimed in the Old Testament as the revelation of God's holiness, i.e., of his essential deity (*Gottsein*). And the miracle of his holiness occurs in that through judgment he accomplishes the work of salvation. He achieves the impossible, the communion of sinners with the Holy One. His grace, through which his own people come to fall, heals them at the same time.

This is God's eschatological deed in Jesus Christ. In him God encounters the men of the Old Testament. They sin against him, and out of God's forgiveness in him they all live. Their rebellion against God puts him to death. Yet it is for his resurrection that they hope as they nevertheless put their trust in God.

For this reason *the New Testament directs believers continually to the Old Testament.* There they find manifold examples of what it means in Jesus Christ to be loved by God and to love him, to become guilty before him, to be judged and yet to be sustained by him. In this sense, we ought to stay close to the Old Testament, as Bultmann correctly maintains, "in order that we may obtain understanding for our situation and for the Word of Christ which is spoken into this situation" (p. 34). Are we thereby taking a risk, as Bultmann thinks, when he says, "Faith seizes the Old Testament and . . . , dares to direct to us the words of the Old

Testament which once were not spoken for us" (p. 34)? St. Paul tells us differently, "These things (which are told in the Old Testament) happened to them as a warning, but they were written down for us (*pros nouthesian*) upon whom the end of the ages has come" (I. Cor. 10:1–13). Thus we are not to see in the Old Testament the reflection of our life but to find examples for the situation of faith.

Such examples from the early period of the people of God would have no meaning for Christians if Bultmann were right in his view that "the new people of God has no real history, for it is the community of the end-time. The consciousness of being the eschatological community is at the same time the consciousness of being taken out of the still existing world."[7]

St. Paul and the rest of the New Testament agree with the Old Testament that the people of God live in time and in the existing world with its tasks and its temptations. And the life of this people, lived under the Word of God, is from beginning to end a continuous history; it constitutes one single whole. Each generation participates in the whole in its own unprecedented and unrepeatable way. The Epistle to the Hebrews compares this to a relay race. This comparison also shows how much the responsibility increases with the last runners who are taking up the race close to the goal. The beginner and perfecter of the whole race of faith is Jesus who guarantees the victory. His course on earth was witnessed by his contemporaries in Galilee and Jerusalem, and he is present with each group and with every individual, wherever and whenever it is their turn. Jesus Christ, the same yesterday and today and forever.

The encounter with Jesus Christ is truly the encounter with the eternal God. For this same reason, it is truly an encounter in time. Neither in the Old Testament nor in the New does God meet men at a point beyond their historical existence. Today he meets us in our situation. Therefore we must not "apply" anything in

---

[7] Bultmann, *History and Eschatology* (1957), p. 36.

the Old Testament by abstracting it from its original relation to the biblical history. Otherwise we would allegorize, that is, we would have it say something other than what it intends to say (p. 33). We are to listen to what God told men at that time, and to their more or less adequate response. With this in mind, we must try to meet the demand of faith in our situation.

The dialogue with the Bible is a continuous acceptance and rejection in the obedience of faith. Therefore, we are not to decide in advance what for us now can or cannot be God's Word, perhaps by selecting what is "authentic," or by adopting it "only in so far as it is actually promise." For God's Word does not only promise; it also commands, it warns, it admonishes, it punishes, it comforts, it forgives. It allows us to know the truth but also to perceive the lie.

If one were to grant the two "inviolable conditions" stated by Bultmann at the end (pp. 34 f.), then the Church indeed would "find again what is already known" (p. 32)—but not from the revelation in Jesus Christ, whom she cannot know apart from the Old Testament. Rather, in this case she would find what every man can say to himself, not what only God can tell us time and again.

6 The Significance of the Old Testament for Christian Faith in Roman Catholicism

JOHN L. McKENZIE, S.J.

Catholic scholars of the last generation have more and more clearly perceived that the significance of the Old Testament for Christian faith is the fundamental problem of biblical interpretation and theology. Catholic interpreters have always affirmed the unity of the Bible; and we know that a naïve affirmation of the unity of the Bible is not enough. Contemporary efforts to give content and clarity to the affirmation go back to the years immediately following World War II. The men chiefly responsible for this work have resolutely attempted to recapture the concept of biblical unity which they find in the New Testament and in the Fathers of the Church.

A return to the past, in this as in other areas of human activity, has proved to be neither as easy nor as profitable as many expected. The more we have studied the New Testament use of the Old Testament and the interpretation of the Fathers, the more it becomes evident that one must be a member of these ancient cultures in order to think like ancients. A modern interpreter can explain Paul's allegory of the two wives of Abraham, but he can scarcely construct such an allegory in his own name. Must he, therefore, feel that he is rejecting the New Testament interpretation of the Old Testament? To this writer, at least, no rejection of the New Testament is implicit in my own inability to think about the Old Testament in allegories. Without making any value judgments, the modern writer is antecedently bound to the patterns of thought of his own culture; they need be neither better nor worse, but they are different.

One must perceive the difference, but it does not solve the question. Can we even speak of an agreement in principle between the New Testament authors or the Fathers and the modern interpreter? Community of purpose does not mean much; certainly all students of the Bible intend to ascertain its meaning. But unless there is some basic unity of understanding between the New Testament interpretation and our own, unless there are some common principles of interpretation which we share, however widely we differ in methods and techniques, it would seem pure equivocation to say that modern interpretation is an organic development of the interpretation of the early Church. Recent writers, therefore, have attempted to isolate these common principles. Two schools deserve mention: one has pursued the principles of spiritual interpretation, the other has proposed the principle of the fuller meaning (*sensus plenior*). It is impossible to summarize either of these schools briefly, as I do here, without distortion, especially since I am not sympathetic to either school. One who wishes to see these movements in their true dimensions should study them in the writings of those who defend them.[1]

Spiritual interpretation is a modern return to the exegetical

---

[1] The literature on spiritual exegesis and on the fuller sense is too extensive to be listed here. The best summary of the principles of spiritual exegesis has been proposed by Henri de Lubac in *Histoire et Esprit* (1950). On the fuller sense, one may most usefully consult Joseph Coppens, *Les harmonies des deux Testaments* (1950); Raymond E. Brown, *The Sensus Plenior of Sacred Scripture* (1955); Pierre Benoit, "La plenitude de sens des livres saints," *RB*, Vol. 67 (1960), pp. 161–96, summarized in *TD*, Vol. 9 (1961), pp. 3–8.

principles of Origen. It is a Christological interpretation of the Old Testament, using *Christological* in the broad sense to designate the Christian mystery. Spiritual interpretation presupposes that the Old Testament always has a spiritual meaning, that is, a reference to the Christian mystery. The defenders of spiritual interpretation believe that the Old Testament is meaningful for Christians only if this mysterious meaning is made explicit. How is the spiritual meaning ascertained? Critics of the theory find it weak at this point. They can see no methods and principles which secure spiritual interpretation against fancy. The proponents of the theory affirm that sound spiritual interpretation must take its departure from literal, critical, and historical interpretation; but they do not believe that scientific exegesis can discover the spiritual meaning. They are confident that the knowledge of the Bible as a whole, enlightened by the habit of faith, is a sure guide which includes its own restraints. And they appear to suggest at times that the habit of scientific exegesis may be an obstacle to spiritual understanding. It must be conceded to them that the history of Catholic exegesis for the last fifty to sixty years has offered little encouragement to anyone who sought an interpretation of the Bible which was in any sense of the word spiritual. In all fairness to the defenders of the spiritual sense, the spiritual bankruptcy of scientific interpretation must be noted as a fact which can be neither explained nor defended. The impatience with mere historical and critical interpretation has been felt by Protestants as well as by Catholics.[2] One can scarcely blame those who doubted that a truly spiritual interpretation of the Bible would come from more and more historical and critical interpretation. It is too much like throwing good money after bad.

The theory of the fuller meaning of Scripture has been recently and persuasively defended by Pierre Benoit. Benoit distinguishes

---

[2] For a summary of modern developments in Old Testament criticism and a discussion of the various decrees issued by the Pontifical Biblical Commission, see Joseph Coppens, *The Old Testament and the Critics* (1942). See also Jean Levie, *The Bible: Word of God in Words of Men* (1961).—ED.

the literal meaning, the meaning of the words of the Bible, from the spiritual meaning, the meaning of things. The spiritual meaning he defines more precisely as the typical meaning: the meaning God gave to those persons, things, or events which prepared or announced the divine economy of the New Testament. These meanings, Benoit believes, are not complete and adequate in themselves; in addition there is a fuller meaning which comes from the fact that the written book is distinct from the internal thought of the writer and is capable of an increment which transcends his conscious intent. The book takes its place among a collection of books which add a vast landscape of foreshadowings and prolongations to the original scope of the book. The fuller meaning arises from the continuity of religious significance between events. The fuller meaning is the enrichment of objective meaning which the words of the Old Testament receive when they are used again in the New Testament.

Benoit calls this the theological meaning of the Old Testament; and I wonder whether he has described anything other than the theological meaning. If the theological meaning of the Old Testament can be defined clearly, perhaps we shall have the answer to the question posed by the topic of this symposium. Let us dismiss once and for all several ideas which the word *theological* may imply. I do not mean by the theological meaning of the Bible the use of biblical texts as proof texts. With most contemporary exegetes, I believe that this antiquated use of the Bible should be abandoned in theology. With Benoit, I do not have in mind a typological or allegorical exposition of the text. What I have in mind seems very close to what Benoit calls the fuller meaning. I differ from him in believing that the fuller meaning is the meaning of "things"—which must include persons, events, and ideas—and not the meaning of words.

Rudolf Bultmann has exhibited his genius for locating the problem precisely where it lies. The significance of the Old Testament for Christian faith is determined by what one's Christian faith is. The existentialist faith of Bultmann is not the faith of Roman Catholicism; and his own exposition of the significance of the Old Testament, consequently, is not the exposition which a Roman Catholic would present, even if the Roman Catholic were existentialist in his thinking. "Faith in Jesus Christ" is altogether too vague a definition of Christian faith to be meaningful. I do not wish to minimize the degree of community of faith among the many Christian denominations. Polemic has often obscured the fact that the community of the separate churches in their Bible and in the Christian traditions which they have maintained is greater than the differences that divide them. Scarcely any church which thinks it is Christian denies that Jesus Christ is the fulfillment of the Old Testament. Whatever "fulfillment" is taken to mean, it does not appear to be an idea about which a specifically Roman Catholic Christian faith in Jesus Christ differs deeply from the faith of the Protestant churches. It seems to me that the theories of spiritual interpretation and of the fuller meaning which I have outlined above would be accepted or rejected by Protestants on methodological rather than theological grounds; and it is for the same reasons that Catholic scholars accept or reject them.

The Catholic Church has never defined her own belief that Jesus Christ is the fulfillment or the fullness of the Old Testament. She has left the exposition of this belief to her scholars. We have arrived at a point where it is now possible to see why the belief has never admitted definition. The incorporation of the Old Testament into Christian belief has always been contingent upon the spiritual needs and the intellectual resources of the time. Theories which were satisfactory in their time, in the sense that they answered the most urgent questions, failed to answer questions which arose from further development of culture and of biblical and theological study. For this reason, it is impossible for me to set forth here a Roman Catholic answer to the question of this symposium; and it is impossible at the present time even to present an answer which would express the consensus of contemporary scholarship. Anyone who faces this question now must answer it by a personal synthesis which, if he is prudent, he recognizes as provisional.

The theories of spiritual interpretation and fuller meaning are both intended to make the Old Testament more meaningful through the perception of its relation to Jesus Christ, its fullness. Attention may also be drawn to another emphasis: the Old Testament makes Jesus Christ more intelligible. Failure to attend to this emphasis is a serious defect in Bultmann's treatment. There is no question that Jesus Christ belongs to the world, and that his message is addressed to all men. Nor can anyone deny entirely the existential reality of Jesus Christ, who comes as Savior to each generation and to each individual and poses a question to which each must give an answer. Christians who hide behind the answer which has already been given by the Church are in danger of becoming merely conventional Christians. Bultmann's insistence upon the personal encounter and the personal commitment is an element of primitive New Testament Christianity worthy of all the emphasis we can give it. Bultmann fails, I think, when he divorces Jesus Christ, or seems to, from the concrete historical reality with which he is identified. This is to dehistoricize rather than to demythologize the New Testament.

Does not Bultmann, like all who find it difficult or impossible to make the Old Testament significant for Christian faith, propose a faith which is exactly that which Bultmann wishes to avoid? What issues is a Christ who is an abstraction and an ideal, a philosopher and a teacher; it is faith in a doctrine rather than in a person. Is this doctrine really the doctrine of the New Testament? Is it not rather a construction which is thought to respond to contemporary needs better than the historical person of Jesus Christ, who is thought to be too deeply rooted in space and time and too deeply enmeshed in a historical culture which we cannot make our own? And if it is such a construction, no matter how much it draws upon the New Testament for its material, is it more properly Christian than anything else?

The historical Jesus Christ, born of a woman and made under

the Law, was a Jew who spoke only to Jews; the group which became his *ekklesia* were Jews. There is here at least a cultural and
theological background which cannot be ignored. No Christian,
least of all a Roman Catholic, denies that this originally Jewish
community had the vitality to transform itself into a world religion. Are Christians equally certain that the transformation was
effected without loss of identity and continuity? Identity and
continuity go deeper than patterns of language and thought. The
language and the basic religious ideology presupposed in the
New Testament are the language and ideology of the Old Testament and Judaism. The Church learned to speak Greek and Latin
and ultimately all the languages of the world; but there are dangers in translation. The New Testament presents Jesus as the
fullness of Israel. I shall not distinguish here between Jesus himself and the primitive Church which preached him, because I
know Jesus at all only through the preaching of the primitive
Church. If this Church was unable to present him in his true
reality, then I cannot speak of a Christian faith at all. But it follows from the conception of Jesus as the fullness of Israel that
one does not know Jesus Christ very well if one does not know
Israel.

One might dispute, if one wished to be precise to the extreme,
whether Jesus was the Messiah of Israel. All the evidence indicates that he himself was at least extremely reserved in his own
use of the term; and the Messianism of the Old Testament is so
transformed in the New Testament that Jesus can hardly be said
to correspond exactly to any messianic conception of the Old
Testament. But the evidence is also convincing that Jesus and the
primitive Church believed that Israel would have no other Messiah, no other fulfillment. In his coming Israel had its final and
decisive encounter with God. The conviction of the New Testament is that the history of Israel, which is the history of its encounter with God, should have brought Israel to the point of
recognition. By implication, it is suggested that this same history
should bring anyone to the point of recognition. It is the history

of Israel that isolates Jesus Christ from any figures in the ancient and modern world who might wear enough of his features to confuse those who seek vaguely what he brings. It is the history of Israel that sets Jesus apart from all culture heroes, king-saviors, cosmic men, and mythological bearers of life; or, in more modern terms, from political saviors, economic prophets, scientific sages, military heroes, psychotherapist bearers of life. It is remarkable, it is even sharply surprising, when one reflects that only as the Savior of Israel can Jesus be recognized as none of these other things. If this be mythology, make the most of it!

One may conceive that the apostles of the primitive Church preached Jesus as the Savior of Israel even to the Gentiles, quoting the Old Testament to show the meaning of his person and mission, only because as simple and uneducated Jews they knew no other resources upon which they could draw. If one conceives them so, he should reflect that he may be too patronizing towards a group of men who initiated the most powerful movement in recorded human history; and he should be assured that whatever these men were, they were not simple. The story of Paul at Athens (Acts 17:16–34) may illustrate the adventure of one of these men in presenting a non-Jewish Christ to a more sophisticated audience, an adventure which he recognized as a failure. I suggest that they preached Jesus in this way because Jesus is the answer to questions and the solution of problems which are perceived only in the Old Testament. Men do not seek a savior until they feel the need of a savior. The apostles seem to have enjoyed greatest success among the poor and the slaves, to whom they promised neither wealth nor manumission; and it is a vast and classic distortion of Christianity to sum up their message as the opium of the poor or as a promise of pie in the sky. One need not read much of the New Testament to see that it makes demands as much as it promises, demands which historic Christianity has not yet succeeded in meeting fully. What could Christianity offer which made it possible to impose these demands?

Christianity offered the salvation which is described and

promised in the Old Testament, and which is not described and promised in any other religion or philosophy of the ancient world. To grasp the full meaning of this salvation, one must consider both its terms: from what man is saved, and for what man is saved. Briefly, man is saved from sin for life with God in Christ. Here we can refer again to a formula of Bultmann: the Old Testament shows the meaning of human existence. It is unfortunate that Bultmann did not tell us clearly what he thinks the meaning is as shown in the Old Testament. Since he did not, I shall venture to use a common phrase and say that the Old Testament shows man under judgment, and under judgment for his sins. The New Testament affirms this, of course, but it affirms it in Old Testament language and with Old Testament presuppositions. At the base of biblical religion is a conviction of the reality and the malice of sin and of man's powerlessness to redeem himself from sin. Where Bultmann fails, I think, to present the biblical message adequately is in his emphasis on forgiveness. The salvation which Jesus brings is more than forgiveness from sin; it is power over sin, victory over sin. It communicates to men a new life which is not merely a life of grace in the sense that man becomes a child of God in spite of his guilt; but he is enabled to live in a manner fitting to the sons of God by the vitality of the grace which he receives through the Son of God. Baptism is death to self and sin; it is also a resurrection to a new life. But the promises are meaningless without a recognition of the radical defect in man, the only defect from which Jesus redeems him.

This, I observe, must be learned from the Old Testament; or at least it is not learned well and existentially except through the Old Testament. Because the Church has always incorporated this in her teaching, Christians have always been aware of it; but this is an awareness which can fluctuate from greater to lesser intensity. Historical generalizations are always dangerous and often false; but does not the history of Christianity show a curve of rising and falling interest in the old Testament which corresponds to world crises? And is not a *krisis* a judgment? The more we become aware of our guilt, the more we turn to those books which have revealed man's guilt to himself.

The revelation of man's guilt, I think, can be adduced as an element of the Old Testament which makes it the Word of God even for modern man, as Bultmann puts it. In Roman Catholic belief it is the Word of God because it is uttered by God. But placing the discussion for the moment on the existentialist background of Bultmann's thinking, the Word of God in the Old Testament which demands a response and initiates a dialogue is not the revelation of law nor the moral imperative of the prophets; it is the revelation to man of just how wicked he is. It is biblical belief that man cannot recognize the depth of his wickedness unless God reveals it to him. God has revealed it in the history of his encounter with Israel.

I choose to call it the history of Israel rather than the revelation or the doctrine of Israel. If one begins to think of the Old Testament as a doctrine, one inevitably finds much of the Old Testament which is practically irrelevant in the sense that it is never read. Rarely one meets a man with the courage and the candor of Bultmann who tells us that what we treat as practically irrelevant is theoretically irrelevant and should be so designated. But one does not select *summa capita* from history; history is life in the concrete, in its existential reality, and no detail fails to enlarge and deepen understanding. The whole Old Testament is relevant to Christian belief only as a story. In the story, not all incidents and characters and documents are equally relevant; but no single incident or character or document is irrelevant. In the story of Israel, God has revealed his encounter with sinful man, in which both he and man are recognized in their true reality; and by revealing it in a story, it is presented with a reality and an urgency which philosophy fails to achieve.

The revelation of man's guilt would be the utmost of gloom and despair, beside which the *Angst* of the existentialist would pale into an annoying cheerfulness, were it not at the same time a revelation of the power and will of God to save. Here also we deal with a living person and not with a doctrine. Man must be convinced that he cannot save himself; he must also be convinced that God can and will save him. Yahweh of the Old Testament is a saving God and besides him there is no other. The personal reality of God breaks through in the Old Testament with convincing immediacy. Jesus could speak of him as the Father with no further comment; Jews should be able to recognize the Father of whom he spoke, and Greeks could not unless they learned the name of the God whom he called his Father. This is the decisive encounter, the moment when God has revealed himself to the point where further revelation is neither necessary nor possible. When the word which God speaks has become incarnate, God has spoken his last word, and the revelation has reached a point of no return. Man has met God, and a decision is imperative, a decision which is total.

I have chosen to emphasize the Old Testament as a means of understanding Jesus Christ because I have seen this emphasis less frequently stated, and because I believe it is an important part of the significance of the Old Testament for Christian faith. I wish to emphasize further that in this emphasis the Old Testament retains its specifically Old Testament character and all its elements. The historian often comes to think that the only reality is historical; he suspects abstractions and generalizations to the point where he appears to his friends to be a positivist. Here the historian will say that God has never encountered "man"; he has encountered men, and he has revealed himself in the historical experience of men in space and time. We can know him only by what he has said and by what he has done, and no generalizations about him can carry conviction unless they are solidly founded in the particular data of *Heilsgeschichte*. In the Christian scale of values, it seems that Jesus Christ is to be understood through the Old Testament; if he is conceived as the key to the understanding of the Old Testament, sooner or later one begins to ask why we should have to understand it at all.

Speaking specifically as a Roman Catholic, I ought to call attention to one Old Testament idea which receives particular emphasis in the Catholic Church. Contemporary Catholic theology has successfully presented the idea of the Church as the Body of Christ. The Catholic laity has received the idea with joy; it has given them an insight into the nature of their Christian community. They cherish the idea even more when they learn the roots of the Pauline idea in the corporate personality of the Old Testament which H. Wheeler Robinson expounded in a now classic essay.[3] The precise metaphor of the body, to be sure, does not appear in the Old Testament; but the idea of the person who incorporates in himself the group which he heads, who illustrates in his person and in his life the ideals which the group professes, and from whom the group derives its life and its distinct identity —this is an Old Testament idea; and the Church recognizes in herself the fulfillment of the Old Testament conception of society.

I do not intend to imply that the fullness of the Word of God, who is Jesus Christ, does not illuminate the Old Testament; I said that one cannot know Jesus Christ fully unless one knows historical Israel, and it is a Christian belief that one cannot know historical Israel fully unless one knows Jesus Christ. It is not really a matter of two distinct realities illuminating each other, but rather of a single reality known entirely. It is, as I have said, first and foremost a story. The historian can neither rewrite the history nor regret that it happened the way it did; he can only study and understand. The Old Testament is complex and confusing. It contains the sublime and the trivial; it can be poetic and creative and it can be dull and pedestrian; it is the Word of God written by men. And it is all these things because life is all these things. One who selects the sublime and the creative may be studying something, but he is not studying human existence. The reader of the Old Testament, when he is baffled by its inconsistencies, remembers that Ezekiel said, speaking for Yahweh, that

---

[3] "The Hebrew Conception of Corporate Personality," *Werden und Wesen des Alten Testaments, BZAW*, Vol. 4 (1935), pp. 49–62.

it is not my ways that are crooked, but your ways. When the Christian meets elements of the Old Testament which seem to lack significance, should he not ask himself whether the significance has escaped him? And if it has escaped him, is it perhaps because he has not grasped the totality of Old and New Testament, and sees details as insignificant because he does not put them in broad perspective?

And so to return whence I began, the exposition of the significance of the fuller meaning of the Old Testament is theological; by which I mean that it accepts the unity of the process of salvation and of its themes and strives to make each of them meaningful as a part of the process. What seems irrelevant may be an insight into human malice or ignorance which one would not otherwise gain. What seems petty may be an insight into the truth that while man is often petty, nothing he does is really petty, for it makes him and his society to be one thing rather than another. If the Christian can and ought to identify himself with the fullness of Israel, which is Jesus living in the Church, he also ought to identify himself with Israel under judgment; for the Christian is redeemed in principle rather than in achievement. If he does not recognize himself in historical Israel, he is living a life of remarkable self-deception.

It seems to be agreed in Christian interpretation that we have not yet written a biblical theology. Perhaps we never shall, and certainly we shall never write the definitive work. This is no reason to abandon the attempt. If we do abandon it, our scholarship will be barren for the Church, and the unlearned and unstable will rush in to fill the void which scholarship leaves in Christian life and thought. The interpreter must be happy if he does what he can, and what he can do is to let the Old Testament speak to his contemporaries and forget about literary immortality. But before he can let the Old Testament speak, he must have listened to it, every word of it.

7 The Connection of Primal Events and End Events with the New Testament Redemptive History

OSCAR CULLMANN*

Redemptive history (*Heilsgeschichte*) is not a history alongside history, nor is it simply identical with history. Rather in its center part redemptive history depends on a *selection* of particular events out of profane history which stand in a specific connection with one another. This understanding cannot be deduced by reflecting upon profane history from within and consequently it has nothing to do with a philosophy of history. According to biblical faith it was God who made this selection, established this connection, and imparted it to the bearers of revelation, the prophets and apostles.[1]

---

* Translated by Louis Martyn.

[1] In order more easily to attack me, my critics credit me with various and sundry conceptions of redemptive history which I have never held. In a forthcoming publication I shall present my understanding of redemptive history in a way which I hope cannot be misunderstood. It is to be hoped that this attempt will also clarify the goal which I pursued in my book *Christ and Time,* and which so many people completely misunderstood by thinking I intended to write a book about the "concept" of linear time. Actually I proceeded on the basis of the opposition between linear and cyclical time-concepts only because

Already in the Old Testament this redemptive history is connected with a primal history (*Urgeschichte*) and an end history (*Endgeschichte*) which contain mythological materials. The same is true for the redemptive history proper as presupposed in the New Testament. The extensive center part, however, while it makes use of mythological elements here and there, rests as a whole on the selection of particular historical events referred to above. Not so the primal and end histories. They recount events transpiring beyond historical time, events which cannot be controlled historically, and which therefore belong in the province of myth.

These observations already lead us to a question. What we have here is a vista beginning with Creation events that are mythological rather than historical, and ending with events that transpire for the most part in a cosmic framework and can scarcely be called historical in view of the simple fact that they belong to the future. Are we justified in using the expression "redemptive history" in connection with such a phenomenon? Are not the principles by which one interprets myth basically different from those applied in the interpretation of any history, including the redemptive history which we have characterized above?

Especially the Creation narratives belong for the most part to a complex of myths which can also be traced in the broad stream of extrabiblical religions, and can be interpreted according to the general principles which apply to the investigation of myths. Frequently they present cosmogonies detached from all history.

---

this opposition makes clear what I have always regarded as most important: to show that two ways of dividing time intersect on Christian ground, both of which are valid. The first is the Jewish, according to which the division between this age and the coming one lies in the future; the other is the new, Christian way, according to which the division has already been reached in the center of time, defined by Jesus' life, death, and resurrection. Anyone who read my book carefully to its conclusion could see that, on the basis of this intersection, "linear" time received a quite unique character and cannot be so simply presented as some of my critics have done. I have taken pains to show that now all periods of the redemptive history are oriented to the new center which is Christ. From this arises a complex relationship which, for want of a better expression, I designate by the word "tension."

Indeed for the most part one must consider them as representations of human conditions rather than of actual events, and not even of events outside historical time. It is merely incidental to the naïve picture language of myth that what is communicated is given the character of events. Thus the "demythologization" of true myths would consist in divesting them of this event-character and, as is often said nowadays in the terminology of existentialist philosophy, reducing them to the self-understanding of existence which they naïvely express.

The Bultmann school extends "demythologization" to redemptive history in the proper and narrower sense, and thus does not restrict this method of interpretation to the primal and end myths connected therewith in the New Testament. Such a procedure correctly points, in any case, to the fact that in the Bible the primal and end myths are inextricably linked together with the center part of redemptive history, so as to constitute a unity. But one must ask whether it is justifiable for an interpretation which applies to what is properly mythological to be made the uniform hermeneutical principle for the whole of redemptive history. In the limited space of this article, we cannot enter into all aspects of this question. It must suffice to point out that, according to my understanding, the sequence which comprises the center part of redemptive history in the eyes of the New Testament authors is composed of ontic events, and for them this is so essential that its event-character cannot be eliminated as in the case of myths.

The particular question we are raising here, however, is whether within the *biblical view* the emphasis upon the sequence of events also has to be retained with regard to the *myths* which now are incorporated into the whole of redemptive history. If that should be the case, the way is opened up for a uniform interpretation of the primal and end histories and of the redemptive history which constitutes the center part of the whole; and this way is precisely the opposite of the one employed by the Bultmann school. Is it not apparent that the incorporation of these myths into a redemptive history has so altered their mythological character that a new interpretation is required?

In order to answer this question, we must first grasp what it means that the New Testament has taken what it regards as the center of all salvation and has put it together with these myths. The center of all salvation is an event which was selected by God from among other events as *the* decisive redemptive occurrence: the life, death, and resurrection of Christ. In a later publication I shall show that this event was not understood as punctiliar, in the existential meaning of that term (*punktuell*); rather it is established as redemptive history, in the immediate context with other occurrences chosen from the whole stream of events. Events in the history of Israel constitute the earlier part of this context, while the later part is made up of events in the history of the apostles, together with occurrences having to do with both the Church and the destiny of Israel. Thus the center part of the redemptive history consists of a fixed cluster of historical occurrences grouped around the life and death of Jesus.[2]

The primal and end occurrences, on the other hand, use mythological materials[3] and are made up of events which are not historically controllable. The problem emerges in that these primal and end occurrences are connected to the extensive center part of the redemptive history. This integration is found already in the redemptive histories of the Old Testament and of late Judaism, which were taken over by the first Christians. The significant thing is that, once this integration is made, the myths stand on a level with the historical occurrences of the center part, and ex-

---

[2] It is currently assumed by some that this view of redemptive *history* (*Heilsgeschichte*) originated in opposition to an existential, punctiliar conception of the redemptive *occurrence* (*Heilsgeschehen*). In a later publication I shall show that this *heilsgeschichtliche* view was progressively elaborated in the New Testament but did not originate in opposition to a punctiliar conception. Indeed, I shall show that it is present precisely in the document which is said to demonstrate the opposite of Luke's redemptive history view, namely, the Fourth Gospel.

[3] As I have already mentioned, this is true also of certain elements of the center part.

tend the center part, with which they remain in closest contact, in both directions—toward the beginning and toward the end.

But for the myths to function in this way they must be *historicized*. Consequently, the proper *demythologization* of the primal and end histories was anticipated already by the first Christians (and before them by the Jews), not by asking for the existential meaning, but by *lengthening* in both directions that history which rests upon a selection of specific events, namely, the history which we are calling redemptive history.

The *decisive*, divine act of redemption is the earthly work of Jesus of Nazareth, a fixed occurrence in time. Therefore the redemptive sequence which proceeds from this *unique act* must be established in such a way as to show that all other divine acts of redemption both depend on this decisive event and point to it. That means, however, that beyond the historically controllable events there are others which, though historically uncontrollable, were revealed by God to prophets and apostles and, as events, are to be connected with the historical center part. This connection is so made, however, that here, in contradistinction to all gnostic cosmogonies, the point of departure is the center part of the redemptive history, rather than a speculation which takes its starting point from the primal and end occurrences.

This is sufficient to show that here the myths are divested of their mythical character by being historicized. It is not the myth that lends to the historical center part its significance as redemptive occurrence. Just the opposite. It is the revelation of what is meant by the selection and interconnection of the center part's historical events that lends to the primal and end occurrences a new significance, namely, as redemptive history. We have noted above that in early Christian thought all redemptive events are seen in the light of their culmination in the earthly work of Jesus of Nazareth. Since this is so, every redemptive event is a Christ event. In the Old Testament the cosmogonic myths were historicized by being connected with the history of Israel. Now in early Christian thought they take the form of an affirmation concerning

Christ as the mediator of Creation. Thus in the prologue to the Fourth Gospel the Old Testament story of Creation is recast in the light of him of whom the succeeding twenty chapters present God's *decisive* deeds of redemption. So also Paul sees the story of Adam's fall in the light of him who comes as the second Adam (I Cor. 15:46; Rom. 5:12 ff.).

Therefore the myth ceases to be myth. It has been divested of its mythical substance, we may say, by being interpreted within the frame of an ontic sequence of historical events, and has therefore lost the character of a self-contained myth. Hence, just as in the case of the center part, this myth is not to be removed from its connection with the biblical sequence of events, nor is it to be reduced to "historicity" in the existential, punctiliar sense, so that the decision demanded of me by the individual event would be more important than a sequence of redemptive history with which I align myself. The New Testament as well as the Old points in precisely the opposite direction, in that it has relieved the original myth of its punctiliar meaning.

In so far as these myths are employed in the Bible, therefore, it is exegetically unjustifiable to seek their essence in the understanding of existence which they are said to express. Their specifically Christian meaning is to be sought in an ontic occurrence which is placed in closest relation to the decisive events of redemptive history and which is interpreted on the basis of the meaning established by this context.

The procedure employed by the Bultmann school is really not demythologizing, but rather de-historicizing, and therefore in regard to *these* myths, *remythologizing*. For in the Bultmann school the myths are once more considered as self-contained entities (*Einzelmythen*) which express a specific understanding of existence.

It must be admitted, however, that the historicizing of myth is carried too far in the New Testament. New Testament authors draw no distinction between events which are historically controllable and those which are not. In the Jewish as in the early Christian view of redemptive history, there is no essential distinction between the historical center part and the primal and end occurrences. The absence of this distinction may appear justified to a degree since, according to the New Testament, the selection of those events which form the center part of the sequence is communicated by divine revelation in the same way as are the primal and end occurrences. Nevertheless, modern interpreters cannot overlook the distinction between the two categories of events, even though for New Testament authors Adam belongs on the same plane with Jesus of Nazareth and the genealogy of Jesus is traced back to Adam without hesitation (Luke 3:23 ff.).

Here we must raise the question whether or not this point at which we cannot simply take over the biblical presentation is essential. In so far as we exegetes want to render the New Testament redemptive history accessible to modern thought, we must first of all be quite clear that for us Adam is *not* an historical person like Jesus of Nazareth. Nor can we seek historical proofs by our interpretation of the primal and end histories under the slogan, "The Bible is right after all."[4] On the other hand, when we see the biblical authors historicizing these myths, it is not their inability to distinguish between historical events and the primal and end myths that is essential. For the theological affirmations which flow from the connection of the primal occurrence to the mid-part retain their full value even when the distinction between events which are historically controllable and those which are not is maintained. What *is* theologically essential is the *event-character* of the primal and end occurrences and their *connection* with the rest of the redemptive history. Thus when we affirm the non-historical character of the primal and end events and adhere to the distinction between them and the center part of the redemptive history, we must take care not to throw out the baby with the

---

[4] Cf. Werner Keller's book, the title of which is the popular slogan, *Und die Bibel hat doch Recht;* Eng. trans. by William Neil, *The Bible as History: Archaeology Confirms the Book of Books* (1956).—Ed.

bath. That is, the biblical authors have already successfully de-mythologized the myths by historicizing them, and we must be careful not to disregard this fact.

To be sure, Bultmann's intention to make the New Testament relevant to modern thought must be carried out. But we should not do this at the price of what is really essential. In other words, we should not disregard the character of the ontic sequence of events as though they were nonessential. The historicizing of the myths by the biblical authors sets a context within which we must respect both the event-character and the sequence of events as essential elements. The New Testament, as indeed the whole Bible, speaks of the *acts* of God, not of his *being*. The two outer limits where the New Testament mentions the being of God, be-fore and after his redemptive activity, are, on the one hand, the first verse of John's prologue, "In the beginning was the Word," and, on the other, the Pauline expression in I Cor. 15:28 defining the end of the revelation in Christ: "God will be all in all." But these limits are not overstepped. The prologue of the Fourth Gospel proceeds immediately from the imperfect to the aorist tense: "through him all things *came to be*." The primal and end occurrences of which the New Testament speaks are *acts* of God, and in this regard they belong together with the decisive act of God that is reported in the center part.

Thus it is necessary for us to accent, over against the New Testament authors, that the primal and the cosmic end occur-rences are not historical occurrences like the history of Israel, the life and death of Jesus, and the life of the early Church. Still, if we want to be true to the New Testament authors' basic intention, we should not disconnect the primal and end occurrences from the sequence of events set forth in the center part of the redemp-tive history. We should not reduce the whole back to its con-stituent parts and treat the mythical elements psychologically or existentially as interpretations of a particular understanding of existence. The first Christians made this mode of interpretation impossible precisely by integrating the myths into the redemptive Christ-event.

There are legitimate limits to the program by which we seek to make the New Testament relevant to modern thought. These limits are overstepped when, for example, in the story of the Fall, as one finds it used in the New Testament, the sin of man is seen psychologically as the timeless condition of all men rather than as original rebellion against God. To interpret the story in this way is to fail to understand sin in the light of the "second Adam" who comes *after* the first. Here too the sequence of events must be allowed to stand. The interpretation of the life of Jesus affects the history of human sin; the efficacy of this life is extended also to the Creation. Thus it is essential to the New Testament view that there are divine primal and end occurrences which have to do with sin understood as a primal event (*Urgeschehen*). There is a cosmic occurrence at the beginning which involves the sin and death of man ("for your sake" Rom. 8:20),[5] and a new Creation at the end, in which "righteousness dwells" and death will be no more.

---

5 See O. Cullmann, *Christ and Time,* Floyd V. Filson, trans. (1950), p. 103.

8 The Historicality of Biblical Language

JAMES M. ROBINSON

Perhaps the most significant fact of Old Testament scholarship in our day is that earlier views of the basic thrust of the Old Testament have been largely superseded by the recognition that the Old Testament itself is concerned primarily (though not exclusively) with *Heilsgeschichte,* the story of the God who acts. This understanding has achieved its classic presentation in Volume 1 of Gerhard von Rad's *Theology of the Old Testament,* entitled *The Theology of Israel's Historical Traditions.*[1] Here we have as basic Old Testament theology the story told in the Old Testament (largely the Hexateuch). This program was no sooner carried through than the resultant problem became painfully visible: is this story history? Von Rad's point of departure had been the insistence that the Old Testament is in intention a "history book."[2]

[1] *Die Theologie der geschichtlichen Ueberlieferungen Israels;* first German ed. 1957, 2d ed. 1958; Eng. trans. by D. M. G. Stalker, 1961. Quotations are from the 2d German ed.

[2] Cf. Von Rad's programmatic essay "Typologische Auslegung des Alten Testaments," *EVT,* Vol. 12 (1952), especially p. 23. Eng. trans. by John Bright in *Essays on Old Testament Hermeneutics* (1963), Claus Westermann, ed., pp. 17–39.

If Old Testament theology is thereby called upon to consist in the narration of Israel's history, the historicity of the Old Testament story becomes a normative theological question from the viewpoint of the Old Testament itself.

This problem is particularly obvious in German Old Testament research, where form-critical studies have indicated that the story is largely a secondary fusion of originally separate units handed down by different groups and at different shrines and festivals, with the resultant implication that the continuous story, though containing various historical materials, can hardly be taken as corresponding to the course of history. This historical implication finds its classic presentation in Martin Noth's *History of Israel*, in which Israel's history begins about where the Hexateuch's story ends. In America the reconstruction of Israelite history, led by the Albright school, has produced a somewhat more conservative picture. Yet in view of the solidly critical approach employed, the distinction between the two schools of thought is one of degree rather than of kind, and consequently the problem is in principle the same. The more radical German position has served to focus attention upon, and thus to call forth discussion of, a problem which is a problem of Old Testament scholarship as such! The assumption that theology can simply wait until the two versions of Old Testament history (*Heilsgeschichte* and modern critical reconstructions) converge and become one, must be replaced by basic methodical reflection upon theologizing in view of the two diverging pictures.

Von Rad conceded that the coexistence of the two diverging versions of Old Testament history was a "difficult problem," but assumed that they could "for the time being" simply stand side by side, with Old Testament theology expounding the one and largely ignoring the other.[3] The "time being" was of short duration. Von Rad's thesis that the Old Testament is a history book in intention was promptly turned against him by Franz Hesse, who argued that the historical-critical history of Israel, not the kerygmatic

---

3 *Theologie des Alten Testaments,* Vol. 1, p. 113.

story of the Hexateuch, should provide the basis for any attempt to do justice to the intention of the Old Testament.[4] Certainly one must concede that the historical-critical version of Old Testament history plays a historic role in our times, and hence any attempt to discuss the Old Testament as a "history book" must include this form of its history. But Hesse's position becomes one-sided when he seeks to attribute only to this form of Israel's history a historic role in New Testament times. "God's history with Israel leading to the goal Jesus Christ is to be traced where history really happened, not where one may point to certain conceptualizations as to occurrence which possibly in some instances turn out to be incorrect."[5] But Old Testament history as it is known in our day was unknown in New Testament times, and hence to relate only this historical-critical history with the goal in Jesus Christ is to conceive of that history in an unhistoric way. The history of Israel had its varying historic form down through the ages, which, though differing from what "really happened" (i.e., from our modern reconstruction), was the form in which that history continued to exist and act, e.g., in New Testament times. It would be a sophisticated form of modernizing to replace the form in which the history of Israel existed and acted in New Testament times with the form in which it exists and acts in our times.

If the historical-critical history of Israel, which methodically and *per definitionem* eliminated the historic form of Israel's history, cannot be simply identified with the form of Israel's history that played a historic role in New Testament times, it has proven

---

[4] Cf. Franz Hesse, "Die Erforschung der Geschichte Israels als theologische Aufgabe," *KuD*, Vol. 4 (1958), pp. 1–19, and "Kerygma oder geschichtliche Wirklichkeit?" *ZTK*, Vol. 57 (1960), pp. 17–26. Similarly Johannes Hempel, "Alttestamentliche Theologie in protestantischer Sicht heute," *BO*, Vol. 15 (1958), pp. 206–14.

[5] F. Hesse, *KuD*, Vol. 4 (1958), p. 11. It is perhaps relevant that Hesse (p. 12) poses rhetorically the critical question "how precisely the Jewish congregation's view of history at the time of the formation of the canon receives the honor of being the bearer of the Christian view of God's action in history." The answer is that history itself gave it this honor: the Jewish picture was the form of Israel's history which was historic in New Testament times. Hence, it was this form which is primarily related to the New Testament.

equally difficult to carry through the case for *Heilsgeschichte*. Not only does the historian question the historicity of the story, but even the theologian has begun to question in his way whether *Heilsgeschichte* is an approach based on history. The theological problem of *Heilsgeschichte* and history becomes apparent in the first programmatic attempt to introduce Von Rad's *Heilsgeschichte* approach to the Old Testament into systematic theology. Wolfhart Pannenberg, spokesman for a group of young scholars emanating from Heidelberg[6] and himself now professor of theology at Mainz, has presented a forceful criticism of current theological positions from the viewpoint, derived from the Old Testament, that "history is the all-embracing horizon of Christian theology."[7] On this basis, he criticizes Bultmann and Gogarten for "dissolving history into the historicness of existence."[8] But it is becoming increasingly apparent that any such anti-Bultmannian polemic can with the same degree of justice (or injustice) be applied to Von Rad's own position, in spite of his (and Bultmann's!) intentions to the contrary. For when Von Rad leaves open the relation of *Heilsgeschichte* to history,[9] *Heilsgeschichte* tends to become *Heilsgeschichtlichkeit,* the historicness of Israel's stance toward the divine. To be sure, this historic stance may be more

---

6 He lists as his colleagues M. Elze, K. Koch, R. Rendtorff, D. Rössler, and U. Wilckens. This group received its main stimulus on the one hand from Von Rad and on the other from the Lutheran dogmaticians Peter Brunner and Edmund Schlink.

7 "Heilsgeschehen und Geschichte," *KuD,* Vol. 5 (1959), pp. 218–37, 259–88. The quotation is the opening sentence of the essay, whose first part is reprinted in *Probleme alttestamentlicher Hermeneutik,* C. Westermann, ed. (1960), pp. 295–318. (See now Westermann, *Essays,* pp. 314–35, Shirley Guthrie, trans.)

8 *Ibid.,* p. 218. I translate *Geschichtlichkeit* as "historicness," to distinguish it from "historicity," which I reserve for the traditional English meaning of "what really happened," equivalent to *Historizität.* My term "historicness" is based on the precedent of R. H. Fuller in *Kerygma and Myth* (1961), who translates *geschichtlich* by "historic" and *historisch* by "historical" (cf. p. xi), a policy which seems to grow easily out of antecedent English usage. For the union of historicity and historicness, I employ in this essay the term "historicality."

9 *Theologie des Alten Testaments, loc. cit.*

than "inner history" (Baumgärtel), in that it arises and perseveres only in relation to historical occurrences. But when this historic stance expresses itself in the narration of stories which may or may not be such occurrences, then the retelling of these stories does not really provide the history to which this stance is related.[10]

Pannenberg himself points to the further problem latent within the *Heilsgeschichte* approach, that the prefix "saving" (*Heil*) tends to introduce a suprahistorical factor which is ultimately unhistorical and which replaces history as the theological center. Karl Barth's *Urgeschichte*, "*primal*-history," is itself not history, nor is Friedrich Baumgärtel's *Grundverheissung*, "*basic*-promise," a specific historical promise; and even the typological approach used by Von Rad to relate the two Testaments relates similar structures found in the type and the antitype rather than relating the historical events themselves. Hence Pannenberg himself takes up Walther Zimmerli's category "promise and fulfillment."[11] without realizing that this "structure," as Pannenberg himself repeatedly calls it, functions in his presentation (though not in Zimmerli's intention) as another instance of a timeless principle being used to replace the actual history. For Pannenberg emphasizes that freeness, creativeness, unpredictability are central in history, but he finds this central aspect of history preserved only in the fact

---

[10] The problem is hardly resolved by the note appended to the second edition (1958) of Vol. 1 (pp. 473 f.) to the effect that "the 'kerygmatic' picture" was rooted in a deeper dimension of historical experience unattainable to historical-critical research; such a "creedal theology" (if one may coin a phrase) is still quite as unrelated to a historian's reconstruction of Israelite history as is—*mutatis mutandis*—Bultmann's "kerygmatic theology." The further discussion in the preface to Vol. 2, *Die Theologie der prophetischen Ueberlieferungen Israels* (1960), focuses upon the Old Testament interpretation vs. the historian's interpretation of historical occurrences whose historicity is not in question (e.g., the fall of Jerusalem in 587 B.C., p. 9). But one may infer that the history Von Rad envisages is also at times not the content of the stories, but rather the history of the tradition (p. 8) or historical experiences influencing the tradition (e.g., the problem of human sacrifice, p. 12).

[11] Cf. Walther Zimmerli's essay, "Verheissung und Erfüllung," *EVT*, Vol. 12 (1952), pp. 34–59; Eng. trans. in *INT*, Vol. 15 (1961), pp. 310–38; reprinted in Westermann, *Essays*, pp. 89–122.

that the fulfillment often involves the "breaking down" of the prophecy as a "legitimate interpretation," a "reforming of the content of prophecy," which is "fulfilled otherwise" than the original recipients of the prophecy expected.[12] Here Pannenberg has unconsciously conceded the incompatibility between history and his structure. For if history is preserved only where his structure is transcended, the structure itself is implicitly conceded to be unhistoric. The logic of his argument should require him to go all the way and reject the structure as another substitute for history, itself unhistoric and at times unhistorical. It is unhistoric in that the structure, rather than the event, is the basis upon which theology builds; it is unhistorical in that even promises whose fulfillment actually never happened are—because of the pressure of the superimposed structure—said to have been fulfilled, and events whose happening was never promised are—because of the pressure of the superimposed structure—said to have been promised. Thus, even in Pannenberg's position, structure and construction tend to replace history.

Pannenberg's position should be regarded as a last and best attempt to give New Testament relevance and modern contemporaneity to the past history of the Old Testament by distilling from it a concept which ultimately replaces that history instead of preserving it. Rather than seeking still another such solution, one should now recognize that here one has reached an end of the road, and that a basically new approach must be worked out. To be sure, the difficulty is so acute that one might well wonder whether the recurrent *metabasis eis allo genos* is not inevitable when one proposes to state in language what once occurred as event. Yet such a conclusion is inevitable only for a rationalistic understanding of language, which conceives of it as consisting of concepts or symbols which are basically different in kind from

---

12 Pannenberg, *op. cit.*, pp. 227, 229. Similarly R. Rendtorff in his "Hermeneutik des Alten Testaments als Frage nach der Geschichte" *ZTK*, Vol. 57 (1960), p. 31, speaks of the fulfillment "outdoing" the prophecy.

history. The historicality of Israelite religion—its fusion of the historical and the historic—could be preserved in language only if here historicality and language tend to coincide.

This problem can be investigated both factually and theoretically. One can investigate whether in fact the historicality of Israelite religion was carried over into biblical language;[13] and one can inquire theoretically into the possibility of understanding language as historicality. It is these two tasks which are to be investigated in a preliminary way in the succeeding two sections. The first will, by the nature of the case, lead more directly to the question of the relation of the Old Testament to the New Testament, the second to the relation of the Old Testament to contemporary theology. But the two forms of the discussion are complementary and together form a whole.

I. *The Historicality of Heilsgeschichte*

One more recent development within the new Heidelberg school of Von Rad has been the recognition of the basic strength of Hesse's position on the part of Rolf Rendtorff,[14] now professor of Old Testament at the Kirchliche Hochschule in Berlin. He proposes to relate *Heilsgeschichte* to the historical-critical history of Israel,[15] for which purpose he envisages a new genre of scholarly literature which would combine what is currently separated into "history of Israel," "history of the tradition," and "Old Testament theology." Since all of this is united in the tradition, he elevates the term "tradition" to the center of his discussion. But, apart

---

[13] The possibility that this is the case has already been suggested by Von Rad in Vol. 2 of his *Theologie des Alten Testaments* (1960), pp. 365 f.

[14] "Hermeneutik des AT als Frage nach der Geschichte," *ZTK,* Vol. 57 (1960), pp. 27–40.

[15] His argument consists in a dialectic: historical fact cannot be disengaged from the history of its transmission in the tradition, and the transmission of the tradition cannot be separated from the course of the history in which it was transmitted. This is a different (and independent) formulation of the same dialectic worked out in terms of "meaningful occurrence" in my article on "The Historical Question" published in the *Christian Century* of October 21, 1959, and reprinted in *New Directions in Biblical Thought,* Martin E. Marty, ed. (1960), pp. 73–94, especially pp. 83–87.

from the fact that this term does not go beyond Von Rad, who even used it for the title of Volume I of his *Old Testament Theology*, it does not adequately suggest Rendtorff's intention to be perfectly open in distinguishing critically the historical and the historic within the tradition, even though holding the two together. For the term "tradition" usually suggests the form in which we have Israel's history prior to the application of critical scholarship to it. Hence Rendtorff's intention could perhaps be better met by speaking of a genre of literature which, by uniting the critical study of *Heilsgeschichte* and the history of Israel, the historic and the historical, is concerned with historicality. The following discussion will seek to approach the problem of the historicality of biblical language in a way illustrative of such a genre as Rendtorff envisages.[16]

As early as the source J (Gen. 24:12–14) one encounters the *berākâ* ("blessing") as an already set formula: an acclamatory *bārûk* (LXX: *eulogētos* or *-menos,* hence the name "eulogy") is followed by the names of the deity, which are in turn usually followed by a relative clause beginning with *'asher* (LXX :*hos*) describing the deity in terms of the specific divine act for which he is being blessed. Since the earliest Berachoth are already fully formed, one may assume the formula to be of considerable antiquity; and since in the Old Testament the formula was more typical of narratives than of psalms or liturgical texts, one may assume that the formula was not primarily cultic in any narrow sense. Of course, the formula was taken up into the liturgy and became characteristic of Jewish worship.

Especially in the Hellenistic period the Beracha is often joined or replaced by another formula which is so common at the opening of Qumran hymns as to have led to their being called after the formula *hôdāyôt* ("thanksgivings"). This formula opens with *'ôdekâ* followed by the name of the deity (usually Adonai), which in turn is followed by a clause normally introduced with *kî*

---

16 The illustrations employed by myself (*ibid.,* pp. 84–87) and Rendtorff (*op. cit.,* pp. 36–39) are perhaps a first step in this direction.

(LXX:*hoti*) stating the reason for thanking God (which can elsewhere be expressed by a phrase beginning with '*al* (LXX: *huper.*)

As primitive Christianity arose from within Judaism, it was a matter of course that these formulae current in Judaism were used. Jesus is represented as saying a blessing when he ate, and Paul's expression "the cup of blessing which we bless" (I Cor. 10:16) reflects the use of the Beracha, which is simply "Christianized" in the formula opening the New Testament eulogies in II Corinthians 1:3; Ephesians 1:3; I Peter 1:3: "Blessed be the God and Father of our Lord Jesus Christ . . ." The introduction of Christian content into Jewish blessings within Jewish worship became such a problem for Judaism that it passed a regulation at the end of the first century A.D. to the effect that one may say Amen to another person's blessing only if one has heard and can accept every word of it.[17] "Normative" Judaism tended increasingly to prefer Berachoth to Hodayoth. Primitive Christianity increasingly preferred Hodayoth, as is attested both by the disappearance of Berachoth and the increasing frequency of Hodayoth, as well as by the tendency—e.g., in the Gospels and I Corinthians 11:24— to replace the verb "bless" by the verb "thank" in describing Jesus' mealtime custom.[18] In the Didache the thanksgiving has swept the field, as is also indicated in Justin's unusual expression: "thanked-for bread and wine and water" (*Apol.* I, 65:5), in its marked contrast to Paul's "cup of blessing which we bless."[19] The LXX verb for thanksgiving is *exomologeisthai,* but this verb is increas-

---

[17] Cf. I. Elbogen, *Der jüdische Gottesdienst in seiner geschichtlichen Entwicklung* (3d ed., 1931), p. 253.

[18] Joachim Jeremias, *Die Abendmahlsworte Jesu* (3d ed., 1960), p. 106, sees here merely a Hellenizing of the verb describing the prayer. But in view of the indications in the source material that the one formula was giving way to the other, the shift from the one verb to the other is probably to a considerable extent a reflection of the shift from the one formula to the other— which is itself partially due to Hellenization.

[19] Just as the Hodaya replaced the Beracha as an opening formula, the doxology built on the basic form *hō hē doxa eis tous aiōnas tōn aiōnōn amēn* (e.g., 4 Macc. 18:24; Gal. 1:5) replaced the Beracha that closed the typical Jewish prayer.

ingly replaced in Christian usage by the newer and more Hellenistic term *eucharistein,* so that the formula ultimately produces the name of the eucharist.[20]

The body of material embraced by the designation "Berachoth and Hodayoth" thus extends over the whole Bible. Since there is continuity of *motif* and function even where the formulae differ, and since the formulae are interchanged without difficulty during a long transitional period, the two terms should properly distinguish variant formulae within one body of material, rather than separating into two a body of material which is in a historical continuum. It is this continuous body of historical material that is the subject matter of our present concern. Although it is a narrow cross section of biblical material, it does extend over the whole millennium of the Bible's composition and beyond. Furthermore, it corresponds well to the central thrust of the Bible discussed in the first section. Hence it may serve at least to illustrate the type of research corresponding to the historicality of the Bible as it bears upon the relation of the two Testaments.

The continuity of the formulae from Old Testament to New Testament is itself one of the various instances of historical continuity. The fact that primitive Christianity reflects the stage in the history of the formulae corresponding to the Judaism of its time rather than to the Old Testament itself is just another instance of the fact that the Old Testament, as primitive Christianity was related to it, was the Old Testament as experienced in the first century A.D. That is to say, the relation is in terms of what the Old Testament had become in New Testament times.

It is, however, more important to observe that within this body of material which *Formgeschichte* draws together one has to do

---

[20] The detailed formal analysis of the development of these formulae, of which the above is only a general summary, is to be published elsewhere. One may refer to the instructive article by Jean-Paul Audet, "Esquisse historique du genre littéraire de la 'bénédiction' juive et de l' 'eucharistie' Chrétienne," *RB,* Vol. 65 (1958), pp. 371–399. This essay does not concentrate upon the forms, but rather upon the continuity of *motifs,* which is pressed to the extent of producing a construction from which inferences are drawn which are not supported by the source material.

with the historicality of Israelite-Jewish-Christian history, i.e., with the fusion of its historicity and its historicness. The material presented within the context of these formulae is historical, not simply in that it may preserve historical fragments of a factual kind, but primarily in that the cast given the material by these formulae corresponds to the cast which the history had as it was experienced when it happened; for the formulae arose as part of the original historical events when they happened. Thus the formulae themselves both are a part of the history that happened and preserve the historical mode in which the history happened. But the material brought together in terms of these formulae also presents this history in its historicness. The formulae themselves were called forth and molded by that history and are thus themselves one way in which that history was historic, i.e., survived as a continuing influence. Here *Formgeschichte* is itself part of the historicness of Israelite history. But these formulae are also intimately related to the historicness of Jewish and Christian religious experience, in that they tend to cast this experience into historic dimensions and themselves underwent alteration in terms of whether this experience was more or less historic. For where religious experience became more cultic and less historic, as in "normative" Judaism, the formulae tended to undergo alterations which avoided the need of a specific event; for example, the second line of the Beracha ("who has . . .") could be replaced by a Beracha upon God's name, or the "occurrence" could be vague, general, or unhistoric, such as the provision of food through nature. On the other hand, the formulae served to preserve Israelite history in Jewish and Christian times in its historic dimension (*Heilsgeschichte*), the primary way in which it then played its historic role in relation to the New Testament. It is this group of various relationships of these formulae to the historical and the historic in biblical history—i.e., to the Bible's historicality—which is here to be illustrated.

The occasion for the use of nonliturgical Berachoth and Hodayoth is an occurrence. Abraham's servant finds Rebekah (Gen. 24:27); the Israelites escape from Egypt (Ex. 18:10); Ruth bears a son (Ruth 4:14); Abigail stops David from killing Nabal (I Sam. 25:32); etc. Tobit regains his sight (Tobit 11:17); Lazarus survives death (John 11:41); Paul speaks in more tongues than any (I Cor. 14:18); and so on. It is in each case this occurrence which composes the body of the formulae, e.g.:

> Blessed be the Lord your God,
>> who has delivered up the men who raised their hand
>> against my lord the king.
>
>> II Sam. 18:28

> And Tobit gave thanks before them,
>> that [or: for] God had been merciful to him.
>
>> Tob. 11:17

It is in such formulae as these that one finds the roots of the historicality of the Bible. For here we have to do with the oneness of the historical and the historic: the occurrence to which the formula refers is expressed in its meaning, in terms of an act of God. But this meaning is not a secondary, theological interpretation added belatedly to the occurrence. It is only because the occurrences were—when they happened—experienced as divine act that the participants commemorated them with religious formulae. That is to say, the use of the formula is itself the result of the significance of the occurrence. The use of the formula is thus both a reliable historical hint about the event and itself part of the historic effect of the event. The very structures of the formulae have arisen because of occurrences molding them into the formulae they have become.

What has been said thus far does not imply that the content is in each case historical. The Berachoth, e.g., from the historical books of the Old Testament, share in the problem of the historicity of these stories. If the story of Abraham's servant finding Rebekah and the story of Ruth are only great short stories, the

Berachoth in them are hardly historical; and one may normally assume that the narrators of stories elsewhere in biblical literature composed relatively freely. But the formulae here used in a secondary setting, i.e., in telling a story, none the less reflect accurately a primary setting. For they betray neither a literary origin nor do they suggest an original setting in the transmission of the tradition; rather they are structured as an immediate response to a specific occurrence, and hence are to be understood within the category of acclamations called forth by an epiphany.[21] The storytellers present characters in the stories using these formulae at important occurrences only because the Israelites who told the stories used Berachoth (and later Hodayoth) in their own daily lives to mark important occurrences which really happened to them. The formulae "Blessed be God who has . . ." and "I thank thee Lord, for thou hast . . ." could hardly have arisen without some occurrences for which one wished to bless or thank God. They did not begin as blank formulae which were superimposed as nonhistorical constructions on history; rather historical experience seeking for adequate expression in language produced the formulae, which hence reflect by their very form the nature of the historical experiences that created them. Consequently, the formulae do not stand as unhistoric and unhistorical structures in tension with the history itself, the dilemma from which Pannenberg did not fully extricate himself; rather the formulae share in the historicality that characterizes their contents.

The fact that these formulae are more directly related to the occurrence they commemorate than to the transmission of tradition means that the historical information they contained is not nearly as fully preserved as are the historic forms themselves. For at each succeeding occurrence the formula which was molded by previous occurrences would be used and thus preserved, but the content would be that of the new occurrence. Hence specific con-

---

[21] Cf. *RAC,* Vol. 1, pp. 216 ff.; *RGG,* 3d ed., Vol. 2, pp. 993 f.

crete instances of the formula would not be preserved in most cases. Yet when the person who used the formula himself wrote the source in which it is recorded, one finds instances where the original content with its historical information is preserved, as in the Qumranian Hodayoth or Paul's passing expression in I Corinthians 1:14:

> I am thankful
>> that [or: for] I baptized none of you except Crispus
>> and Gaius.

And the possibility should not be excluded that historical information, originally commemorated in these formulae, has survived through oral transmission. The following discussion may illustrate this possibility.

Blessings were pronounced upon humans as well as upon God, and the two types of blessing were similar in form and even in function. Often they occur side by side in commemorating the divine and human sides of an occurrence (Gen. 14:19-20; I Sam. 25:32-33). Hence the blessing upon the human can assume a form which suggests also an interest in his God, as in the case of Melchizedek's blessing upon Abraham:

> Blessed be Abram by God Most High,
>> maker of heaven and earth; . . .
>>> Gen. 14:19

Or, conversely, the blessing upon God may assume a form which reveals an implicit blessing upon the human,[22] as in Genesis 24:27 (cf. further II Sam. 18:28; Dan. 3:28; etc.):

---

[22] This may be the correct explanation for the problem in Gen. 9:25-26, where the Masoretic punctuation pairs a curse upon Canaan with a blessing upon the "Lord God of Shem," an apparent incongruity leading to the repointing presupposed in the RSV: "Blessed by the Lord my God be Shem." The difficulty with this repointing of the text is the absence of the lamedh ("by") which normally accompanies this form of blessing (e.g., Gen. 14:19; Jud. 17:2; I Sam. 15:13). Thus the repointing calls for a conjectural emendation, all of which becomes unnecessary when one recognizes that a blessing

Blessed be the Lord, the God of my master Abraham,
who has not forsaken his steadfast love and his faithfulness toward
my master.

This latter form of blessing names the deity in the construct state
followed by the person who worships that deity. This is the same
kind of designation of a *numen* which Albrecht Alt identified under the term *theos patrōos,* and to which he gave credit for having
preserved for posterity the names of the patriarchs.[23] As various
individual *theoi patrōoi* were merged in the "ecumenical" movement leading to the amphictyony, harmonistic terms arose such
as "the God of Abraham, Isaac, and Jacob." Such late terms are
frequent in Berachoth, e.g., "the God of Israel" (I Sam. 25:32;
I Kings 1:48; 8:15; Lk. 1:68; and the Mishna tractate "Berachoth"), or "the God of our fathers" (Ezra 7:27). But Alt's
thesis is that originally the *theos patrōos* of each patriarch was
separate, with a separate name for the *numen* followed by the
name of one patriarch. This thesis is attested in the case of Isaac
("the Fear of . . . Isaac" in Gen. 31:53b) and Jacob ("the
Mighty One of Jacob" in Gen. 49:24; and so forth). But in the
case of Abraham, Alt can provide no instance which survived the
harmonistic movement, but can only conjecture, from the analogy
in other cases and on the basis of Gen. 15:1 ("Fear not, Abram,
I am your shield"), that the *theos patrōos* must have been "the
Shield of Abraham."

This conjecture finds striking confirmation in one of the oldest
Berachoth to have survived through oral tradition, in the first
(and one of the oldest) of the "Eighteen Petitions" in the Jewish
prayer of that name:

---

upon a person's God functions as a blessing upon the person, and hence may
stand in fitting antithesis to a curse upon a person. A similar role is played in
epistolary thanksgivings by a phrase such as *peri humōn,* which gives a
thanksgiving to God the function of expressing thanks to the recipients of the
letter. Cf. Paul Schubert, *Form and Function of the Pauline Thanksgivings,*
BZNW, Vol. 20 (1939), pp. 59, 150, 169, etc.

[23] "Der Gott der Väter," *Kleine Schriften,* Vol. 1 (2d ed., 1959), pp. 1–78.

> Blessed art Thou, Yahweh (our God),
> God of Abraham, God of Isaac and God of Jacob,
> God Most High, Creator of heaven and earth,
> Our Shield and Shield of our Fathers.
> Blessed art Thou, Yahweh, Shield of Abraham.[24]

This first "petition," since it opens the prayer as a whole, begins with a Beracha, and then, like each of the other "petitions," closes with a Beracha in which the gist of the whole "petition" finds expression. The various elements in the body of this "petition," which on first glance seem so heterogeneous, are on closer examination seen to have been drawn together by the idea of Abraham, which unites the Melchizedek blessing ("God Most High, Creator of heaven and earth") with two late harmonistic versions of a blessing upon the *theos patrōos* of Abraham, one of which preserves his name ("God of Abraham, God of Isaac, and God of Jacob"), and the other of which preserves the designation of his numen as "Shield" ("Our Shield and Shield of our Fathers"). From the point of view of the history of tradition one would conclude that alternate Berachoth are sensed as relating to Abraham, and are hence conflated in the body of the petition and summarized in the closing Beracha to the "Shield of Abraham." It seems hardly probable that the compiler of this "petition" would have—via some train of thought remarkedly analogous to that of Alt—created the term "Shield of Abraham" as his summary, after having drawn together the body of the "petition." It seems more probable that the closing Beracha ("Blessed art Thou, Yahweh, Shield of Abraham") was itself either a traditional Beracha,[25] or

---

[24] This is the part of the first "petition" held to be oldest by G. Dalman, *Worte Jesu*, Vol. 1 (1898), pp. 299 ff.; he is followed by Paul Fiebig, *Jesu Bergpredigt* (1924), p. 108. W. Staerk, *Altjüdische liturgische Gebete* (*KlT* No. 58, 2d ed., 1930), omits from the oldest form the second line but includes in its place "our God," which Dalman had omitted.

[25] Since the form of the *theos patrōos* (name of the deity in the construct state followed by the name of the worshiper) coincides with the form of the divine name in the type of Beracha now under consideration (i.e., the Beracha which refers formally to God but applies actually to God's man), one may

at least contained a traditional divine predicate, which provided
the compiler with his point of departure. For it is the only unit in
the first "petition" which can satisfactorily explain the attraction
of each of the others. Thus the first of the "Eighteen Petitions"
preserves in a striking fashion the successive layers in the transmission of the *theos patrōos* largely responsible for the preservation of the historical fact of a patriarch's name, together with the
tradition's oldest form, which previously had been only hypo-
thetically reconstructed.[26]

Such a discussion should indicate that the formulae under consideration may not only have survived as forms in which new content from occurrence to occurrence could fit, but that in some
cases occurrences of basic significance could be commemorated
in Berachoth which would retain their contents and be transmitted with these contents through tradition, eventually to play a
historic role in Judaism and Christianity, and in our day to provide the historian with historical information. One could recall
with sharpened historical interest the opening of the Beracha in
the short story in Genesis 24: "Blessed be Yahweh, the God of
my master Abraham."

Perhaps of more importance than the possibility of the formulae
preserving details of historical information is the fact that the
formulae were part of the historical occurrences themselves, and a
part which would give these experiences their particular historic

---

suspect that this type of Beracha was the original setting of the *theos patrōos*
"Shield of Abraham." This would be all the more probable if one were to
follow the suggestion of Walther Zimmerli, "Verheissung und Erfüllung," *EVT*,
Vol. 12 (1952), pp. 34 f.: "The sociological type of these groups, which are
to be regarded as half-nomadic, shifting their pasturing area from the steppe
to the arable land, suggests the conjecture that the promise of possessing a land
of their own already played a role in the original form of this tradition." The
simplest form in which one could conceive of such a promise would be in a
blessing of the following type:

> Blessed be the Shield of Abraham
> who has promised him [us] this land.

Cf. also the Greek thanksgivings preserving the names of *theoi patrōoi* in in-
scriptions cited by Alt, *op. cit.*, pp. 73 ff., Nos. 32, 39, 53, 55.

[26] *Māgēn 'abrāhām* in Alt, *op. cit.*, p. 67 and W. Staerk, *op. cit.*, p. 11.

cast. The formulae were a regular part of Israelite, Jewish, and primitive Christian life, and hence entered with persons into their experiences (a "pre-understanding" present as language), to color those experiences with a particular mode suggested by the formulae, a mode which itself was a reflection, and hence a historic form, of the antecedent history in which the formulae arose and were preserved. This may be illustrated from the Book of Tobit. For here one can clearly see to what a great extent Berachoth (and to a lesser extent the emerging Hodayoth) were a constant concomitant of the daily living of the godly Jew at the opening of the second century B.C. This may not only be inferred from the incessant Berachoth in Tobit, but is also made explicit in the *dénouement*, when the angel Raphael lays aside his disguise and gives God's opinion on the way man should live, namely, in the constant stance of blessing and thanksgiving (Tob. 12).[27] It is this "understanding of existence" that the preceding story had illustrated and that the ensuing psalm of Tobit (chap. 13) implements. This particular historic stance revealed in Tobit is a historical fact about the Maccabean period of no little importance for understanding the origin and nature of that historical movement. (Cf., e.g., the Beracha ascribed to Judas Maccabaeus as he goes into battle, I Macc. 4:30–33, quoted below.)

This historic consciousness, itself an effect and a cause of Israelite history documented and fostered by the formulae under consideration, plays via the formulae a considerable role in the

---

[27] In anticipation of the discussion of Section II, one may observe that the angel of Tobit, in which the understanding of existence inherent in the formulae finds expression, is identified by Rilke (cf. "Duino Elegy" II, 3–6) with his symbol of the angel, in which he seeks to regain that wholeness which we have found inherent in the formulae: "The Angel of the Elegies is the creature in whom that transformation of the visible into the invisible we are performing already appears complete . . . The Angel of the Elegies is the being who vouches for the recognition of a higher degree of reality in the invisible—therefore, 'terrible' to us, because we, its lovers and transformers, still depend upon the visible" (*Briefe aus Muzot* [1935], p. 337.) This wholeness described by Heidegger as a square uniting as its sides the divine, the mortal, earth and sky, is called forth by language, of which a basic instance consists in the formulae hypostasized in Tobit's angel.

Jewish and primitive Christian presentation of their own history. To this the discussion now turns.

Already in the Old Testament historical books Berachoth seem to provide a setting for historical narration, which tends to overflow the original limits of the formula; i.e., there is a tendency to produce a narrative form of the formula. In I Kings 5:21 (5:7 RSV) Hiram blesses God for Solomon's ascension to the throne:

> Blessed be the Lord this day,
>> who has given to David a wise son to be over this great people.

In II Chronicles 2:12 this blessing has been expanded both by inserting a prefatory line referring to Creation and by appending allusions to the building of the Temple and palace:

> Blessed be the Lord God of Israel,
>> who made heaven and earth,
>> who has given King David a wise son, endued with
>> discretion and understanding,
>> who will build a temple for the Lord,
>> and a royal palace for himself.

Another illustration of this trend toward narrative expansion is found in Tobit 11:16, where the text reads according to B and A:

> And Tobit gave thanks before them
>> that [or: for] God had been merciful to him.

To this the S text adds:

> and that he opened his eyes.

In such instances one has to do with rather wooden insertions of the material from the surrounding narrative into the formulae. One nevertheless observes a tendency to expand the second line of the formulae giving the historical occasion, by a third parallel line completing the historical statement. This led to the pattern ". . . who has . . . and has . . ." or ". . . for thou hast . . . and hast . . ." whereupon one might come to a grammatical halt and begin a new sentence, if more narrative were needed, as in I Samuel 25:39:

> Blessed be the Lord
>> who has avenged the insult I received at the hand of Nabal,
>> and has kept back his servant from evil;
>> And the Lord has returned the evil-doing of Nabal upon
>> his own head.

In all these instances of the growth of the formulae toward fuller narration one has to do with the problem of the influence of the secondary setting of the formulae in narrative books. Is this longer, narrative version of the formulae due to the fact that these instances of the formulae are composed by the narrators of the books or of their sources, who had at their disposal quantities of story material and skill at narrating? Or is one to assume that the formulae in their original acclamatory setting tended to include more narrative?

For the earlier period this may perhaps remain a moot question, somewhat analogous to that concerning the more narrative form of the kerygma in the sermons of Acts. But when we subsequently come upon the formulae in their original setting, as we find them, e.g., in Qumranian hymns and primitive Christian texts, the longer narrative form is fully developed, perhaps due to the more hymnic use of the formulae. It is this longer, narrative form of the formulae that is used by Qumran and primitive Christianity to express the new occurrences which are constitutive for them. For example, the hymn 1 QH 2, 20 ff. begins:

> I give thanks unto thee, Lord,
>> for thou hast put my soul in the bundle of life
>> and hedged me against all the snares of corruption.

The hymn then proceeds to narrate in detail what is here summarized in the formula.

Precisely the same structure occurs in the primitive Christian Hodayoth, the best examples of which are Revelation 11:17–18 and Luke 10:21–22 (Matt. 11:25 ff.). The first is as follows:

We give thanks unto thee, Lord God Almighty, who art and who wast,

that [or: for] thou hast taken thy great power
and begun to reign.

And the nations raged,
but thy rage came,

and the time for the dead to be judged,
and for giving the reward

to thy servants, the prophets and saints,
and to those who fear thy name, both small and great,

and for destroying
the destroyers of the earth.

The second, from Q, is as follows:

I give thanks unto thee, Father, Lord of heaven and earth,
that [or: for] thou hast hidden these things from the wise and
understanding
and revealed them to babes.
Yea, Father,
for such was thy gracious will.
All things have been delivered to me by my Father;
and no one knows who the Son is except the Father,
or who the Father is except the Son
and any one to whom the Son chooses to reveal him.

Here one has reached the point at which the formulae have been
extended into hymnlike kerygmatic summaries, quite reminiscent
of the hymns in Philippians 2:6–11, Colossians 1:15–20, and
I Timothy 3:16,[28] which could originally have arisen in connec-

---

[28] In I Esd. 5:58 (LXX; RSV 5:61) one finds the Hodayoth formula with
the verb *homologein* rather than *exomologeisthai* (cf. also 4:60 and Philo,
Legum allegor, I, 82). This makes it possible for Günther Bornkamm ("Das
Bekenntnis im Hebräerbrief," *Studien zu Antike und Urchristentum* [1959],
pp. 188–203, especially 195 f.) to identify in Heb. 13:15 with its *homolo-
gountōn* an allusion to eucharistic hymns, one of which he suspects is used
at the opening of Hebrews, in view of its similarity to the hymn in the Preface
of Hippolytus' church order. This conjecture is strengthened when one observes that the *thusia aineseōs* of Heb. 13:15 is the LXX equivalent to the

tion with these formulae, as Colossians 1:12–14 (cf. *1 QH* 11, 3–14) and Ephesians 1:3 ff. suggest.

These formulae have here become means for expressing the saving event central to Christianity, and thus were a context in which the linguistic formulation of its historic significance could take place. But this context for the growth of Christian *Heilsgeschichte* was also the context in which daily occurrences were experienced, and it is in the interaction of the two that the historicality of Hebrew and Christian religious experience consists.

---

later term *eucharistia* preferred by Aquila, which thus forms the missing link to the *gratiās tibi referimus* in Hippolytus. Hence one may also wonder whether the *homologoumenōs* introducing the hymn of I Tim. 3:16 reflects the Hodayoth formula. For in I Tim. 3:16 one must somehow explain the fact that the introduction to the hymn and the hymn both belong to the liturgical unit used, since the scheme "the mystery once hidden but now revealed" (cf. N. A. Dahl, *Neutestamentliche Studien für R. Bultmann* [1954], pp. 4 f.) straddles the introduction and first line of the hymn. Here, as in Col. 1:12–20, the formula is apparently separated from the hymn (beginning with *hos*) by intervening liturgical material (Col. 1:12–14; Heb. 1:1–2). This could perhaps be a reflection of the style in the narrative forms of the formulae discussed above, where the hymnic narration follows upon an initial pair of lines which summarized briefly what is then more fully narrated. This could also explain the odd situation in Eph. 1:3 ff., where the two strophes whose opening is marked by the participles in vss. 5 and 9 (cf. Ernst Käsemann, RGG, 3d ed., Vol. 2, p. 519) seem to be inseparable from the liturgical Beracha in vss. 3–4. The motifs of deliverance from evil and assembling into the kingdom are so frequent in Berachoth and Hodayoth (cf., e.g., Didache 9–10; I Clem. 59:2; 60:3) that their recurrence in Col. 1:13 would tend to confirm that the opening formulation in vs. 12 (*eucharistountes tō patri* . . .) reflects the opening of a Hodaya. In view of the custom (Justin, *Apologia*, I, 65) of following baptism directly with the eucharist, the allusions back to baptism sensed here by Käsemann (*Exegetische Versuche und Besinnungen* [1960], pp. 43 ff.), and indirectly attested for I Tim. 3:16 by the baptismal homily imbedded in the parallel hymn in I Pet. 3:18 ff., need not contradict the assumption that these hymns are eucharistic. Since Jewish hymns beginning with the formulae tend to return to them at the close (cf. Sirach 51:1, 12; Martyrdom of Polycarp, 14), one may wonder whether such a sensitivity led to the inclusion of the quotation from Isa. 45:23 in Phil. 2:11, with its *exomologēsetai*. (Cf. the comparable problem in the prayer of I Clem. 59–61, whose formal opening has been bypassed but whose final summary may reflect with its *exomologoumetha* an opening Hodaya.) Bultmann has conjectured (orally) that the awkward opening of the hymns with *hos* reflects the Beracha formula. Somewhat similarly Joachim Jeremias (*NTD: Der Briefe an Timotheus und Titus* [1948], p. 22) had conjectured that the hymn of I Tim. 3:16 was prefaced with a line such as "Praise and honor be to him who . . . "

The nonliturgical, autobiographical Beracha in II Corinthians 1:3 ff. and the liturgical, doctrinal Beracha in Ephesians 1:3 ff. belong together, as do the idiomatic and casual expressions of thanks in I Corinthians 1:14; 14:18, and the liturgical, Christological thanksgiving and hymn in Colossians 1:12–20. For historicality does not simply consist in a canonical *Heilsgeschichte* in which the historical and the historic are fused, but also in the fact that this canonical *Heilsgeschichte* is transmitted by a people whose contemporary experience is characterized by meaningful event. Present occurrences experienced within the framework of blessing and thanksgiving hinder *Heilsgeschichte* from degenerating into an unhistoric rationalistic scheme of the ages; the historicality of present experience is both the result and also the continuing sustainer of the historicality of *Heilsgeschichte*. It is this dialectic which is now to be illustrated.

One setting in which the longer narrative formulae occur is that of prayers of petition. In a given situation one prays for God's help because one believes God helps in such situations, and one believes this because one believes God *has* helped in such situations. One prays in a given situation because of the historicality of one's faith which is rooted in *Heilsgeschichte;* and one's situation in turn colors the form in which one narrates *Heilsgeschichte*. A poignant illustration of this is found in the Beracha spoken by Tobias (Tob. 8:5 ff.), as he prepares to consummate his marriage with Sarah, whose seven preceding husbands had been killed by an evil demon in the bridal chamber. Understandably enough, he petitions: "Grant that I may find mercy and may grow old together with her," to which she adds her hearty Amen. But this petition is prefaced by a Beracha including a narration of God's having made mankind for marriage.

> Blessed art Thou, O God of our fathers,
> and blessed be thy holy and glorious name for ever.
> Let the heavens and all of thy creatures bless thee.

Thou madest Adam and gavest him Eve his wife
   as a helper and support.
From them the race of mankind has sprung.
Thou didst say, "It is not good that the man should be alone;
Let us make a helper for him like himself."

The shift from the standard Creation line "Creator of heaven and earth," mentioned previously, to this particular narration of a part of the creation story is clearly the result of Tobias' situation, in terms of which he narrates (cf. similarly the *Genesis Apochryphon,* col. 20, lines 12 ff.).

Perhaps the most striking instance of this interaction between the historicality of one's faith with regard to the present situation and one's narration of *Heilsgeschichte* is found in Judas Maccabaeus' prayer as he leads his army into battle, I Maccabees 4:30–33 (cf. also vss. 8–11, 24–25):

Blessed art thou, O Savior of Israel,
   who didst destroy the attack of the mighty warrior by the hands of
      thy servant David,
   and didst give the camp of the Philistines into the hands of Jonathan,
      the son of Saul, and of the man who carried his armor.

Likewise do thou hem in this camp by the hand of thy people Israel,
And let them be ashamed of their troops and their cavalry.

Fill them with cowardice;
and melt the boldness of their strength;
and let them tremble in their destruction.

Strike them down with the sword of those who love thee,
and let all who know thy name praise thee with hymns.

Here the choice of a segment of past history and the way in which it is presented are clearly determined by a desire to correlate it to the present situation. For the actual wording of the petition for God's present action and the recollection of God's past action are

made to coincide, and the correspondence is expressly stated:
"Likewise do thou . . ."

This interaction of the recollection of *Heilsgeschichte* and the
petition in terms of one's own situation is clearly evident in the
hymn of blessing and thanksgiving in Sirach 51:1–12, whose
central verses 8–9 read:

> Then I remembered thy mercy, O Lord,
> and thy work from of old,
> that thou dost deliver those who wait for thee
> and dost save them from the hand of their enemies.
>
> And I sent up my supplication from the earth,
> and prayed for deliverance from death.

This pattern can include a rather full narration of God's past acts
which one "remembers," as in the psalm of thanksgiving in
I Chronicles 16:8 ff., leading to the prayer for deliverance in vss.
35–36. The outline—Beracha, narration, petition, as well as the
interaction between the recollection and the petition—is also indirectly attested in Judith 13:18–20.

It is upon this pattern that the prayers in Didache 9–10 are
built, where the petition for God's deliverance of the Church
from evil into God's kingdom follows upon thanksgiving for the
saving event of Christ. But when one examines these prayers more
closely, he finds not only this striking instance of continuity with
Judaism, but also an illustration of the way in which primitive
Christianity preserved the historicality of religious experience at
the point at which it was fading away. For the thanksgivings of
the Didache are "Christianized" versions of the Jewish mealtime
blessings, such as are attested in the Mishna tractate "Berachoth."
The most striking thing about these standardized blessings of
"normative" Judaism is that they have lost their historicality and
are merely blessings for the gifts of nature in food and drink. Just
as ancient Israel had once "historicized" the nature festivals of
Canaanite religion in terms of God's deliverance from Egypt into

the promised land, so the Didache shows primitive Christianity "historicizing" these expressions of gratitude for nature in terms of God's deliverance in Christ.

When the Jewish mealtime blessings are historicized in terms of the saving event of Christianity, their correlation to the petition for eschatological deliverance is strengthened, and this correlation restores the historicality of daily experience. For the primitive Christian, caught up in the eschatological process whose inauguration is commemorated in blessings and thanksgivings and whose consummation is sought in petitions, finds here the understanding of his daily existence. The eschatological deliverance is "realized" in daily deliverances, as their commemoration in the context of blessings and thanksgivings indicates. It is hardly coincidental that the allusion to deliverance in Asia in II Corinthians 1:10 is in a context beginning with a eulogy in 1:3 and leading to a call for prayers of thanksgiving in 1:11. Similarly the allusion to the deliverance from the "mouth of a lion" in II Timothy 4:17 serves as the transition to the conclusion of the book, which consists in the typical conclusion to the Christian prayer: the petition for eschatological deliverance and the doxology, corresponding to the beginning of the epistles with the prayer's opening Hodaya or Beracha.[29]

Thus these formulae, used daily by the historical Jesus, developed hymnically to express the historic significance of Jesus, and actualized in connection with the various experiences of primitive Christians as the historicality of Christian existence, present a central segment of the history of primitive Christianity. The historicality of Israelite religion, caught up in these formulae, is thus through them a constitutive part of the historicality of Chris-

---

[29] The examination of these formulae suggests that the thesis of Paul Schubert's *Form and Function of the Pauline Thanksgivings* needs modification in two respects. The thanksgivings opening the Pauline epistles do not simply reflect Hellenistic epistolatory style, but also primitive Christian liturgical style. Hence, especially in view of the Qumranian Hodayoth, they do not prove Paul to have been a "Hellenist of the Hellenists," as Schubert one-sidedly concludes, but rather to stand in the merger of the two cultural backgrounds. (Cf. my article "Liturgie NT" in *Biblisch-historisches Handwörterbuch.*)

tianity. Here, then, one has an illustration of what is perhaps the central "relation" of the Old Testament to the New Testament.

II. *The Historicality of* Lichtungsgeschichte

In each generation one theological discipline seems to move beyond its own boundaries and call forth such a response from the general cultural environment as to elevate it to the center of theology. This was the case with Church History prior to World War I, when Harnack, with his insistence upon historical-critical method free of dogmatic construction, seemed to give theology its standing and its relevance in the culture. After World War I it was dogmatics that assumed this central position, as it combined new elements ranging from the thought of Kierkegaard to eschatology into "dialectical theology." More recently New Testament research has provided a focal orientation for theology as a whole, as Bultmann made use of the categories of Heidegger's *Being and Time* to state the New Testament kerygma in a way accessible to a postmythological age.

At the present moment there are indications that Old Testament scholarship could move beyond its departmental confines into such a central theological position in the coming generation. Certainly Old Testament scholarship in our time has at its disposal both a series of significant breakthroughs in its field and outstanding scholars capable of producing a synthesis on the basis of them. Consequently there are already tendencies toward an Old Testament orientation from within other departments. Not only is there the young group of German scholars formed in Heidelberg under Old Testament influences, which has carried Old Testament theology into systematics, especially in the person of Pannenberg. Also the later Barth, whose original affinity to Bultmann ended in antithesis, has expressed approval of the current trend of Old Testament studies.[30] And Ernst Käsemann, who has led the movement

---

[30] "How My Mind Has Changed," *The Christian Century,* January 20, 1960, p. 75.

away from Bultmann within the Bultmannian school and is now the most influential New Testament professor in Germany, has moved via a joint seminar on Romans 9–11 with Walther Zimmerli into a more positive relationship to Old Testament scholarship and its *Heilsgeschichte* orientation. Whether such auspicious indications will in fact lead to a new synthesis with the Old Testament as its center depends to a considerable extent on whether Old Testament scholarship can relate itself significantly to broader cultural or philosophical currents of the day, in terms of which the Old Testament position could be expressed in the other theological departments and even outside of theology proper. It is the purpose of the present section to suggest one such correlation.

In Heidegger's early work *Being and Time* (1927) he rediscovered the central problem of ontology: Why is it that things exist at all, rather than there being nothing? This problem, that things are, the problem of their "is-ness" or "being,"[31] is the question of being which Heidegger insists has long been obscured by metaphysics, in that it assumed their being and went on to classify the things that are into their proper categories. Heidegger proposed to reawaken the more basic question, with the long-range goal of producing a general ontology. The first step was a regional ontology, an ontology based on just one kind of beings. He chose that kind of beings for which the problem that they are, the ontological problem, is a constitutive part of them. The kind of beings,

---

[31] One needs to note that the term "being" (*Sein*) is used in a verbal sense, to refer to the fact that things are, rather than in a purely substantival sense as a designation for a thing (*Seiendes*). Werner Brock in his introduction to the volume of Heidegger's essays *Existence and Being* capitalizes the former (*Sein* = "Being") and pluralizes the latter (*Seiendes* = "beings"), so as to distinguish them. The capitalization seems to me misleading, in that it invites the general reader to hypostasize and the theologian to deify "the fact that things are." To avoid this misunderstanding I have not capitalized, but have tried in usage to give a verbal ring to *Sein,* first by using the awkward coinage "is-ness" or a clause "that things are" as translations, with the hope that this verbal ring can be then carried over to the term "being," especially if this term is used so as to suggest the verbal meaning, e.g.: " 'the fact of their being' is what concerns us," i.e. " 'their being' is what concerns us."

for which the problem as to whether they are or are not is "built in," is man. For he is the being which is always and inevitably involved in becoming himself or losing himself. The question "to be or not to be" is a part of man's inescapable constitution, not only in that he must face death, but also in that he is by his very nature concerned with "self-realization," with being what he potentially is. In that man grapples constantly with whether he has or has not attained authentic existence, he is constantly involved in the ontological problem. Hence Heidegger devoted the first (and only) volume of what he intended to be a much longer work to a structural analysis of man's "is-ness," his "being." It is this analysis that Bultmann used in his translation of the New Testament kerygma into existentialistic categories.

Although it may be no coincidence that Heidegger presented his analysis of the categories in which man grapples with the problem of being just at the time when existentialism was becoming the vogue, he did not write from an existential concern, but rather from a philosophic concern for ontology as such. Hence it is to be considered as a consistent continuation of that basic concern when the later Heidegger[32] moved beyond an analysis of man's being as his center of orientation. He now emphasizes that the "is-ness" of things or their "being" unveils itself from time to time in history, so that history, not anthropology, has become the basic dimension of his thought. This history is termed *Lichtungsgeschichte.* Heidegger may envisage a play on words with *Lichtung,* a term which can mean simply a clearing in the woods where light breaks through, hence an area which has become light, whereas Heidegger seems to use the term verbally to refer to being emerging from the obscurity of forgetfulness into clear light within thought. Perhaps the English term "clearing" best catches these

---

[32] The basic shift in Heidegger's philosophy justifying a distinction between the "early" Heidegger of *Being and Time* and the "later" Heidegger is analysed in *The Later Heidegger and Theology* (1963), Vol. I of the series of symposia *New Frontiers in Theology.* My introductory essay in that volume on "The German Discussion of the Later Heidegger" is a fuller and more recent presentation than the present essay.

facets of the German expression, so that one might translate "clearing-history."[33]

This *Lichtungsgeschichte* is not confined to the history of thought. For Heidegger has repudiated the autonomy of thought in which a "subject" uses his categories to classify and thus know an "object"—a procedure which Heidegger argues is the one massive subjectivism of Western thought that has prevented reality from unveiling itself and has produced the age of the "worldview," in which our views of the world obscure reality itself. Hence Heidegger rejects the "subject-object" pattern of thought in the interest of greater objectivity, an objectivity in which the "object" unveils itself, i.e., functions as the subject with freedom to speak for itself, and should hence better be termed the "subject matter" rather than the "object." Truth is more basically an "unveiling" (*a-lētheia*) than a correlation of objects to a subject's patterns of thought. Hence the history of thought is itself only a reflection of the history of the subject matter unveiling itself. The task in studying the history of thought is thus to move through the thoughts themselves to the subject matter from which the thoughts arose and to which they refer. One should observe the structural similarity to the position of Von Hofmann which gave rise to his term *Heilsgeschichte:* the prophecy is not the saying of the prophet; rather the prophecy is the history whose inherent prophecy the prophet merely expresses in language. Hence, Von Hofmann argues, we should move through the prophet's prophecy to the prophetic history, which is what is fulfilled in Christ. This is what led to the recognition that the center of the Bible is *Heilsgeschichte.* In the case of being for Heidegger, its history is not just a history of thought about the problem of being, but rather its history is this subject matter, the "is-ness" or "being" of beings, forcing itself in upon thought. *Lichtungsgeschichte* is here the history of "being" itself.

The recognition of the historicality of "being" is at the center of the thought of the later Heidegger.

---

[33] Cf. Jakob Ludwig Karl Grimm's *Deutsches Wörterbuch,* 1854–1919.

Our talk about "being" never understands this term in the sense of a category under whose empty generality the historically conceived doctrines about beings belong. "Being" speaks from time to time as it is given to it to do so, and hence is permeated by tradition . . . One has "being" only from time to time, in this and that formulation given to it to have: *Phusis, Logos, Hen, Idea, Energeia,* substantiality, objectivity, subjectivity, will, will to power, will to will.[34]

Hence Heidegger infers that the study of "being" must take the form of studying Western philosophical thought, to move through it to its subject matter which has unveiled itself in such classical philosophical terms. But the odd omission from this list of concepts in which being has been unveiled is that unveiling of "being" which is central for Heidegger, namely its historicality. Is not this omission due simply to the fact that this central unveiling of "being" does not derive from the Western philosophical tradition, but rather from the historicality of biblical thought? If this be true, it is logically inconsistent with Heidegger's premises to take this historicality only as a thought, as an "empty" category, apart from the tradition with which it is permeated, i.e., apart from the specific subject matter which gave rise to this thought. It is precisely because Heidegger has recognized in a basic way the historicality of *Lichtungsgeschichte* that he should be logically required to concern himself with the history which was the subject matter which called into thought the historicality of being. This is all the more obvious when one notes his concession that the Western philosophic tradition is more characterized by forgetfulness of "being" than by awareness of it. And as a matter of fact he concedes that biblical language was at the origin of his philosophic thought.[35] Hence one may say that Heidegger has in prin-

---

[34] *Identität und Differenz* (1957), pp. 47, 64; author's trans.; cf. Eng. trans. by Kurt F. Leidecker, *Essays in Metaphysics* (1960), pp. 44, 59.

[35] Cf. *Unterwegs zur Sprache* (1959), p. 96: "The term 'hermeneutics' was familiar to me from my studies in theology. At that time, I was especially stimulated by the question of the relation between the word of the Holy Scripture and theological speculative thought. It was, if you will, the same relation, namely between language and being, only hidden and inaccessible to

ciple (though not in practice) provided the avenue through which Old Testament research may move beyond the confines of its discipline into a central role in theological and philosophical discussion in our day. What is now needed is for biblical scholarship to make use of this opening. If a generation ago Barth showed the relevance of Paul's Epistle to the Romans to man as man, and thus freed it from its previous limitation to the pious or officially "religious"—a limitation which in a "world come of age" is quite confining—it may be the task of our generation to free the Bible as such from this limitation. Dietrich Bonhoeffer's parting call for a "nonreligious interpretation of biblical concepts" relevant to a "world come of age" could find here its answer.[36]

Although it does not fall within the scope of the present essay to carry through such a program in detail, the proposal may be made somewhat more concrete by observations relative to the central segment of biblical material discussed above. The awareness of being which Heidegger wishes to revive—namely, amazement that things are rather than there not being things at all—is an awareness inherent in the biblical concept of Creation. Here if anywhere wonder that things are rather than their not being is expressed in eloquent language. But it is not simply in the Creation narratives that the "being" of things is experienced numinously, rather than taken as a matter of course. The Creation narratives are a stage setting for the biblical story which has been cast back from the story itself upon the backdrop. It is Israel's experience of its history as God's creation which is logically prior

---

me, so that I sought a guiding thread in vain on many detours and false leads . . . Without this theological origin I would never have arrived on the path of thought. But origin always remains future." At the meeting of "Old Marburgers" in October, 1960 at Bethel, Heidegger proposed an "analogia proportionalitas" (*A:B :: C:D*). As philosophic thinking is to being (in that being unveils itself to thinking), so is believing thinking to the revelation (which comes to faith as the word).

36 Cf. Bonhoeffer's *Letters and Papers from Prison,* published posthumously (1954), also under the title *Prisoner for God,* ed. by Eberhard Bethge; trans. by Reginald H. Fuller. His scattered remarks have led to considerable discussion, published largely in symposia under the title *Die mündige Welt,* I (1955), II (1956).

to its adaptation to its purposes of the Creation narratives current in its environment. For the wonder that Israel is, rather than not being at all, is the basic experience of Israel in all its history. It is this wonder at being that brings occurrences to expression as unfathomable events whose ground is designated with the term God. The reference to the living God, in distinction from a *prima causa,* does not so "answer" the question of being as to end the wonder and amazement in the question, but rather "answers" the question precisely by pointing to the God before whom this wonder at being is constant and inescapable. This is what is implicit in its experience of occurrences in the stance expressed by the formulae "Blessed be the God who has . . ." or "I thank Thee, Lord, for thou hast . . ."[37] It is not inappropriate that Berachoth commemorating specific occurrences should on occasion attract to themselves a parallel line commemorating God as "Creator of heaven and earth." The function of the prophetic message is again and again to recall Israel from presuming upon its existence— which presumption is a religious parallel to what Heidegger condemns in his rejection of "metaphysics"—back to an awareness of the questionableness and contingency of its being at all, i.e., to that which in religious language is described as its dependence upon the living God for its being. This function was also performed to an extent by the formulae which built ontological awareness of the question of being into Israelite history, an awareness which is a basic and pervasive point in which the *Heilsgeschichte* story is quite historical. Berachoth and Hodayoth are the language of being, which, in view of their historicality, means that Israelite history is a history of being, history experienced in the

---

[37] Heidegger himself (*Was ist Metaphysik?* [8th ed., 1960], p. 49) can speak of "the hidden thanking which alone shows due appreciation to the favor involved in being entrusting itself to man's nature to be thought, in order that he may with regard to being take over the guardianship of being." This is wrongly translated in *Existence and Being,* W. Brock, trans. (Chicago: Gateway Paperback Edition, 1960), p. 358. Ernst Fuchs, *Hermeneutik* (1954), p. 72, ends his discussion of Heidegger with the remark that man is "the being that thanks." "Where this thanksgiving becomes audible from the depths the word has 'succeeded,' for there the question about God has found its answer."

wonder of its being, i.e., experienced as God's act, as *Heilsge-schichte*. This *Heilsgeschichte* rooted in the formulae is then also *Lichtungsgeschichte*, a history of being unveiling itself in numinous language through which its subject matter entered Western thought, and through which modern thought can rediscover that subject matter.

According to Heidegger, language is not to be understood as arising basically from the thinking subject, man, but rather as arising from "being" unveiling itself, speaking to us, giving rise to language which calls "being" into thought. This has been the historic function of Berachoth and Hodayoth, and is illustrative of a deeper dimension in the relation of the Old Testament to the New Testament. Old Testament *Heilsgeschichte* as *Lichtungsgeschichte* expressed in such language as Berachoth and Hodayoth reaches its climax in the New Testament, where being is unveiled as the basic miracle of resurrection or new creation. It is the function of such language, according to Heidegger and the Bible, to call forth man's wholeness, his *Heil* (German *heil* = English "whole," "hale"). Such wholeness Heidegger describes formally in terms of a square, in which the divine, the mortal, earth and sky touch. This concept of wholeness, so much more analogous to the Bible than to the otherworldly "salvation" of the mystery cults which Bonhoeffer insists our world has outgrown, is the sense in which *Lichtungsgeschichte* is for Heidegger *Heilsgeschichte*. As such *Lichtungsgeschichte, Heilsgeschichte* could play a historic role in our culture today.

From here perspectives for systematic theology open, which cannot be pursued in the present essay on the relation of the Old Testament to the New Testament. But perhaps a few may simply be listed. The current correlation between the kerygma and existentialism may broaden into an ontological dimension of the Christian message without surrendering the historicity of existence. For the relation between the God who raises the dead and the God who calls that which is into being, a relation sensed by Paul (Rom. 4:17), may become clearer. As a designation for the being of "that which is," which keeps prominent a wonder at the fact that things are, the theological concept of the *Creation of creatures* may gain new relevance. And as the biblical term in which the question of being is answered without stultifying the awe inherent in the question, and thus without obsuring the question itself (the fate of philosophy as ontology fell into metaphysics), the term *God the Creator,* as a nonmetaphysical term, may again become useful in theological discourse. The concept of language as not deriving from man's subjectivity but rather coming to him from its subject matter, most basically as being unveils itself to thought, may prove a new medium of intelligibility for the concept of the *Word of God.* And in view of the wholeness language calls forth as it unites the divine and mortal, earth and sky, the preaching of *salvation* may be able to put aside its otherworldly religiosity which seemed to Bonhoeffer so out of date, and regain some of its biblical down-to-earthness. *Hermeneutic,* as the continuation in our day of the biblical event of language, could provide common ground in terms of which the various theological disciplines could meet.

The prolegomenon to any such theology, i.e., the transcendental condition of its possibility, is the correlation of the historicality of *Lichtungsgeschichte* with the historicality of *Heilsgeschichte.*

9   Revelational Discernment and the Problem of the Two Testaments

JOHN DILLENBERGER

I

The Christian claim that the new reality has become manifest and is continually known through proclamation and reception in the mystery of faith raises the inevitable issue of the role of an antecedent or contributing reality or realities. It is the problem of the relation of the Christian faith, anchored in the New Testament, to the Old Testament. The formal interrelation is obviously attested in that the Christian Scripture contains the Old and New Testaments. This, however, does not settle the question of the diverse range of interpretation. On the one end, the Old Testament is interpreted as a precursor, now no longer valid or relevant except as an historical past that is entirely overcome and therefore to be abandoned. On the other end, it is said to have essentially the same content as that of the New Testament. Then the two Testaments represent a different "administration" of the same reality.

Circles of the early Church, as in Alexandria, stand near the first alternative, not in that antecedent realities are denied but because other avenues of knowing, such as gnosis, were preferred by

159

the Greek mind. The consequence was that the New Testament was read with the categories appropriate to gnosis and with attendant disregard of the Old Testament. The recognition that this happened in the early Church, and that similar cultural categories all too often adversely conditioned the understanding of the New and Old Testaments, has led to the contemporary accent on Hebraic ways of thinking and to affirming the historical nature of biblical faith. The issue is not that there are ways of thinking which in and of themselves are Christian. Rather, there are ways of thinking which include insights, nuances, aspects of life and meaning which are essential to the riches of the Gospel; and, on the other hand, there are ways of thinking which do not and cannot carry these dimensions, and thereby subvert the fullness of Christian understanding. The latter was a serious problem in the early Church.

It is also the problem in the contemporary Church. The exposition of the New Testament in terms of moral and/or spiritual insights destroys the understanding of both Testaments through categories inadequate for expressing the central dimension of faith. The existential interpretation of Scripture, more adequate in its categories of understanding than the previous view, has not given evidence of doing justice to the full dynamics of life and faith.[1] A simple recovery of Hebraic and allegedly historical ways of thinking will not in itself solve these problems. Indeed, for theology, more richness and diversity are essential than such a recovery would provide. But it is also true that to ignore Hebraic ways of thinking is to subvert Christian understanding all the more. Herein lies the significance of the Old Testament for Christian life and thought: while the new reality in Christ is central to Christian understanding, its full comprehension demands the articulation of life and the problems of God's dealing with the world, both of which are exhibited with great poignancy in the Old

---

[1] See, for example, Amos Wilder's criticism of the position of Ebeling and Fuchs in the forthcoming volume, *The New Hermeneutic*, John Cobb and James Robinson, eds.

Testament. The message of the New Testament may grasp and transform one's life without reference to the Old Testament; but the riches of that message will not be apparent without the whole range of possibilities—those both of God and of man—exhibited in a pilgrimage which, however interpreted, is unique in history. The riches of faith demand the Old Testament. The theological delineation which follows in the next section is designed to show on a crucial level how the riches of faith demand both Testaments.

II

Revelational discernment is a category drawn from and applied to the biblical heritage as a key to its meaning. As such, its content is continually open to correction and reformulation through the light that breaks forth out of this double or dialectical encounter. In terms of content, it refers to the utilization of the known gift of grace or forgiveness and its implications—understood as the heart of the New Testament message—toward the enrichment of life and understanding by discerning retrospectively the heritage of both Testaments. The actual, though not necessarily chronological, starting point is the faith engendered through the New Testament. But it is fructified by discerning its antecedent forms in the Old Testament and its context.

This approach excludes all direct and abstracted or extrapolated ways of knowing God or speaking about God. The knowledge of God is not self-evident. There is no direct testimony, no way of utilizing nature and history as direct pointers to the actuality of God. Such an immediate use of nature and history is indeed the expression of man's religiousness. But, as Calvin has indicated in accord with Romans I, while this approach expresses a haunting recollection of God, it nevertheless turns the truth of God into a lie. Man is said to be without excuse, for "ever since the creation of the world his invisible nature, namely his eternal power and deity, has been clearly perceived in the things that have been made" (Rom. 1:20). But this knowledge cannot be turned to advantage or made into a virtue. The process is not reversible.

Indeed, the content of such knowledge is directed to the creature rather than the Creator (Rom. 1:25). That is why a natural theology is inevitably an idolatry.

Although the knowledge of God is not self-evident, and therefore God faces the consequent risk that he may not be readily known properly or at all, there are resources in God's being for encountering man. Knowledge of God is the fruit of God's wrestling and struggling with man, not merely of man's struggling with himself or with God. Man has only known God as God's possibilities have become actualized.

The concept of God's possibilities is not to be identified with a theory of development or evolution. That would return us to direct testimony. Nor is the stress upon God's possibilities to be understood as a limitation of the nature of God. That would again be direct evidence. Rather we are speaking about God's way of dealing with us as discerned in faith in the light of Scripture. God's possibility is his self-chosen way of communicating with man, namely the struggle to be known of man, as man authentically remains man. While man has violated his relation to God and therefore distorted his own being as well, God has not chosen to violate or destroy us, but to make himself known to the world in ways which eventually elicit a particular kind of faith and understanding. Surely that is a clue to the reality of God.

Nature and history are the matrix of God's possibility for man. What is God's possibility in nature? Assuredly primitive man's temptation was to multiply the powers of divinity in proportion to the powers of nature. There was a power, or demigod, or god, for wind and rain and vegetation and fertility, and for those complex junctures where nature and the events of history seemed to coincide or coalesce. And primitive man undoubtedly hoped that the powers might be influenced in order to bring about a meaningful structure of existence, a pattern analogous with the cosmos and the dependability of sun and moon and stars. It is no wonder that there was a penchant for order in ancient life and religion; it was order that was longed for in the face of the immediate vagaries of nature and of history. While we moderns rebel against order because we have encountered its over-rigidities, we must remember how redemptive a structure of order appeared to primitive man.

When the powers were consolidated and the gods diminished, no basic change in conception or orientation occurred. That development expressed the increasing cohesion of man's social existence. But Israel's religion is ultimately to be understood at another level without denying the cultural factors. The question has been asked, for example, whether it is accidental that the God of Israel emerged from the desert. The desert stands for the monotony of nature, where the powers and forces of nature have been reduced in number. The monotony of the desert is like the monotony of monotheism. Could it be that God's possibility of moving ahead another step in the enterprise of being known occurred in the monotheistic impulses stemming from the desert? This does not imply that the desert always produced the monotheistic tendency or that pure monotheism emerged from the desert.[2] The monotheistic direction was assuredly established to such an extent that conflict emerged between the God Yahweh or the tribal god or collective tribal gods and the gods of Canaan. Eventually the God Yahweh emerged and took on the legitimate functions and powers of the gods of nature. The history of Israel therefore does not represent a simple development from henotheism to monotheism, a process in which the powers of gods are consolidated under one God who eventually becomes the supreme God. Rather, the monothesim of Israel is the fulfillment of the monotheistic impulse from the desert situation and its actualization in the domains of Israel's history.

It appears that God's possibility received a new thrust in the desert where, in this limited way, his lordship became apparent. Of course, one can interpret the matter quite differently. From a

---

[2] The emergence of Israel's monotheism is a debated scholarly question. But it should always be kept in mind that even fairly conservative scholars date it comparatively late.

sociological and psychological orientation, the materials can be read as the social conditioning of the gods in which monotheism eventually emerges. But from another angle, the social process is God's opportunity. The insights of sociology and psychology may be used to illumine processes, such as the emergence of the God of Israel. The validity of believing in the God of Israel is called into question only where the insights of other disciplines serve doctrinaire explanatory functions. Theologically, it can be said that the God of Israel broke the forces and powers of nature and in principle made it impossible thereafter to confuse nature and the powers of nature with God. Therefore, for Israel, "the heavens declare the glory of God" (Ps. 19)—they do not prove or argue his existence, as Pascal has so movingly indicated.[3]

The God of Israel also broke the forces of history. God entered into covenant with Israel. He succeeded in shaping a people particularly and uniquely related to himself. He would be their God and they would be his people. But the question immediately arose, "What does it mean to be his people?" Surely if they are his people and live reasonably in terms of what he requires, God will appropriately reward them, for such is the nature of justice and of God. Nor should it be too difficult to obey God, for the law makes the requirements of the Covenant concrete, and the prophets remind those who follow the law that it must be understood from its covenantal foundation. For a time it appeared as though this reasonable expectation would prevail. The Israelite nation was gradually formed; there was a semblance of justice and order; and the nation bade fair to have a place among the nations of mankind. The situation of Israel was not simply that she had enemies, as all people do, but that in relation to them she had a special role to play, for she stood related to God. Surely God could be identified minimally with comparative justice in the world, and therefore Israel's historical life could show the way of this God.

The events of history, however, were not to support this way

---

[3] *Pensées,* No. 243.

of viewing things. A full-fledged nation had been formed, but catastrophic events ensued: the kingdom was divided, the northern kingdom fell, the southern kingdom also fell, and many of the inhabitants were carried into exile. And while the political situation under the Greeks was tolerable, they profaned the Holy of Holies, the central religious symbol of integrity. In this process the role of Israel in the world increasingly became a problem to faith. The overly pious understood the disasters in the history of Israel to mean that the people were not obedient enough. The prophetic counsel to trust Yahweh, however, clearly did not mean that if he were trusted everything would turn out all right, as the pious always tend to believe. Trust Yahweh, not the chariots of Egypt, was a counsel for allegiance and not a stratagem of victory. Indeed a case could be made that the righteousness of Israel was clear enough when compared to the rest of the nations. The taunt of Israel's enemies in the midst of each defeat—"Where now is your God?"—must have wrung the heart of every Israelite, for it was reasonable to believe that God is a God of Justice, a God who is good for something.

Given the historical destiny, it is no wonder that messianic expectations intensified. No good could be expected from the historical drama. Perhaps only a transcendent Being who combines power and goodness could bring historical affairs to their fulfillment. The Israelites knew that the good people in the world apparently had no power and that the powerful people were scarcely good. Only God could combine power and goodness. This seemed to be the lesson of Israel's history.

The situation was no different in individual terms. Like Israel, Job was comparatively righteous. In fact he was attested to be "blameless and upright." Like Israel, he had his troubles; and in the midst of them he, too, was confronted by the ever-present counsel that the misfortunes of one's position in the world must be due to his sins. Like Israel in her saner moments, Job was willing to admit his sin. The problem, however, was the disproportion between virtue and suffering in the world. The wicked prospered, the innocent suffered. The times were out of joint. Job had only the alternatives of absolute rebellion or of affirming a righteousness which was entirely incomprehensible to him. Whatever the historical judgment on the happy ending of the story,[4] it is theologically not worthy of the poem. If the answer to Job's question depended upon the ending, one might blasphemously reject God.

In the context of the previous delineation, the Old Testament is the history of why it does not make sense to believe in God. A God ought to be good for something; but in both social and individual life there is only defeat, agony, and suffering. In the history of Israel and in the person of Job, comparative righteousness has no future in history.

The New Testament related that Jesus of Nazareth, a totally righteous man, was crucified. In him the dramatic problem of Israel in the world is intensified. That which the Christians claim to be the resolution of the issue could only be viewed, from the standpoint of Israel, as the final traumatic expression of the problem. In the words of St. Paul, this is a stumbling block to the Jew, for instead of even partial vindication there is only the absurdity of total suffering. For those who, like the Greeks, had no expectations, the affirmation concerning Jesus of Nazareth could only be folly (I Cor. 1:18–26).

It is at the point of the Cross, however, that the center of Christian meaning rests. Perhaps God could not become known as God except in the midst of suffering. Perhaps only suffering, and nothing else in all Creation, could be free from being confused with God. Everything else in human existence came out of the positive aspects of nature or history and was in danger of becoming identified with God. In the latter case, the question of God was always posed through something positive which argued for him, or in terms of purposes which were to be fulfilled. If one were to look for a God, it would hardly be in the midst of suffer-

---

[4] See, for example, Aage Bentzen, *Introduction to the Old Testament*, Vol. 1 (1957), pp. 175–77; Robert H. Pfeiffer, *Introduction to the Old Testament* (1941), pp. 667–75.

ing. A God is meant to deliver from suffering. In Christian understanding, on the contrary, it appears that God could only be disclosed as God if he were encountered where the temptation to confuse anything in the world with him was removed. One could say that the Cross is the point at which the full wrestling of God with the world becomes apparent—where, therefore, God is known as God and where man's appropriate place in the world is set forth in the context of suffering.

The problem of the Christian movement has always been that the notion of suffering has been open to being domesticated and distorted. A major part of the history of the Church in the early and the medieval periods was the attempt to explain suffering and to set it within a wider context in which everything was given its appropriate place. The radical element of the Reformation revolt consisted in putting the Cross again in the center of Christian understanding and meaning. The truth that God could only succeed in making himself known in the midst of suffering had been discussed in previous periods when Christians, by turning suffering into a virtue, almost destroyed the possibility of God becoming known. There was considerable courting of martyrdom in the early Church. The adage that the Church was built upon the blood of martyrs is not necessarily a positive fact. For the ancients, as we know, to die well was a goal devoutly to be desired, for through such death one could erase a miserable life. Thus it is an open question whether some of the early Christians who sought martyrdom so consciously and precipitately were not themselves pagan in this orientation. The problem of suffering in the world is that there may be no escape of martyrdom. Said Augustine, what if we were not permitted to die?

In Protestant history, as well as in certain aspects of the previous mystical tradition, the tendency has been to oversentimentalize the Cross, to have either a sentimental pietism concerning the Cross as in the hymn, "The Old Rugged Cross," or to verge on an erotic, and perhaps neurotic, attitude toward the Cross, as in certain intense forms of the mystical tradition.

It may be that the Cross, which stands at the center of the

Christian movement, is the reminder of the harsh reality of suffering from which no one is excluded in principle. In itself, suffering is not a good thing. To declare it good is to distort it. It may correct some people; it may drive others to the edge of existence and to destruction. It may divide the faithful from the unfaithful; but this is not its reason for being. Suffering is the absurdity, the absurdity beyond all the sin of man. It is the absurdity which cannot be comprehended and for which no explanation suffices. It is the absurdity which is God's opportunity.

There is no answer to the problem of suffering. The only possibility is to declare in faith that God may be known in suffering, for indeed God has been there all along. The Cross is the silent reminder that one may not escape the vicissitudes and suffering of life. Even those who relatively escape the agony of the world must know that the Cross is the mark of their existence as well. There but for the grace of God go they. This is the meaning of the injunction to take up one's cross and follow Jesus, the Christ. The injunction does not refer to false manufactured crosses but to bearing the cross, to knowing God through the joyful agony of the world even when its burdens do not press in upon one in all their urgency. The Cross, therefore, belongs to the utmost of joy and of suffering. The revelation of God and the life of men in faith coincide at the point of suffering.

The consequence of suffering is the emancipation of man from attributing ultimate meaning to his own involvements and achievements in history. To ascribe such meaning to them is idolatry, and it subverts even the normal possibilities of man by tempting him either by perfectionism or opportunism. Indeed, all the programs of life have to be laid down in the light of the Cross. But the act of laying them down, in this instance, is not their abandonment; abandonment refers only to the ascription of meaning which such programs cannot bear. That which is laid down is, in the light of the Cross, in fact taken up again. This is the freedom of the Christian in the world. The programs and possibilities of existence have lost their ultimate meaning. They now take on meaning in the light of the Cross; that is, their fragmentary but positive significance is seen in the context of their proper limitation. Programs of life, therefore, are opportunities in which the Christian struggles and works for justice; they are not courses of action for reaching ideals that are final, but they provide contexts where one obediently struggles and lives. This indeed must be the dynamics of action under the Cross. The achievements of history stand under the Cross. Standing under it, they participate in the agony of suffering, incompleteness, distortion, and perverseness of human existence. To deny this is to attempt to be as God has not chosen to be—the God who has encountered us in the agony of suffering and of defeat, and whose victory is apparent in the base and weak things of existence.

Where God's possibility becomes actualized in that God is known as God at the edge of suffering, man discovers his freedom and true being. Such a total biblical faith, dramatized in the history of Israel and in the Cross itself, has the possibility of setting man free from himself—from the burdens of his existence and from the need to make his activity count with finality even as a contribution to the total development. Such a man holds all things lightly, but wrestles to be obedient to the Source of his life. He lives by a power not his own which transforms everything that he touches, whether it be with reference to a discernible achievement in history or the word of comfort spoken in the midst of situations where no margins of change remain. This is the man who measures the height and depth and whose understanding of the love of God breathes freedom into his being as he exercises his energies in the choices and struggles that are set before him.

It is surely clear that such a faith is grounded and nourished in the Gospel of the New Testament. But it is equally clear, if the present exposition is valid, that its contours and scope of meaning demand and include the Old Testament. Indeed, two major affirmations concerning the place of the Old Testament are indispensable. First, faith's appropriation of the revealing of God as God includes the discerning of his revealing possibilities and activities. Second, the New Testament faith, for its fullest appropriation, includes in its own horizon the actuality and awareness of genuine and false alternatives. For in the Old Testament the range of human possibilities and of existence, apart from and in faith, are delineated. And the New Testament faith can be seen in its fullness only as these possibilities, as well as man's existence in the present, are taken into account.

III

The theological-historical position outlined in the previous section and designated as revelational discernment provides the frame of reference from which observations are made concerning the positions of contemporary biblical scholars on the relation of the two Testaments. Thus the issues are not joined at the technical and critical levels of Old and New Testament scholarship. They are joined at the point, rather, where theological discernment affects what is seen at technical levels. The critique proceeds from a theological-historical orientation, the net effect of which is the reinterpreted incorporation of motifs in biblical scholarship. One cannot speak of revelation as history (*Offenbarung als Geschichte*), or the history of salvation (*Heilsgeschichte*), or typology, or promise and fulfillment, or historicity, as interpretations able to bear by themselves the full weight of God's becoming known as God through the media of the biblical heritage. Such concepts do express motifs of understanding adequate for aspects of the total problem but not adequate as such for the wider dimensions envisaged in the concept of revelational discernment.

Bultmann has seen the radicality of New Testament faith—that its full dimensions are not to be found in the Old Testament and, indeed, are grounded in proclamation and the attendant event of grace. The Old Testament, therefore, is the history of failure.[5] Even its aspects of promise are to be understood in this negative

[5] R. Bultmann, "Prophecy and Fulfillment," *Essays Philosophical and Theological*, James C. G. Greig, trans. (1955), p. 200. Reprinted in *Essays on Old Testament Hermeneutics* (1963), Claus Westermann, ed., pp. 50–75.

role, contrasting to the New. Hence there can only be a backward glance to the Old Testament. It does form a part of our history, but in the same way as does Socrates.[6] A critical understanding of past history is always illuminating. But essentially the Old Testament must be abandoned in the light of the New.

The history of failure, if one were to regard the Old Testament as such, need not be as negatively understood as Bultmann sees it. If, as has been suggested, God could only have become known as God in the midst of total failure, exemplified in suffering, then Cross-Resurrection takes on its full contours only from the light of failures which have become God's opportunity. Indeed, without a constant retrospective appropriation of the history of failure, faith and a mode of existence can be so readily identified as to preclude reference to the God who is continually making himself known.[7]

Precisely in that Bultmann rejects the Old Testament as theologically necessary, he has shown the radical possibility of starting with the New Testament faith in looking toward the Old. The interpretations with which we are concerned do affirm that the Old Testament can only be seen in the light of its end or fulfillment: Christ. But the decisive issue in interpretation is whether this is said in a retrospective or prospective sense. While categories such as prophecy and fulfillment are understood from the standpoint of their fulfillment, they do pose the issue in terms of a past actuality which has been verified or completed. But is it not the case that the New Testament, convinced of the new reality, speaks of the prophecies and promises now in the light of fulfillment? Indeed, this it does precisely because only by the new reality is the prophecy so transformed as to be acceptable. This retrospective vision must be strictly adhered to in theologically interpreting the relation of the two Testaments.

---

6 Cf. *supra* pp. 31 f.

7 The full grounds of this statement cannot be entered into in the confines of this essay, for that would demand an extensive theological exposition. But the theological thrust of Section II surely shows the affinities and decisive differences with respect to Bultmann.

The forms of New Testament understanding are forged in the Old Testament. Gerhard von Rad has shown that crucial categories—election, fulfillment, God's acts, wrath, righteousness, faith—have a special character in the Old Testament not found elsewhere, and that they forge the context in which the New Testament equivalents, in the light of the new reality, transform their meaning.[8] The new reality breaks all these common bonds; but the previous failures are nevertheless the formal context for new understanding. Perhaps God's possibilitiy of being known in this new way was facilitated by the Hebraic-Greek juncture, when the power of the Hebraic was still pervasive but no longer able to dominate the scene because of the widespread Greek language and culture.

This formation of concepts which move from Israel into the New Testament world can obscure the decisive difference if the new reality is not firmly grasped and used as the angle of vision from which the Old Testament is understood. The failure to grasp this rigorously has led to the concrete difficulties in the interpretation of prophecy and fulfillment. In the present discussion, Bultmann's understanding of prophecy and fulfillment in terms of prediction and fulfillment need not detain us.[9] Undoubtedly such elements are present; but they are part of the world view of the time and can be interpreted rather than abandoned. Such interpretations stress the promise side of prophecy rather than the predictive categories. The nonliteral approach is reflected in the thought of individuals as diverse as Gerhard von Rad, Walther Zimmerli, Brevard Childs, Wolfhart Pannenberg, and so on.[10]

---

[8] Gerhard von Rad, *Theologie des Alten Testaments,* Vol. 2 (1960), pp. 367–68.

[9] Bultmann, *op. cit.,* p. 188. (Westermann, *Essays,* pp. 54 f.)

[10] Gerhard von Rad, *op. cit.,* pp. 340–43, 398–99; Walther Zimmerli, "Promise and Fulfillment," *INT* (1961), pp. 310–36 (Westermann, *Essays,* pp. 89–122); Brevard Childs, "Prophecy and Fulfillment," *INT* (1958), pp. 259–71; Wolfhart Pannenberg, "Heilsgeschehen und Geschichte," cited from *Probleme alttestamentlicher Hermeneutik,* Claus Westermann, ed. (1960), pp. 295–318 (Westermann, *Essays,* pp. 314–35). See also Pannenberg's sections in the book he has edited, *Offenbarung als Geschichte* (1961).

In different ways, they distinguish the content of prophecy from its form. Moreover, they both identify and distinguish the content of the Old and the New. For Gerhard von Rad the Christ event is beyond all its anticipations, but there are analogous realities in the Old Testament. God's Word and his acts belong to both Testaments, and the prophetic word reaches to Christ and has its authentic expression in him.[11] Frequently this is expressed typologically, as for example in the conclusion of the story of Joseph and his brethren, where it is declared the brethren meant it for evil but God meant it for good (Gen. 50:20). This word receives its genuine content and full meaning in Christ but is prefigured in the Joseph story.[12] Given the fulfillment in Christ, the two Testaments can be said to substantiate each other.[13]

For Zimmerli, the relation of prophecy and fulfillment rests not in the coming to pass of concrete events, but "in the promise of the divine person, about which all Old Testament promise revolves . . ."[14] For Brevard Childs, "word and fulfillment are part of the self-same reality. However they do not have the same wholeness." Indeed, "the witness of the Gospels is that in Jesus Christ the prophetic word of the Old Testament is filled."[15] Hence, Childs sees the relation as one of filling, making full, total, and whole with the riches of Christ. Pannenberg, too, uses the categories of promise and fulfillment, insisting that they be understood from the standpoint of completion.[16] He insists that there must be some genuine identity in essence and content, although the details which connect the two need not bother us.

Indeed, the God made known in Jesus Christ is the God of Abraham, Isaac, and Jacob. That statement rests on the New Testament confession. The movement must be from the New

---

[11] Von Rad, *op. cit.*, pp. 396, 398 f.

[12] *Ibid.*, p. 382.

[13] *Ibid.*, p. 400.

[14] Zimmerli, *op. cit.*, p. 337. (Westermann, *Essays*, p. 121.)

[15] Childs, *op. cit*, pp. 267, 269.

[16] "Heilsgeschehen und Geschichte," *op. cit.*, p. 299. (Westermann, *Essays*, pp. 317 f.)

Testament to the Old Testament for understanding it in the Church. As a scholarly, historical, theological enterprise, the Old Testament can be understood in its own light, with all the forms of faith and unfaith which it conveys. As a book understood theologically in the Church, the same contours of faith and unfaith disclose God's impossibilities and possibilities with man, now seen in their full intensity in the Cross. It is because of this that the categories of promise and fulfillment are not adequate for the whole picture. They distort through an analysis of the part and the whole, and by laying aside what in the Old Testament does not contribute to this end.

The categories of promise and fulfillment as well as typological exegesis are related to *Heilsgeschichte,* in which the development of Israel's history is the medium of God's revelation and the movement toward its culmination, Christ. Therefore, it, too, falls into the category of the part and the whole. In the case of Gerhard von Rad, the full articulation and attention to the wide range of New Testament thought make the theology of the Old Testament stretch, if not break, the contours of *Heilsgeschichte,* even though he is considered one of the chief exponents of this view. Walther Eichrodt, though less centrally associated with this movement, more typically elaborates the position in terms of the concept of covenant, which he vigorously applies to the materials of the Old Testament.[17] The fullest development of a theological position built upon *Heilsgeschichte* is the position represented by Pannenberg and the group surrounding him. The history of Israel

---

[17] In the English edition of his *Theology of the Old Testament,* Vol. 1, J. A. Baker, trans. (1961), Walther Eichrodt has added an excursus (pp. 510–20) in which he objects to the theological determination of historical materials in Von Rad's work and virtually places him adjacent to Bultmann. But the matter can be interpreted otherwise. The interpretation and reinterpretation going on within the Old Testament may find its analogue and completion in further reinterpretation from the standpoint of New Testament faith. A suggestive approach standing between Bultmann and Von Rad seems to be that of Friedrich Baumgärtel, "Das hermeneutische Problem des Alten Testaments," cited from *Probleme alttestamentlicher Hermeneutik,* pp. 114–39. (Westermann, *Essays,* pp. 134–159.)

is the history of God's self-revelation, seen in all its manifestations in the indirectness of disclosure and finding its fulfillment in Christ. History—and that means the whole complex of historical events as distinguished from historicity—is the comprehensive category of interpretation. Revelation as history has its original expression in the events of Israel's history and reaches universal scope in the development of apocalypticism.[18] "History is reality in its totality"[19] and the medium of God's activity and disclosure.

Pannenberg's concern is surely to see the entire biblical material as part and parcel of the revelation of God which is brought to fulfillment in Christ. As with Von Rad, all the materials must be included.[20] But in the rightful regard for the totality of the history, God's revelation is too directly and positively identified with the block of history that Scripture represents. In contrast, a concept of revelational discernment which is anchored in the New Testament faith and which appropriates the Old from that standpoint, can include the variety of Old Testament theology and see in it God's possibilities with man.

---

[18] Pannenberg, "Heilsgeschehen und Geschichte," *op. cit.*, p. 300 (Westermann, *Essays*, p. 319); also *Offenbarung als Geschichte*, p. 96.

[19] Pannenberg, "Heilsgeschehen und Geschichte," p. 301. (Westermann, *Essays*, p. 319.)

[20] Pannenberg's biblical orientation has the range of Von Rad; but the type of approach appears closer to Eichrodt.

10 History and Reality

The Importance of Israel's "Historical" Symbols for the Christian Faith

G. Ernest Wright

The relation between the Old and New Testaments is a problem which must be investigated simultaneously on two different levels. One is exegetical and "phenomenological"; that is, it involves the attempt to ascertain and describe the actual use of the Old Testament by the New, and also the thought world of the early Church, in order to see just what were the dominant structural influences from the world of old Israel in the life and work of the new community. The second level is the hermeneutical and theological question as to what role the Old Testament should actually fulfill now in the Christian's life and thought, and in the mission of the Church. Dr. Bultmann's essay, with which this volume begins, proceeds at the second or hermeneutical level—if we understand by hermeneutics the Church's (or the Christian's) attempt to proceed from textual and historical exegesis to the present situation in which the interpreter lives. That is, hermeneutics involves the constant attempt to comprehend the old within the context of a new situation. It, therefore, is always concerned with reinterpretation, whereby a creative past is brought into meaningful relation to a present in which, without such interpretation, the power of the past event is lost.

To discuss the significance of the Old Testament within the scope of hermeneutics as here defined cannot proceed, then, apart from the context of one's theological outlook as a whole, a theology which articulates the faith meaningfully in the time and place where one exists. Hence it is inevitable that what one sees as basically important in the Old Testament will be determined ultimately not simply by what exegesis discovers, but by what one now thinks can and should be affirmed. A predetermined theology leads one to articulate what is conceived as revelation in the Old Testament, and in the Bible as a whole, a revelation in which the writer or speaker is personally involved and which he is prepared confidently to affirm as "the Word of God" for our day. It is the purpose of this paper to inquire whether Bultmann has exhausted the theological possibilities for our time. If other approaches are permissible, one of which will here be suggested, then as a matter of course different views of the importance of the Old Testament for the Christian faith will be affirmed. In other words, one's theological understanding of the meaning and significance of the Old Testament is simply an integral part of his theological position as a whole, and cannot be separated from it.

I

If the procedural analysis given above is correct, then one cannot simply raise questions about Bultmann's exegesis and by this means hope to establish a different view. Bultmann's basic question cannot be answered by simply quoting and expounding New Testament texts; for it is not so much, "What does the Bible say?" as "What can I believe?" Yet it is inevitable that one's theological position and tradition will influence even his exegetical discoveries. In Bultmann's case one may note the following things among others:

1. In his first footnote (*supra*, p. 8) he indicates by implica-

tion his *historical* assessment of the New Testament in relation to its environment. The religious movement depicted in the Christian canon is referred to in the plural ("both religions") and is said to have both continuity and discontinuity. It is discontinuity which is emphasized, however, so that the Old Testament is no more than one among many phenomena in a complex background. In one sense no historian can object to such a statement. Yet if upon it a whole structure of exegesis is erected, then the Old Testament scholar must object that it lacks precision. From a purely descriptive standpoint the canonical Bible, taken as a whole, displays an inner movement and an interrelatedness of its parts which are far more characteristic of itself than anything either of its two main sections has in common with their environment. From the comparative religion standpoint, if from no other, this point seems obvious, though it is frequently obscured in scholarly writing. Furthermore, it must be recalled that behind Bultmann's statement lies his interpretation of the powerful influence of "Gnosticism" on the New Testament, especially on the Johannine literature, an interpretation which Old Testament scholars generally have long regarded as far too conjectural.

2. Further, Bultmann's Lutheran background comes out, perhaps, in the amount of space he gives to the Law–Gospel problem. To one raised in another tradition, particularly the Reformed or Calvinistic, this problem does not assume the centrality that it does for the Lutheran. Paul's letters to the Galatians and Romans can be viewed either as central to the understanding of the Bible as a whole, or as primarily an attack on Judaism and not actually an interpretation of the religion of the Old Testament, at least as the latter is known by modern research. What we choose to emphasize at this point may be determined by our unexamined presuppositions. Furthermore, one's background may even influence his understanding of Old Testament law so that it is regarded as little more than a concrete expression of a general sense of unconditional moral obligation, though like Old Testament "religion" as a whole it is shut up within the history of the

"Jews" and conceived as applying only to them. In other words, background presuppositions may lead to *emphases* totally foreign to what was central to Israel herself.

3. The perspective in which one interprets the person and work of Christ is also influenced by theological presuppositions. Thus central to Bultmann's presentation of Christ are the concepts of revealer, Word, and God's eschatological deed of forgiveness. In the essay before us in this volume it is the last mentioned which receives most emphasis, because of the Lutheran's absorbed fascination with the Law-Gospel problem. The complexity of the New Testament's own presentation, and particularly its elaborate use of Old Testament analogical expressions, is consciously neglected. At one point only, in reference to a saying of Luther, is an analogy permitted: ". . . Jesus, in so far as he engaged in teaching, is not different from the Old Testament prophets; rather, like them, he proclaimed the Law and consequently belongs within the Old Testament" (p. 12). Here almost unconsciously a "bias" or "leaning" is disclosed that cannot be supported by careful exegesis: namely, that the Old Testament and law are almost synonymous, and that the prophet is a teacher of *torah*—though the teaching office in Israel as a matter of fact was primarily a function of the priesthood, not of prophecy. The statement can only be comprehended when the term "law" is understood not in terms derived from exegesis, but as a generalized expression for obligation.

II

Of more fundamental importance is the question as to what theological possibilities exist for the modern man who would take his Bible seriously. Central to Bultmann's view is a sharp reaction against "historicism," that is, against the whole attempt to interpret the Old Testament simply as the history of a past religion. If one would be "genuinely historical," he will not read the Old Testament "as the document of a bygone time" but as a literature which presents the possibility for a relevant understanding of human existence now, of what I am and how I am to exist (pp. 13 f.). The true function of religion, and therefore the function of scriptural study, is not an objective understanding of what *once* happened in history, but a personal concern for how the past events illumine my self-understanding at this moment of time.

This attack on "history for its own sake" on behalf of an interpretative procedure concerned with the "genuinely historical," as Bultmann defines it, is very important and suggestive. It surely has implications, not least in importance for the teaching of the historical disciplines in theological education. Yet, when all is said and done, what really is the "genuinely historical" for Bultmann? In the final analysis, does not the existentialist background of the viewpoint actually dissolve the historical, so that one lives, alone, in the presence of the new existence, the eschatological deed of forgiveness wrought in Christ? Is not the fulfillment and the "eschatological event" the end of significant history in this perspective? If so, then the conclusion is almost inevitable from the beginning: the Old Testament is not revelation for the Christian except in a very limited and provisional way. It is not God's Word in the Church except as one finds in it "what is already known from the revelation in Jesus Christ" (p. 32). It is helpful only in the sense that it makes God's Word in Christ understandable.

If, however, the Old Testament is continued in the Church's proclamation, the inviolable conditions are the rejection of every form of allegory in interpretation, and the acceptance of only that understanding of it which prepares for "the Christian understanding of existence" (pp. 33 f.). By implication, then, one must conclude that the Church's vast expenditure of money for Old Testament departments, for Old Testament scholarship, for historical and archaeological research, for the teaching of Hebrew —all of this in the last analysis can only be viewed as very problematical.

The implications as thus stated may be unfairly and extremely drawn, because they represent the "bias" of the present writer. Yet to one who has so recently supervised the expenditure of some $90,000 in an archaeological expedition, with more yet to come, the essay makes this impression! And the question arises with even more urgency as to whether the "genuinely historical" of Bultmann is actually a valid assessment of the role of the past in the present, of the Old Testament in the New, or of the Scripture in the Church.

In Bultmann's program for demythologizing the New Testament he is deeply concerned, as all of his critics ought also to be, that the Bible be read in a truly meaningful way, for the repetition of past formulae will not necessarily proclaim the saving power of the Gospel in our time. Hence, quite appropriately, he insists that biblical cosmology must be translated for a world which has no geography for heaven or hell. As he proceeds, however, it becomes clear that the true aim of demythologizing is not simply to state cosmology in a meaningfully anthropological fashion, but also to eliminate virtually all symbolical and analogical language as appropriate to man's understanding of himself. In so doing he does not wish to make the distinction, which Reinhold Niebuhr deems so significant, between the *permanent* and the *primitive* myth "in every great mythical heritage. This deals with aspects of reality which are supra-scientific rather than pre-scientific. Modernistic religion has been so thin on the whole because it did not understand this distinction and thus sacrificed what is abiding with what is primitive in religious myth."[1]

To this writer the primary question in Bultmann's "genuinely historical" understanding is whether or not the nonsymbolic is ever a way to true self-understanding. Is it not instead a highly sophisticated abstraction which bears little real relation to the life-world in which I live?

In the words of a former colleague:

---

[1] "The Truth in Myths," *The Nature of Religious Experience: Essays in Honor of Douglas Clyde Macintosh* (1937), pp. 118–19.

I am a network of intentions or references which radiate out from my body into the past which I have been and am, into the future which I project ahead of myself, and into the life-space around me. These intentions reveal ranges of independent things and persons which are open to other perspectives than my own . . . In this lived existence, I am not only aware of objects of different kinds. I am also aware of the intentional attitudes with which each of these objects is necessarily correlated, such as love-hate, hope-despair, and the disinterested observation which is characteristic of what we call *reason* and *science* . . . Thus *my* world transcends itself and points to a further horizon, *the* world . . . In my personal existence I am a living bias, opening into a moving world-horizon that is filled with ambiguity, and where even the urge towards clarity and objectivity represents a choice ruling out other possibilities, and therefore bearing with it a certain risk. For a human person to give up all bias is simply to commit suicide. To be alive is to pursue certain values rather than others, and these values cannot be placed in a separate realm or region of their own. They are necessarily involved in the act of existing.[2]

The terms "value" and "bias" in this quotation would appear to have the same range as the term "meaning" when applied to my life-world. But how do I perceive these "meanings" or "values," and how do I attempt to articulate them? Only in my most sophisticated moments do I try to abstract them, state them nonsymbolically, lift them from my actual living world, and view them as objects. When I do so, strangely enough, they no longer have power over me; they lose their reality. For this reason, if I am really to penetrate the springs of my existence, I must deal with the whole symbolic structure of reality in which I live—or more precisely, with the competing symbolic structures. A certain friend, my car, Genesis 3, my desk, a loved teacher, the Cadillac of Professor X, Christ on the Cross, a certain book—these are "known" by me, not simply as objects in themselves, but as realities which are a part of my life and which come to mind when facing other realities, often of a completely different character.

---

[2] John Wild, "Existentialism as a Philosophy," *JPh,* Vol. 57 (1960), pp. 45–62.

The latter is possible only because they exist as images in my mind through which I face and interpret other objects or persons. They are encounters, or "events," in my personal history, a selection of which is preserved within me as images which determine attitudes and actions.

Thus the human being lives, and his actions are impelled, by images, which become symbols: that is, realities in which meaning coheres and which are the interpretative forces in the facing of present and future. One does not encounter the world directly. He creates, or has created for him, a world of symbols through which he experiences, interprets, and perceives "truth" in the objects, processes, people, nations, and cultural heritage in the midst of which he lives. A religion is the structuring of a certain group of symbols which are understood to portray ultimate reality and the manner in which meaningful life is to be lived in relation to it. By its very nature, therefore, a religion involves an articulated system of meanings within which a people finds its life. Conversion involves the restructuring of a person's existence within that particular structure of meaning. A particular "truth" only has meaning in a particular structure. To "demythologize" it, when this involves desymbolizing, is to rob a religion of its very being. In the life-world of the human being no knowledge of the Ultimate is possible in the last analysis, whether one approaches it scientifically, artistically, or religiously, except by means of a structure of symbols through which the Real communicates or makes itself known. Or, in Christian terms, God has revealed himself to us through his gracious condescension, through the accommodation of his infinity to our finiteness, so that "we speak of these gifts of God in words found for us not by our human wisdom but by the Spirit" (I Cor. 2:13, *NET*).

If there is a measure of truth in the above statements, then one could further assert that a human being who seeks self-understanding does not have the option of choosing between "mythical" and "nonmythical" conceptions of reality—using the term "myth" in the very generalized, imprecise manner now fairly common in theology. One has only the freedom of choice between rival symbolic structures. If so, then a "genuinely historical" understanding of the Old Testament should begin at this point.

III

In attempting to state positively the significance of the Old Testament for the Christian Church the point of beginning must be at an objective level. That is, with all of our limitations and environmental-theological predilections we must at least *attempt* to bridge the gap between ourselves and the ancient writing, in order to be sure that we get the central point, that we understand it as depicting a movement external to ourselves. If I am to find meaning within it for my own self-understanding, then it must not be because I appropriate it as I see fit, but because I initially attempt to understand and to find myself caught up within it. Bultmann's "genuinely historical" understanding is not stated in this manner. Does not his view prompt the query as to whether I am only a *prisoner* of my own self-understanding and that *self-transcendence is an impossibility?* If "the concept 'existence' must be the methodical starting point of theology,"[3] and if the concept is to be analyzed practically as an object of logic without any reference to the living world of images in which a person "exists," then the conclusion follows as here suggested. The kind of self-transcendence involved in the attempt to understand a people far removed from oneself is not emphasized. Does this suggest by implication, if not by direct statement, that the importance of historical research and of historical criticism in areas not conceived to be specifically "Christian" is of questionable worth to a Christian's self-understanding? *Heilsgeschichte* as kerygma is sometimes divorced from history, is dissolved into theology by means of a radical program of desymbolization, and thus is reduced to little more than a modern pietistic version of Gnosticism

---

[3] R. Bultmann, "The Historicity of Man and Faith," *Existence and Faith,* S. M. Ogden, ed. and trans. (1960), p. 92.

which is concerned not with history but with creation (life) in the presence of death (nonexistence).[4]

Modern historical research, allied with form criticism, has introduced fresh perspectives, and indeed radically new emphases, into biblical scholarship which are beginning to have profound influence on the "younger" theologians, at least in the United States. We now perceive that the first main point about Israel in her world is her peculiar interest in her history, the use her writers made of her historical traditions, the manner in which both public and private worship, and the proclamation of the divine Word by prophets, is firmly fixed within these historical traditions. Archaeological endeavor, furthermore, has shown that even the patriarchal and Mosaic narratives derive from actual historical eras, that the basic traditions, beginning with the Abrahamic, preserve authentic memories of actual ages whence they ultimately derive, even though in their present form they are far removed from their points of origin and have been interpreted and reinterpreted for religious[5] usage in later ages.

The Hebrew concern with a selected group of events which

---

[4] W. Pannenberg, with considerable justification in my opinion, has argued that the existentialist procedures of Bultmann and Gogarten dissolve the historical into historicity, while the *heilsgeschichtlich* emphasis of Barth and others tends to dissolve the historical into a sort of primal history, both representing a retreat from the ambiguities and uncertainties of historical criticism. See his essay, "Heilsgeschichte und Geschichte," in *Probleme alttestamentlicher Hermeneutik*, Claus Westermann, ed. (1960), pp. 295–318; Eng. trans. by Shirley Guthrie in *Essays on Old Testament Hermeneutics* (1963), Westermann, ed., pp. 314–35.

[5] This fairly neutral term is used here in order to avoid the term "cultic" now so popular in the circles of biblical scholarship. We are likely to conceive anything "religious" in antiquity as cultic; but this does not mean that ancient man would have seen the matter that way. In any case, in Israel literature arose in a variety of ways and with a variety of interests, as was the case also in Babylon, where the evidence is much clearer. Parts of literature could be used, redrafted, or recapitulated for cultic and other usages, even as the elements behind it had a variety of backgrounds. The term "cultic" ought to be used with much greater caution, because a national tradition, even in Israel, had a more complex origin and transmission than the one-sided emphasis on cult and liturgy suggests. Here is another point where archaeological investigation into contemporary cultural areas can assist in matters of perspective and generalization.

alone explained the Israelite's identity and provided the clue to the interpretation of present and future; the new understanding of time; the verbal structure of the Hebrew language with its emphasis upon occurrence in contrast to a noun-centered language with its interest in universals—these have all been much commented upon in our generation and are adjudged to possess critical importance for the method and mode of Christian theological expression. Various factors have influenced this current emphasis, but of basic importance has been historical and archaeological research which, by providing background, enables the interpreter to focus squarely on those central points which characterize the literature. Without reviewing further the current insights into the theological significance of Israel's event- or history-centered mode of religious expression and involvement, let us turn briefly to a consideration of its significance for a "genuinely historical" understanding of the Bible.

1. Is the biblical Word of God to be conceived as the Word which one existentially grasps, the proposition which illumines self-understanding? Obviously, the biblical Word is not primarily a truth, but an event which people met or encountered on the level of daily life, completely and entirely within history. There was no spiritual realm of "faith" which transcended earthly existence; the two-realm order of reality was rejected. Life was to be found in God's creation, the sole arena for which man is responsible. The Tree of Life, life beyond death, whatever is previous to time and whatever will come after time—these are God's prerogatives, withheld from man's responsibility. The biblical event, then, is an occurrence in the realm of human living which structures life, which produces in the community of the individual and in the individual himself a new conformation or *Gestalt*. The event brings into being, and is remembered in such a way that it continues to form, a powerful *image*, a creative image, which cannot be reduced to an abstraction, whether as principle, law, grace, or forgiveness. Jesus Christ, who was born, who suffered, and who died under Pontius Pilate, is recalled as a

real person in a particular history. His image or picture as an
actual person is the creative center of the Christian's life. To
possess that image is to be "in Christ," to follow Christ, to take
up my cross as he carried his, *to become involved in my history
as he was in his.* Christ is the historical event—in this instance a
person with a history—who forms a powerfully creative image
which would restructure the self in history to conform to him.[6]

2. By what means is the historical person, Jesus, to be understood in relation to ultimate reality? I am inclined to begin by
laying far more emphasis on a dynamic view of the *canon* of
Scripture than seems to be found in Bultmann's presentation. Is
the canon little more than a historical accident, so that method-
ologically one can disregard it and *begin* with the assumption of
two radically different entities in its two parts? Has the Church no
valid theological point in its attempt to articulate a doctrine of
the canon? Is not the canon as a whole[7] the prerequisite for a
"genuinely historical" knowledge of Jesus Christ? Without elaboration I shall simply assume the validity of the biblical canon for
reasons which may be clearer below.

Moreover, it must be admitted that one's theological position
as a whole will determine the context within which he discusses
the matter. For my part I have never been able to follow those
who emphasize the Person of Christ in such a way as to occasion
a radical displacement of the doctrine of the Trinity, or to sub-
sume the Trinity under or within its second "Person." In this
connection, where the canon is assumed, I would not attempt
any further definition of the Trinity than the general statement
that it does not represent in the *first* instance an abstraction concerning substance, hypostases, persons, but instead the Church's

---

[6] For a description of what this biblical manner of presentation means for
theological method, with particular application to theological ethics, see the
very original work of Paul L. Lehmann, *Ethics in a Christian Context* (1963).
An important implication is that the event of Christ in its totality suffers a
radical reduction when confined to "God's eschatological deed of forgiveness."

[7] I speak here of the canon dynamically without reference to the ancient and
modern discussion about marginal books which may be omitted or admitted
without changing anything essential.

attempt to summarize the complexity of God's presentation of himself within the canon's historical progression. And the purpose of this presentation is truly "historical" only when it provides the structure within which my own life is reformed. In the words of Calvin, the Scripture in this sense becomes the spectacles whereby "the otherwise confused notions of Deity" are dispelled and we are provided "a clear view of the true God."[8]

Finally, in an attempt to suggest the theological stance from which the meaning of Christ may be discussed, one must ask whether the initial assumption, namely, that the starting point of theology is existence, also presupposes that the only truly meaningful categories for self-understanding arise from within the psyche, from the human fate of death, from anxiety and dread. The criticism of this basing of theology on existential philosophy has been that, like pietism and revivalism in Christian circles, it neglects man's social involvements, his nature as known from, and formed within, social and political groups.

In any case, the categories of understanding in the Bible are drawn for the most part from the political and social spheres, and they are understood to have had their original setting within the great Old Testament events to which allusion has already been made. They involve powerful historical images, creative of society and selfhood. They are coherent, particular, and structured, even within the great historical variety and movement of biblical history. As such, they have little to do with the archetypes of C. J. Jung which have their origin in the depths of the individual and in the collective unconscious. Instead, certain concrete images have been chosen and others rejected because of Israel's understanding of the singularity of her history.[9] As a result the individual is transcended, overarched. Self-transcendence is expected

---

[8] *Institutes of the Christian Religion*, Bk. I, Chap. VI. In a discussion of the Trinity in dynamic terms the precise number "three" is sometimes questioned; but I should be inclined to insist on at least three over against the common use of the term improperly as a surrogate for an actual or implicit Binitarianism of Father and Son.

[9] So, more fully expounded, Bernhard W. Anderson, "Cosmological and Historical Imagery in the Bible" (unpublished).

of him. He is required to turn his eyes initially from his own existence to contemplate not his own possibilities, but the possibilities within a life not his own to which he is related. *The primary question, then, is not the importance of Israel's history for our history, but whether the God of Israel is the God and Father of Jesus Christ and our God.*[10]

In sum, then, it is here assumed that the Person of Christ is to be understood in the following terms:

1. To speak of him is to envisage the whole New Testament story about him—his life, death, teaching, and actions—as forming one whole event. This event has the effect of creating fresh possibilities. It becomes a powerfully creative image which recreates life in both the individual and the community who participate in it. The event is pictorially preserved in the mind, and as such is a source of power, while reduction to theology and the nonpictoral can rob it of its power. Ideas in themselves rarely move the soul until they are presented in living, pictoral form, that is, in historical images.

2. To understand the meaning of Christ requires attention to the Christian *canon* of Scripture, for the Church's doctrines of both canon and Trinity place the person of Christ within a context of divine activity in history. The meaning and mode of this divine action is the central content of the canon of Scripture through which God is revealed as *our* God and in the form by which he would be known as our God. Therefore the biblical language, or mode of knowing, is of basic importance for the Christian faith. Its symbolic patterns provide the sole means by which Christian truth is finally to be grasped meaningfully even in this present. Translation into other patterns must constantly be attempted, but in the last analysis the communication of the

---

[10] So also Anderson, *ibid.:* "If, as a matter of fact, the historical images of the Old Testament are theologically indispensable, then the question, 'Is Israel's history *our* history?' should be interpreted to mean, 'Is the God who is described in the Old Testament our God?' " For an excellent treatment of the subject under discussion by a Reformed theologian, one with which I would be inclined to associate myself, see Arnold A. van Ruler, *Die christliche Kirche und das Alte Testament* (Beiträge zur Theologie, Vol. 23; 1955).

Gospel is possible only by means of a core group of historically derived images—or events which produce both the images and the appropriate language whereby the faith is articulated.

IV

If this is true, then the following affirmations could be supported.

The function of our cultural and religious past is to provide the context, the spectacles, wherein or whereby one finds it possible to interpret—to see meaning in—the present. Past events, and the images they have created within a community, must constantly be reinterpreted in any present. Otherwise their power is lost, or they are set within a special realm of their own, apart from lived history. In this manner, for example, there has been separation of Gospel from world, of grace from nature, of *Urzeit* and *Endzeit* (the primeval and the eschaton) from that arena which is properly our real concern, the present with its challenge to responsible vocation by the way of the Cross.

The function of the Old Testament in the Christian Church, then, becomes of profound importance, though in a very different dimension from that described by Bultmann. The faith of Israel has provided for Christian theology that "doctrine" of God; that view of time and history; that view of man in history as creature who, though a sinner being redeemed, is charged with great responsibility and vocation; that view of community created for vocation within which the individual finds his own calling and true individuality—in other words, the basic elements of Christian theology within which alone the figure of Jesus the Christ can be grasped. At the same time these elements provide the bulwark against the naturalistic, nonhistorical views of reality which would turn the biblical doctrine of God, and therefore the understanding of Christ, into something other than it is.

An approach of this sort is very different and, in my judgment, far more "genuinely historical" than the assessment of Christ as the eschatological event of forgiveness, an event which in effect sets aside past events as really meaningful for self-understanding because they are transcended. Here the emphasis is on the fact that a creative past provides the manner and mode in which truth is grasped and by which the present and future are interpreted. Every present, of course, poses a hermeneutical problem: the language or symbols of understanding in terms of which past action and past adjustment have successfully been undertaken must be reinterpreted constantly. Thus the elements available for understanding will be far more complex in the first century B.C. than in the time of Isaiah, even as the latter period is more complex than the time of Israel's tribal league (period of the Judges). Yet this necessity for reinterpretation inheres in the biblical view of existence under God. *The hermeneutical process, however, is not the rejection of the originally creative events, but the searching out of the various facets of original meaning in order to lay emphasis upon that which is still of basic importance. Reinterpretation of images is not their denial but their interpretation in relation to present historical realities.* Furthermore, the self-transcendence involved and required does not first of all turn the eyes of faith within, but without, to the deeds of God and to the world. The individual is thereby delivered from the prison of self and the almost neurotic fascination of the self with its internal problems, including its ultimates of life and death.

In brief compass, I would single out the following structuring elements which gave form to the Old Testament images and which become constituents of the Christian faith:

1. The great events known as God's "mighty acts" (call and promise to the Fathers, deliverance from slavery, preservation in the wilderness, gift of a land) are all interpretations of historical memories and data which envisioned ultimate Power at work to save the weak and the oppressed. Here, in one series of human happenings, Power is seen in relation to right, compassion, and salvation, with the result that righteousness proceeds not from norms or principles, but from Power acting in compassion to save those unjustly deprived of right. Righteousness in the Bible, springing from this rootage, will move in the direction of saving-

suffering love (Christ on the Cross) which at any one moment exists in tension with justice, though never setting it aside.

2. This directing and saving Power has created a people out of the lost, and by this act has established a particular type of relationship. With unexpected and unmerited kindness the ultimately Superior has granted life, land, and government to those who are inferior. Hence the latter are bound by ties of gratitude to this great One in a relationship which he has initiated. Worship will center, therefore, in praise of him who has so acted, and in confession of unworthiness by the recipients of the action. Ethical obligation will then be understood as the proper right of the Superior and the grateful response of the recipients. In its deepest sense sin will be seen as betrayal of the relationship, as disloyalty and ingratitude. It is guilt, and only the action of the Superior in atonement and forgiveness can repair the breach.

3. Two basic structures, drawn by analogy from political life, were employed to give formal expression to the type of relationship thus established. Both are treaty (covenant) forms of a type which contain no specified means of legal enforcement—like international treaties generally. Recently it has been shown that the Mosaic covenant was adapted from the second millennium B.C. vassal treaty, in which the emperor or "king of kings" establishes a relationship with a vassal. The first part of the treaty, composed in the first person, is free narration, never stereotyped, describing the suzerain's benevolent acts to the vassal. Then follow the covenant stipulations, detailing the interests of the suzerain which the vassal vows to observe. The treaty includes the list of witnesses and also the statement of the advantages and disadvantages of obedience ("blessings and curses"), the sanctions in every case being religious. Israel used this type of covenant form to present in objective terms the mutual relation between God and people. Thus obligation was formally set in the context of grace. Indeed this is the only treaty form that permits this rather unique relationship to be expressed in a formal way. Under this analogy, therefore, God appears to Israel as the

sovereign of the world who has entered into a special treaty relation with one people, though at the same time his royal relation to all peoples is affirmed.

The other treaty form is a very special type which probably had its origin in the ancient theologies of kingship in western Asia. According to these theologies, the divine council members selected and empowered the king and committed themselves to support him in the office. In Israel this treaty form found expression in God's covenant with David, wherein God committed himself to sustain the dynasty. This covenant was considered an act of pure grace on God's part; its analogue was found in the Abrahamic covenant—that is, in the interpretation of the old tradition concerning the relation of the patriarchal "God of the Fathers" to the patriarchal clan. God makes a promise and seals it by a vow; the recipient of the promise is not required to take an oath, although it is expected, of course, that he will fulfill the office to which he has been appointed. God is also pictured in sovereign terms, though his royal relation to the people is mediated through the king. It should be observed, however, that the Mosaic covenant provided the governmental structure of the Israelite tribal league in which leadership was charismatic. This covenant form was prior to monarchy. The monarchy, therefore, had to adjust itself to the pattern already established. The charismatic rule of God was continued in the office of prophecy, an office which ran parallel to that of the monarchy.

Two main histories of the people in their Promised Land survive, and each uses one of the two covenants as the means for interpreting Israel's history. The Deuteronomic history (Deut.–II Kings) sees the whole meaning of Israel's series of crises in terms of the broken covenant and the action of God both to repair it (charismatic leaders, the monarchy, prophets, many saving acts) and to take appropriate action against those who have violated the relationship and broken their vows. The Chronicler's history (I–II Chron., Ezra–Neh.), on the other hand, was written after the disasters had fallen, at a time when attention was on a small group of survivors who were seeking to rebuild in Palestine. Central to this history is the Davidic covenant which gives assurance of an eternal and most gracious commitment of God upon which the community may rest its hope.

These considerations indicate that two main factors are fundamentally important for understanding Israel's images of reality: first, the interpreted traditions which suggested the type and direction of the divine action in history, and second, the covenant forms which by analogy furnished the structures for the conception of the Real. These structures, derived from historical *political* patterns, signified that the primary sphere of divine interest was the world of human life; God will appear in the guise of a sovereign ruling this world, and by his marvelous acts will determine to make it his kingdom. The earth as his Creation is the good earth, a fit setting for the good life. But the dominant language for communicating meaning will be derived from historical forms, and more especially from the two primary spheres of social life: law and government. The family pattern will be used repeatedly, but only as a way of illuminating particular implications in the Ruler-servant pattern, or, as in the case of the fatherhood of God, only to stress the personal relationship of the monarch to his people as fatherhood was commonly used by ancient monarchies.

Biblical theologies have not sufficiently emphasized the necessity for language analysis in order to understand the particularity of this religious view of reality over against other views contemporary with or subsequent to it. Each major attempt to interpret ultimate reality, and life in relation to it, has a language appropriate to its understanding of the truth. Because the apprehension of meaning is truly conveyed only by appropriate language, certain words are chosen and others set aside, a particular structure of images is evolved and another is rejected as wrong. The type of truth involved depends upon this symbolic structure. It is grasped only by him who finds his life restructured within the framework of the religion. In the Bible as a whole, truth has its own particular setting and definition. Whether it be seen as the person, Jesus Christ, or as the knowledge of God in the prophet, it involves the assertion of the sovereign claim of God and the necessity of an appropriate response at the moment in which one lives. Thus biblical "truth" employs a certain group of nouns, adjectives and verbs, descriptive of or derived from historical realities, which alone are believed to be adequate depictions of God. While a profound sense of humility before God's ultimately mysterious being is always present, what God has revealed of himself is believed sufficient for us to speak and live meaningfully in his presence. Moreover, it is characteristic of the history-centered language of the Bible that nearly all of the so-called attributes of God are at the same time descriptions of the life of him who "knows" God: e.g., righteous, holy, redeeming, faithful, just, gracious, loving, merciful, "slow to anger," compassionate, zealous, and so on. Among the exceptions we may note, as an example, the Hebrew conception involved in the word, *nāqām,* poorly translated as "vengeance." This is not a description of the good life because it refers to both the judging and redeeming activity of the sovereign Lord of history who bears ultimate responsibility for justice and salvation. Hence it is a prerogative of God alone. Hope is an example of a term not applied to God. In the biblical setting hope involves a conception of time to which God as sovereign is not subject and provides an exception to the historical and anthropomorphic images otherwise used of God.

Hence it can be affirmed that the basic language of Israel, given content by a certain group of events (or interpreted occurrences) and derived from the political, legal, and social spheres, is the basic language of the Church also. Though the New Testament is in Greek and not Hebrew, its conceptual language is largely a translation of an approach to reality, an understanding of truth, that is non-Greek. A long history of interpretation lies behind the evolved language; various "foreign" elements have been introduced; the new Event exhausts linguistic limits and requires experimentation. But truth as grasped through the images of the

Hebrew sense of reality, and through the language appropriate to it, is the only truth that is really adequate to the understanding of Jesus Christ.

V

To return to the beginning of this discussion, it may again be affirmed that one's understanding of the importance of the Old Testament for the Christian faith is simply one element in, and a derivative of, his theology. This essay suggests that a theology is possible which is based more on a study of the creative symbols and the language appropriate to them than on existentialism which rests its theological case on a language abstracted from a study of the psyche. If such a theology were given developed expression, then the importance of the Old Testament would be so obvious that it need not be argued. Instead, the more important task would be the meaningful exposition of the Old Testament in the Church in the knowledge that the Bible is ultimately a unity and that each part "makes full" the other.

The preservation of the historical language and symbols is of such basic importance, I maintain, that apart from them the Christian faith would be turned into a different type of religion, concerned primarily with the individual's search for ultimate security. In the Bible's view, whether in Genesis or in Paul, this ultimate security, the search for which is characterized by anxiety about death, is beyond our grasp. Indeed, it represents an area that is not in our control; it is something God has separated as his own preserve. The follower of Christ need have no fear of death, but nevertheless death is his lot—"dust thou art and to dust thou shalt return" (Gen. 3:19). Death is the measure of man's time, the time for which he is responsible. His community and he himself in the context of that community have been given a vocation within history, and God holds him accountable for his responsible use of this allotted moment of time. Such a view of time, of the meaning of life in history, of the directing hand of God over all human affairs, of his redemptive power at work in a struggle in which alone my life can find its meaning—this, as I see it, is what is centrally biblical, whether in Israel or in Christ. And it is precisely what existentialism, at least as Bultmann employs it, fails to make central. Indeed, it can never be central without the use of the Bible's own mode of language. Yet the use of the Bible's language is never uncritical. Every age, beginning with the tenth century B.C., has participated in the reinterpretation of faith's symbols—interpretation here being defined as the inquiry into the fundamental meaning of the image and its origin so that its contemporary importance can again be affirmed in relation to the events of our time. This procedure has always involved an element of selectivity. To refer to an example already given, the postexilic period placed its hope in the Davidic covenant. It was believed that the community had been destroyed in the requirements of the Mosaic covenant, and a major effort was undertaken to see that it did not happen again. The great accumulation of "Mosaic" laws was codified into a constitution, something previously unknown in the cultures of western Asia, and Mosaism was reinterpreted as life within the constitution. This is the setting of the New Testament's breach with, and critique of, Judaism. Hence the term "covenant" does not have as profound a use in the New Testament as it does in the Old. To recapture its original center the Apostle Paul was forced exegetically to go behind Moses to the faith of Abraham, for the current understanding of the Mosaic covenant as simply "the Law" made it irrelevant to his case. Later ages, particularly early Protestantism, made much greater use of the term. Modern historical criticism has recovered its original form and content, indeed its singularity as a profound religious conception in its time, and thereby has made it available for even more significant theological use. In other words, the historical context of the interpreter has much to do with the particular things in the Bible which he chooses to emphasize. Although historical criticism acts as an aid to the interpreter in his task, it also acts as his critic when his interpretation departs from the faith's central and characterizing structure and content.

While insisting on the basic importance of the Bible's historical symbols, and therefore of the Old Testament, we are nevertheless continually faced with various biblical conceptions which are problems to us. This is particularly true in the area of cosmology, in terms of which God is conceived as ruling from his heavenly throne, surrounded by his council of ministers (angels). Obviously, such views can no longer be taken literally. Yet is it not possible to preserve the historical symbols apart from the cosmology in which they had their original setting? This is the problem, formulated by Reinhold Niebuhr, of separating the permanent or the structurally basic from the temporal elements which have to be laid aside.

More fundamentally important is the question of the relation of the symbols to the Real. If the historical is so basic to the Christian's knowledge of God, and if the historically derived symbols for understanding are crucially important for the Christian's apprehension of truth, what is the relation of the historical to God? Israel's historical understanding of the "living God" must be taken seriously as more than simply metaphorical because the ultimate Mystery, the ultimately Holy, the "ground of being," actively reveals itself historically. Yet in what sense may it be affirmed that Reality is truly historical?

One mode of expression is the biblical term "glory of God." In the Old Testament the "glory" (*kābôd*) is the revelation of God's presence in the world, or, specifically in a large group of passages, "the shining, refulgent envelope which surrounds God's being" (Albright). This term indicates both the reality of God's presence in the world of which he is sovereign, and his mystery, which hides him from human sight, handling, materialization, manipulation. According to Paul God has given us "the light of the knowledge of the glory of God in the face of Jesus Christ" so that we "are changed into the same image from glory to glory" (II Cor. 4:6; 3:18). Here is one striking term which suggests the hiddenness and mystery of ultimate meaning beyond our grasp and at the same time the actual appearance of the Real behind this mystery within human history so that we are changed to conform to the image which it reflects.

The central issue in Christian theology, in the words of a colleague, can never be "elevation from the finite to the infinite dimension, but *restoration to the unhindered rule of God, i.e., the kingdom of God*. This restoration encompasses both the vertical and the horizontal dimensions, truth and salvation, conversion and social righteousness. Redemption is not a mere spiritual deliverance *from* the categories of time and space, but restoration *in* these categories which are constitutive of the human existence and man's history."[11]

The Christian's knowledge of God, then, is a saving knowledge within time and space. There is no other realm to which one can turn; there is no possible knowledge of an Absolute beyond and apart from history. Instead, history supplies both the arena and the mode of revelation. One can logically deduce that God as he is in himself is not bound, determined, or exhausted by the forms of the biblical revelation. The Christian affirms, however, that no knowledge of him is possible except within the realm where he has chosen to make himself known; and this involves the full use of analogical language. In other words, the historical process may not be identified with God; neither is it permissible to assume uncritically that one can arrive at the very being of God by the biblical analogies, any more than by the existentialist's reduction of the historical and social through the analysis of existence. Yet the Bible may be viewed as God's manner of making himself known as *our* God. Here he has accommodated himself to our finitude within the forms of time which are lived and filled by human action and emotion, affirmation and denial, love and hate, joy and sorrow. In so doing he has created the vision of true community in the people of God; of the true humanity in the person of Jesus Christ; and of the purpose of both in a temporal context of the now and the not yet; of the present which is filled with the excitement of the action of the living God, and of the coming time in which the fulfillment of promise assures direction and hope.

---

11 Heiko A. Oberman, "Protestant Reflections on Church and State," *TL*, Vol. 4 (1961), pp. 60–65.

11 The Way of the Promise through the Old Testament

CLAUS WESTERMANN*

There is complete agreement among modern Old Testament scholars that the event of the Exodus from Egypt is of fundamental importance.[1] As yet no such unanimity has been reached concerning the effect of this basic act of God in the history of Israelite faith and worship. One line which runs through the whole Old Testament and in addition indicates the clearest and most important point of transition to the New Testament is that designated by the two concepts, promise and fulfillment. In recent decades it has evoked extensive discussion.[2] This discussion has been impeded, at least in the German-speaking world, by the vagueness and ambiguity of the terms employed: announcement (*Ankündigung*), promise (*Verheissung*), prophecy (*Weissagung*). While Bultmann, for example, begins with the concept of

---

* Translated by Lloyd Gaston and Bernhard W. Anderson.

[1] "The liberation of Israel from the Egyptian 'house of bondage' is and remains fundamental for the religion of the Old Testament." See G. Quell, *TWNT*, Vol. 3, under *apokaluptō*, p. 574. "We must start from the fundamental belief of Israel that Jehovah saved them out of Egypt." See N. Snaith, *Mercy and Sacrifice: A Study of the Book of Hosea* (1953), p. 53.

[2] See the collection of essays entitled *Probleme alttestamentlicher Hermeneutik*, Claus Westermann, ed. (1960), where the most important literature between 1950 and 1960 is brought together. Eng. edition, *Essays on Old Testament Hermeneutics* (1963), ed. by James Luther Mays.

prophecy, Zimmerli puts the entire emphasis upon the concept of promise. Baumgärtel does the same, but his understanding of "promise" is quite different from that of Zimmerli. Precise definition of these terms is of little avail because they are so deeply rooted in the history of theology that they have frequently undergone change and hence a univocal meaning cannot be derived from the history of their use. Also, to begin with the terms used in the New Testament would present difficulties because they already give expression to a particular interpretation of the relation between promise and fulfillment. This has been shown especially by the discussion of the theses of Bultmann and Baumgärtel. [3]

We can attain clarity on this matter only by beginning with the situation in the Old Testament, and not just with the terms used for promise and fulfillment but primarily with the events themselves. Zimmerli has done this in his article, "Promise and Fulfillment,"[4] and it seems to me that we must continue in this direction.[5] How fundamentally our understanding of the relation between promise and fulfillment has changed vis-à-vis the earlier view can be seen by comparing Zimmerli's article with the book by F. Delitzsch, *Messianic Prophecies in Historical Succession*.[6] The most radical change is seen in the fact that formerly those who inquired into this relationship within the Old Testament concentrated only on specific *utterances* (*Worte*); which utterances of the Old Testament have the character of promise or prophecy and therefore can be brought into relation with the *act* of fulfillment reported in the New Testament? By contrast we see today that the promissory or prophetic utterances of the Old Testament

---

[3] Cf., *ibid.*, the articles by Bultmann, Baumgärtel, Von Rad, H. W. Wolff, Eichrodt, Pannenberg, and Westermann.

[4] *Ibid.*, pp. 69–101; Eng. trans. by J. Wharton in *INT*, Vol. 15 (1961), pp. 310–38; reprinted in Westermann, *Essays*, pp. 89–122.

[5] So also, for example, Pannenberg, *op. cit.*, p. 311. (Westermann, *Essays*, p. 329.)

[6] In German, *Messianische Weissagungen in historischer Folge* (1st ed., 1890; 2d ed., 1899; Eng. trans. by Samuel Ives Curtiss, 1891).

are not to be understood apart from a series of acts of God reported there; that is, they are a constituent part of a history reported in the Old Testament and can be brought into connection with the final fulfillment in the New Testament only in the totality of this history.[7] This is based on the simple methodological axiom that the individual utterance of the Old Testament must be first understood in its own context, in order then to become a word directed to us over the intervening historical interval.

I

In the events reported in the Old Testament (the history of God with his people) an important place is given to that correspondence of God's speaking and acting which is designated by promise and fulfillment. Such correspondence is already inherent in the act of God which provided the basis of the history of the people of God, for in the Book of Exodus this act is portrayed as the fulfillment of a promise (in other words, the keeping of a pledge or a vow):

> I have seen the affliction of my people who are in Egypt,
> And I have heard their cry because of their taskmasters;
> I know their sufferings,
> and I have come down to deliver them out of the hand of
>   the Egyptians,
> and to bring them up out of that land
> to a good and broad land, . . .

Ex. 3:7–8

The encounter thus portrayed by the Yahwist is a beginning not only in the sense that Yahweh here meets Israel for the first time, but also in the much more radical sense that both become in this encounter what they are from now on: Yahweh, the God of the people Israel, and Israel the people of Yahweh. Quite aside from

---

[7] "When we survey the entire Old Testament, we find ourselves involved in a great history of movement from promise toward fulfillment" (Zimmerli, *op. cit.,* p. 91; Eng. trans. [Westermann, *Essays*], p. 111).

the question of the historicity of Moses and his work, the significance of this event positively demands that it could not have happened wordlessly. It is unthinkable that this beginning occurred without words, as a more or less fortuitous happening which only subsequently was given the meaning that it has in the "historical credo."[8] To this act of deliverance belongs necessarily some event of speaking (*Wortgeschehen*). In the Yahwist's presentation God promises deliverance to those crying out of their affliction. The story begins, then, by relating that *a Word* comes to the slaves in Egypt, a Word promising deliverance. Only on the strength of this Word do the people set out from Egypt; and then along the way comes the mortal danger from which Yahweh delivers the helpless: he does what he promised them.

In the formulation of the Yahwist the promise that God gives has two parts: one in the perfect tense and one in the future. Moses first of all hears from God something that has already happened: "I have seen . . . I have heard," and only then does the announcement proper follow: "to deliver them . . . to bring them up . . ." As the grammatical formulation shows, the future (or imperfect) statement is subordinate to that in the perfect. The first, the primary, utterance is the sentence in the perfect, in which Yahweh is the subject. This is the form of the *assurance of salvation* (*Heilszusage*):[9] it announces something coming in such a

---

[8] Gerhard von Rad has shown that in the period before the monarchy Israel's faith was confessed in terms of a "historical credo," a brief recitation of Yahweh's mighty acts as found, e.g., in Deut. 26:5–9. See G. von Rad, *Genesis* (1961), pp. 13–23.—Ed.

[9] Professor Westermann uses the German word *Verheissung* ("promise") to include three forms of promise. To preserve this distinction we reserve the English word "promise" for the broader meaning. For the first form of promise (*Zusage*) of salvation we use "assurance," not in its subjective sense of certainty (e.g., assurance of faith) but in the sense of God assuring or promising an event. For the second form (*Ankündigung*) we use the English word "announcement" (cf. "the Annunciation"), that is, an announcement or prediction of what is to happen. And for the third form (*Schilderung*) we use the word "portrayal" in the sense of a description of the shape of things to come. It should also be kept in mind that the German word *Heil* (cf. "hale," "hail," "whole," "holy") has a broader meaning than English "salvation" and includes such ideas as health, wholeness, soundness, welfare, victory.—Ed.

way as to assure that with God it has already happened. This salvation-assurance in the perfect tense, with the two characteristics just indicated, is found throughout the whole Old Testament. It corresponds most clearly with the assurance of deliverance addressed to Israel in exile in the prophecy of Deutero-Isaiah.[10]

> But now thus says Yahweh,
> he who created you, O Jacob,
> he who formed you, O Israel:
> Fear not, for I have redeemed you;
> I have called you by name, you are mine.
>
> Isa. 43:1

Here, too, the salvation-assurance in the perfect is combined with an announcement of salvation (*Heilsankündigung*) in the future tense:

> When you pass through the waters
> I will be with you;
> and through the rivers, they shall
> not overwhelm you;
> when you walk through fire you
> shall not be burned,
> and the flame shall not consume
> you.
>
> Isa. 43:2

The situation in which this salvation-assurance is given to Israel corresponds to that of Exodus 3. Here, as there, the people suffer affliction; here, as there, the saving God encounters the people in their affliction first of all in a *Word*, a Word which assures them that with God deliverance has already been determined.

Between these two liberations from captivity at the beginning and at the end, each of which embraced the whole people, the salvation-assurance (formulated in the perfect tense) persisted in various forms. It received its clearest and most palpable expression in the salvation-assurance of the Yahweh wars.

---

[10] Cf. J. Begrich, *Studien zu Deuterojesaja* (1938).

> And Yahweh said to Joshua:
> Do not fear or be dismayed! . . .
> Arise, go up to Ai!
> See, I have given into your hand the king of Ai, . . .
>
> Josh. 8:1

Gerhard von Rad has shown the importance of this assurance given in the Yahweh wars and its survival far beyond the time of the "Holy War."[11] For the history of the promise in the Old Testament it is important that the response of faith belongs originally to this form of the salvation-assurance in the perfect tense, as Von Rad has shown. Also the situation to which the assurance of the Yahweh wars is addressed is an acute distress of the people.

Such an assurance in the perfect tense was also given to the individual Israelite during the Settlement; it was a cultic event —the "priestly salvation-assurance" which J. Begrich has deduced from the structure of the "individual lament."[12] The same features apply here too: it is addressed to a particular situation of distress (e.g., that of Hannah, I Sam. 1) as direct speech of God and in the perfect tense. It can also be called an assurance that prayer is granted (*Erhörungszusage*), for in it God says directly or indirectly that he has heard the entreaty of the one who called to him in affliction (corresponding exactly to Ex. 3:7!).

There are further forms such as the salvation-assurance given to the mediator in the story of his call (e.g., Jer. 1:8–10). With respect to their form the whole massive complex of prophetic oracles of judgment also belongs here,[13] in so far as they are essentially in the perfect tense and are the direct speech of God. Here the salvation-assurance has changed into its opposite: instead of God's turning toward his people, his turning away from them is proclaimed as fact, until with the realization of divine judgment full salvation can again be proclaimed.

---

[11] Cf. G. von Rad, *Der heilige Krieg im alten Israel* (Zürich, 1951; Göttingen, 1958).

[12] "Das priestliche Heilsorakel," *ZAW*, Vol. 52 (1934), pp. 81–92.

[13] On this see Claus Westermann, *Grundformen prophetischer Rede* (1960).

II

The promise at the beginning of Israel's history contains a future as well as a perfect aspect: God announces his intervention also in such a way that it reaches out into the historical reality of the people. The *announcement of salvation* (*Heilsankündigung*) can be connected with the assurance in the same utterance, as in Exodus 3:7–8 or Deutero-Isaiah's promise of salvation, or it can stand alone with its own, independent form. The latter is much more often the case. Here belong the majority of the oracles of the "prophets of salvation" which have come down to us (e.g., the words of Zedekiah in I Kings 22:11 or of Hananiah in Jer. 28: 2–4), but also such salvation-oracles (*Heilsworte*) as the prophets of judgment occasionally were commanded to proclaim, as for example Isaiah 8:1–4 or Jeremiah 32:14–15. Often such announcements of salvation for Israel take the form of an announcement of woe upon Israel's enemies, as in Isaiah 7:4–9 or Amos 1–2 and most of the oracles against the nations. The form of these announcements of salvation can be quite varied. They all have in common the future verbal form: something is announced which will come to pass. This can occur in sentences in which God himself is the subject, as in Jeremiah 28:11: "Thus says Yahweh: Within two years I will break the yoke of the king of Babylon . . ." But usually these announcements state in the third person what will happen; e.g., Isaiah 7:7: "Thus says Yahweh: It shall not stand and it shall not be. For the head . . ." An especially frequent feature of these announcements in the future tense is the confirmation by a sign. Thus in the examples just cited Isaiah offers King Ahaz a sign (Isa. 7:14)[14] and Hananiah breaks the yoke from Jeremiah's neck (Jer. 28:10).

In one essential point the announcement of salvation agrees with the assurance of salvation (and therefore in many promises the two can be combined): both are directed to a situation of

---

[14] For this reason it is wrong to see the arrival of the sign, i.e., the naming of the child, as fulfillment of the announcement of salvation!

distress. Both presuppose that the person or community addressed suffers acute, overwhelming distress; and the promised salvation has always, directly or indirectly, the character of deliverance from this distress. Again this can be seen from the two examples adduced: Isaiah 7–8 presupposes the threat to Jerusalem in the Syro-Ephraimitic war, and the situation in Jeremiah 28 is preceded by the first conquest of Jerusalem and the first deportation of 597 B.C.

A clear difference, however, lies in the fact that the assurance of salvation, whether given to the whole people or to an individual, is spoken with an unconditional certainty, while on the other hand the simple announcement of salvation remains throughout the Old Testament in a peculiar jeopardy, or one might even say, in a peculiar uncertainty. This is seen most clearly in the Old Testament's retrospective verdict regarding the prophets of salvation, a verdict which amounts largely to condemnation. Only a very few actual prophets of salvation have been received into the prophetic canon (Nahum, Habakkuk; also sporadic oracles of anonymous prophets). From I Kings 22 to Jeremiah 28 the Old Testament reports again and again the almost unbearable situation that salvation and disaster are proclaimed simultaneously in the name of God; and in every one of these situations, without exception, it is the prophet of judgment —never the prophet of salvation—who is confirmed. How difficult this jeopardy or uncertainty of the salvation-oracle was for the hearers is shown once again by the two examples from the books of Isaiah and Jeremiah: in the one case it was a word authorized by God (Isa. 7), and in the other it was not authorized (Jer. 28), but the word itself had no mark by which the hearer could decide with certainty whether it came from God or not. In addition there also belong to this group of futuristic announcements of salvation those which, at least as far as we can tell, were not fulfilled, as for instance Jeremiah's salvation-oracles for North Israel in Jeremiah 30–31; Ezekiel's announcement that Tyre would soon be conquered by the Babylonians, in Ezekiel 26–27;

or the announcement of Haggai and Zechariah that the time of salvation would begin with the completion of the Second Temple. All of these announcements of salvation have in common that they are addressed to a definite situation of distress and announce the end of this distress in a definite event. In prophecy of judgment the announcement of salvation underwent a radical change when, in view of the coming divine judgment upon Israel, it survived as the announcement of a new, transformed act of divine redemption.

III

To be distinguished from the two types of promise discussed above is a third which is essentially different in kind, the *portrayal of salvation* (*Heilsschilderung*). This no longer connects only two points, a concrete situation of distress and a concrete act of divine deliverance, but rather it contrasts the *external aspect* of the present condition to an *externally* portrayed condition of salvation. The simple announcement has here become a portrayal. The promised salvation does not merely consist of turning away affliction but rather there is promised an extensive change of present reality into a new, basically different reality. A typical example of such a portrayal of salvation is Isaiah 11:1–10. This text shows a characteristic feature by which the portrayal is easily to be recognized: the time of salvation portrayed almost always transcends in some aspects historical reality. In Isaiah 11:1–10 it is especially the peace among the animals that transcends historical reality (vss. 6–8); in other passages it is peace among men as a completely transformed, permanently existing condition (Isa. 2:1–4).

A second characteristic of the salvation-portrayal in distinction to the salvation-assurance and the salvation-announcement can likewise be seen in the example of Isaiah 11:1–10: the situation portrayed reaches beyond the sphere of man and of man's social life to the Creation. The animals' struggle for existence ceases, the desert becomes a garden, an abundance of blessing is spread abroad, and the sun sets no more. This feature is especially developed in the apocalyptic portrayal of salvation, the final stage in the history of the salvation-oracle. Yet this graphic portrayal of a condition of salvation has roots that reach back into the earliest period of Israel, for the very early blessings have a remarkable similarity to late portrayals; for example, the Judah oracle in the so-called Blessing of Jacob.

> Binding his foal to the vine
>> and his ass's colt to the choice vine,
> he [Judah] washes his garments in wine
>> and his vesture in the blood of grapes;
> his eyes shall be red with wine,
>> and his teeth white with milk.
>
> Gen. 49:11–12

Or in the oracles of Balaam:

> How fair are your tents, O Jacob
>> your encampments, O Israel!
> Like valleys that stretch afar,
>> like gardens beside a river,
> like aloes that Yahweh has planted,
>> like cedar trees beside the waters.
> Water shall flow from his buckets,
>> and his seed shall be in many waters.
>
> Num. 24:5–7a

It is clear that the portrayal of salvation has its roots (or anyway one root) in the blessing (or, more exactly, in the oracles that expand the blessing) and that the blessing, which certainly is pre-Israelitic in origin, was taken up into the prophetic oracle (*Seherspruch*) and further transmitted. But whether or not it can be demonstrated that this prehistory lies behind the portrayal of a state of salvation, it is certain that the latter, with respect to both its nature and its origin, is fundamentally different from the announcement of salvation and the assurance of salvation.

IV

The point at which the promise and blessing come together can be precisely determined in the Old Testament. In the passage with which we began, Exodus 3:7–8, deliverance of the people is combined at once with bringing them into the good land: . . . "to bring them up out of that land to a good and broad land, a land flowing with milk and honey, to the place of the Canaanites, . . ." While in this passage the promise of the land fills out and has even become part of the promise of deliverance, in Genesis 12: 1–3 it is the theme proper. Here it is combined with the promise of family increase ("I will make of you a great pepole") and in this form it runs through the entire patriarchal history. Both land and posterity are comprehended under the concept of the blessing.[15] God promises Abraham that he will bless him. Promise of blessing is really a contradiction in itself; what we have in Genesis 12:1–3 is a bold linguistic innovation of the Yahwist. For the blessing is essentially nonhistorical. It can be given to someone or denied to someone (in which case the blessing is always accompanied by an action), but according to the original understanding it cannot be held in prospect for a later time (e.g., Gen. 32 or 27).[16] In Genesis 12:1–3 the Yahwist combines the blessing with the promise and thus joins together two basically different theological conceptions: one in which God's saving action is central and one in which his blessing action is central. The taking up of the blessing into the promise provides the connection between the patriarchal history (which is wholly governed by the concept of the blessing) and the history of the people Israel (which is based on the Exodus deliverance and the confession of this event in

---

[15] "The word of Yahweh to Abraham which introduces the Abraham story indeed sounds the note of land and posterity as elements of promise, but it clearly places them in the shadow of the pledge of a blessing (unmistakeable in the five-fold use of the root *brk*)" (Zimmerli, *EVT*, Vol. 12 [1952], p. 313; Westermann, *Essays*, p. 92).

[16] On this cf. especially J. Pedersen's working out of the new understanding of "blessing" in *Israel: Its Life and Culture*, Vols. 1–2 (1926), pp. 182–212.

faith), a connection which finds literary expression in the placing of Genesis 12–50 before Exodus-Numbers. From this point on the promise of the blessing is included in the history of the promise. This is already evident in Exodus 3:7–8, where the formulation begins to pass over into portrayal: "to a good (= pleasant!) and broad land, a land flowing with milk and honey . . ." The meeting of these two lines is one of the most important points along the way of the promise through the Bible. One can trace these two lines running parallel, but never completely merging together, right into the New Testament.[17]

V

With the determination of the three basic types—the assurance, the announcement, and the portrayal of salvation—the way of the promise through the Old Testament is far from being sufficiently delineated. First of all attention must be drawn to a distinction which up to this point has only been touched upon here and there. In each case the question must be raised, to whom the promise applies—the people of God, the individual, or mankind (perhaps even the whole Creation).[18] Basic to the relationship of these three realms of salvation to one another is a simple observation afforded by an initial glance at the history of the salvation-oracle in the Old Testament: these three realms do not simply run along side by side from the beginning to the end of the Old Testament, but rather they are so interwoven that only the history of the salvation-oracles *as a whole* can answer the question of the interrelationship of the salvation promised to the people of God, the individual, and the world. A second observation follows when

---

[17] God's saving action in Christ is not limited to the suffering, death, and resurrection of Jesus; to his earthly career belong also the giving of blessing and increase through healing, feeding, and preservation of life. The blessing of the children belongs here, too. According to Matt. 10:13 the disciples not only proclaim a message but they also have a blessing to give or withhold.

[18] C. Steuernagel in "Die Strukturlinien der Entwicklung der jüdischen Eschatologie" (*Festschrift Alfred Bertholet* [1950], pp. 479–87), distinguishes between national, individual, and universal eschatology.

one surveys the wealth of salvation-oracles: throughout the whole Old Testament these three realms are related to each other in such a way that one never completely supplants the other. It is true that in some parts of the Bible and in some periods one of these realms of salvation can be so much in the foreground that the others are hardly even mentioned. Nevertheless, to the very end the salvation promised the people of God stands in the center of the two other circles: salvation for the individual and salvation for the world. It is to be clearly emphasized that the promised salvation applies first of all to the people of God. This realm of the salvation-oracle remains central right to the final stage. In Israel neither the salvation promised to the individual nor that promised to the world ever completely took the place of that promised to the people. Even when the "remnant" has taken the place of the empirical people, it still represents the people. Indeed it is precisely the concept of the remnant that shows how firmly faith in the promise clung to the belief that it was directed to the people.

This realm of the promise of salvation, however, was never so absolutized that no more room was left for the individual and the world. This fact, which is especially important for the history of the promise in the Old Testament, is already to be seen in the basic formulation of the promise to Abraham in Genesis 12:1–3. The combination of the deliverance motif with the blessing motif, which the Yahwist accomplishes here (see above), yields the result that the individual as well as the whole of mankind are included in the promise. The promise given to Abraham is directed properly to the people: "I will make of you a great people." Yet on the one hand this promise is given to the individual man Abraham (and the following Abraham narratives show that Abraham is not meant as merely a representative or a forerunner of Israel but rather as an actual individual with his personal destiny); and, on the other hand, the promise to Abraham culminates in the words: "in you all the families of the earth will be blessed." By this means the history of the blessing, which begins with

Abraham, is related to the preceding "primeval history" (*Urge-schichte*) of Genesis 1–11 which concerns mankind and the whole Creation. The history of the people of God, as sketched here in Genesis 12:1–3, remains in the center between God's dealing with the individual and his dealing with the world, right to the Servant songs of Deutero-Isaiah and the Book of Job.

This aspect of the history of the salvation-promise in the Old Testament is important for the fulfillment in the New, because it also holds true for God's final act of salvation in Jesus Christ that this saving deed has happened for the new people of God, for the community of believers. And yet it has happened in such a way as to remain in the center of salvation for the individual and of salvation for mankind and the whole Creation. However, even as in the Old Testament the relationship of these three realms of the salvation-promise cannot be determined once and for all in a timelessly valid way, so also is this impossible for the New Testament fulfillment. We may neither restrict the salvation finally revealed in Christ to the Church (particularism), nor turn it into a salvation only for the individual (individualism), nor disregard the Church confessing her faith and explain it directly as salvation for the world (universalism).

VI

A further differentiation is based on the manner in which the promise is mediated. Here especially the "in many and various ways" of Hebrews 1:1 applies. Promises are given directly by God only to the patriarchs, but in these cases there are wide differences in the way he speaks to them. It can simply be said that "God spoke to Abraham"; or God appears to Abraham, he speaks to him in a dream or through messengers in human form. Human mediators of the promise are never found in the patriarchal history. But from the beginning of the history of Israel onward the promise is given directly only to the mediator: Moses and Joshua, the seers and the prophets, the Servant of the Lord. The promises to the whole people and to individual members of the people are always given through a mediation, in a cultic act or through a prophetic word.

The history of the salvation-oracle in the realm of prophecy has not yet been clarified; we still lack a convincing, comprehensive presentation. The salvation-oracle, however, extends far beyond the realm of prophecy. The cultically mediated salvation-oracle had a far greater importance in Israel than used to be recognized. The salvation-assurance of the Yahweh wars belongs in the framework of a sacred observance. The priestly (or cult-prophetic) salvation-announcement, given in connection with the lament of the people or of the individual, is a constituent part of a cultic observance. The combination of the blessing with the promise gave to the oracle of promise a position in connection with the cultic blessing, as shown by the expanded blessing form in Numbers 6:24–26 and the blessing Psalms such as Psalm 67. From Psalms 91 and 121 and Job 5:18–26 we can deduce the assurance of blessing (*Segenszusage*) to an individual as a special cultic act, in which the blessing is also combined with the promise. In so far as cult prophecy is at the same time prophecy of salvation (*Heilsprophetie*) it points to a cultic situation of the oracle of promise. The many prophetic elements in the Psalms also point in the same direction. Finally, the many salvation-announcements secondarily attached to the prophetic oracles of judgment (as, for example, Isa. 4:2–6) are hardly to be explained apart from the cultic transmission of the oracles of the prophets.

From this may be derived a conclusion which is important for the history of the salvation-oracle in the Old Testament. This history is not completely described by establishing the points along the journey of the people at which some form of a promise was given and then stretching a line from these points to the fulfillment of the various promises. Rather, we must assume a broad, unbroken line of *transmission* of the promises, which, above all, was not a literary but a cultic transmission. If, from the angle of the New Testament, one sees just the individual points of the various promises made at some time or other only from the viewpoint of whether or not they are fulfilled in Christ, then he has not at all seen what is decisive about the life of these promises in the people of the Old Covenant: namely, how they gave constant support to the people of God step by step along their way and thus, being received and passed on from one generation to another, constituted a decisive element in the people's journey toward the hour of fulfillment. This *real* life of the promises is nowhere so immediately apparent as in the portion of the lament of the people (*Volksklage*) which we call "retrospect to God's former saving action." Here the people in their affliction cling to God's former assurances and hold him to his Word. Here it becomes evident that the essential element in the oracles of promise is not at all what can be seen subsequently by observation or reflection: the relation, discernible in the events, between an announcement and the coming of what was announced. Rather, the essential thing is the efficacy of the oracles of promise in their acceptance in faith by those to whom they were given.

VII

This is especially true of the "messianic" promises proper, of which we have not yet explicitly spoken. They cannot be classified unequivocally in any one of the three groups of salvation-oracles. They are all based on the prophet Nathan's oracle of promise for the Davidic royal house (II Sam. 7).[19] In the history of the promise this is just as new and basically as foreign an element as monarchy was for ancient Israel. This promise of Nathan is given at the point where one period of the history of promise and fulfillment is concluded, the period which began with the promise in Exodus 3:7–8. The period that now begins is characterized by the fact that the salvation God assures his people is bound to the institution of the monarchy. Yahweh had given a king to Israel in

---

[19] Cf. L. Rost, "Sinaibund und Davidsbund," *TLZ,* Vol. 72 (1947), cols. 129–34 and G. von Rad, *Theologie des Alten Testaments,* Vol. 2 (1957), pp. 308 f.

order to rescue it from the new political danger. To this extent Nathan's promise is in line with the old assurance of salvation. But in so far as the Davidic royal house, a political institution, receives the promise it is something completely different from, say, the assurance of deliverance in the Yahweh wars. A dynasty, endangered to the extreme by the humanity of its bearers, has become God's means of preserving the people! Hence it is a fact that the fulfillment of this promise of Nathan is not to be discerned in the history of the kings of Judah. On this point we must agree with Bultmann's presentation: the Judean royal history is actually a history of failure and it is portrayed as such in the Deuteronomic History. Out of this history of the failure of Nathan's promise have arisen the messianic promises. Decisively important for understanding them is the fact that behind every oracle in which (as in Isa. 9:1–7 or 11:1–10) a *quite different* king is promised there stands the long, difficult experience of the failure of another promise.[20]

These messianic promises of the Old Testament are not at all understood if their essential character is seen as a mere prediction. They are very questionable as such, for the simple reason that the coming of Jesus Christ largely did not correspond with their literal sense, as shown by the passionate contesting of his messianic claim. The messianic promises acquire their meaning solely from the special historical experience of Israel in which the agonizing contrast between high promise and depressing reality called forth the prospect of a different king. We hear a direct echo of this experience in Psalm 89. Seen from this aspect, the messianic promises are not—as is usually supposed—especially relevant to the fulfillment in Christ; their fulfillment in him is rather an especially broken, an especially hidden and indirect one.

---

[20] Here the question of dating can remain beyond our consideration. Even though today the great majority of scholars assign Isa. 11:1–10 to the prophet of the eighth century, it continues to be questionable whether the formulation "a shoot from the stump of Jesse" could have been coined in a time when the Davidic dynasty was still on the throne.

VIII

The messianic promises, based upon Nathan's promise to David, differ from the promises previously discussed in that here the promise to the people focuses upon an individual man as the mediator of God's promised salvation. Concurrent with the Nathan promise—that is, at the beginning of the monarchy in Israel—the prophecy of judgment begins also. To the same kings who received the promise of God's salvation, God's judgment is announced again and again, from David on to Zedekiah. In this way the whole period of the monarchy is defined by a peculiar tension: in the very same hour an oracle of salvation can be opposed by an oracle of judgment, both spoken in the name of Yahweh; or the prophet sent by Yahweh can oppose the anointed king—in the name of Yahweh![21] The salvation-promises given to the people and assured to the king now become ambiguous and history demands a resolution of this tension.

The consequence of this tension is, first of all, that the prophets as messengers of judgment are persecuted and their message suppressed; in ever-increasing measure they have to suffer on account of their message. This line reaches its high point with Jeremiah. In their very suffering the prophets—as the countertype of the king—also acquire importance as mediators; that is shown in the call of Jeremiah, who receives an explicit promise for his almost intolerable office. The promise is taken up again in answer to the prophet's complaints;[22] the suffering of God's messenger now belongs to his office. Thus the history of the prophets as messengers of God's judgment flows into the activity and suffering of the Servant of the Lord which the Servant Songs of Deutero-Isaiah[23] intentionally describe in a hidden and allusive way. Only this much is clear: the Servant's activity and suffering have as their goal the salvation of the people of God and, further,

---

[21] Cf. I Kings 22; Amos 7:10–17.
[22] Jer. 1:18 and 15:20.
[23] Isa. 42:1–4; 49:1–6; 50:4–9; 52:13–53:12.

the salvation of the nations. And in this activity the royal line and the prophetic line come together again. The Servant Songs cannot be fitted into any of the previous forms of the promise; it is even an open question whether they speak of the past, present, or future. It is clear, however, that in these songs the Servant, who has no power whatsoever and who brings about salvation through vicarious suffering, confronts the king who mediates salvation in the framework of a political institution. It is also clear that the real office of this Servant is an office of the Word and that in this respect he stands in the succession of the prophets.

It is important for the history of the promise in the Old Testament to see here in Second Isaiah each of the two lines of the promise, in which the coming of salvation is connected with a specific person, in its historical context: one line which leads from prophecy to the Servant of the Lord and the other which leads from the Nathan promise over the historical monarchy to the messianic promise. The Gospel of John clearly brings these two lines together in Jesus' answer to Pilate's question:

I am a king.
For this I was born, and for this I have come into the world,
to bear witness to the truth.
John 18:37

IX

The promise of another mediator to come reached its climax with the Servant poems of Deutero-Isaiah. In the postexilic period the promises of a Coming One never went beyond the messianic promise and the poems of the Suffering Servant. To about the time of the Exile also belong the oracles which marked the climax of the promises for the people, of which I mention three examples: the oracle concerning the new covenant (Jer. 31:31–34); the announcement of the resurrection of the dry bones (Ezek. 37), and the invitation of the Gentiles to salvation (Isa. 45:20–24).

The real significance of the oracle concerning the new covenant

(Jer. 31:31–34) lies in the fact that here the covenant is included in the promise. According to its original meaning a covenant can only be concluded, it cannot be promised. With the inclusion of the covenant in the promise the nature of the covenant was radically changed; it now means the end of the previous history of God with his people. But what begins as the "new covenant" can only be intimated from afar off. In this sense, and only in this sense, can it be said that this oracle concerning the new covenant was fulfilled in Christ and his Church—not, however, in the sense that every sentence of Jeremiah 31:31–34 literally applies to the Christian Church. The cessation of tradition (Jer. 31:34) does not hold true for the Church. It is clear, however, that the new covenant has a stronger reference to the individual.

The oracle about the resurrection of the dry bones is, like Jeremiah 31:31–34, one which points to the frontier of the present people of God and hints at something indescribably new lying beyond. Ezekiel 37 is the most powerful Old Testament oracle of promise which points directly to a completely new action of God. But here likewise it holds true that the resurrection of the dry bones can only speak allusively, symbolically, of that which actually happened in the fullness of time.

In Isaiah 45:20–24 Deutero-Isaiah says to the remnant of the destroyed people: the time will come when destruction will also fall upon those who are now your masters. Then, however, the God of Israel will not stand forth triumphantly as the one who finally is proved to be in the right, but rather he will show himself as the one who, from the beginning on, willed the salvation of the world: "Turn to me and be saved, all the ends of the earth!" (Isa. 45:22). But even here, as well as in the commission of the Servant to be "a light to the nations" (Isa. 49:6; cf. 42:4), this can only be hinted at. Even at the conclusion of the great drama of the history of the people of God, what had been said to Abraham at the beginning still remains as promise: "In you shall all the families of the earth be blessed" (Gen. 12:3). Gerhard von Rad's remark regarding the three great groups of salvation-oracles in the prophets, illustrated by the three examples above, applies here: "What differentiates the message of the prophets from all of Israel's previous theology of redemptive history (*heilsgeschichtliche Theologie*) is that the prophets await everything that is decisive for Israel's existence, life and death, from a coming divine event."[24]

X

The history of the promise in the Old Testament cannot be continued through the postexilic period. There are, to be sure, still a great number of individual oracles of promise, but they are largely variations on earlier motifs. From the Exile on clear phases, turning points, and modifications can no longer be established in the realm of the promises.

The only thing that is really new in the postexilic period is the rise of apocalyptic. It is, however, so much a world of its own that it has to be treated as an independent history; in any case, it is by no means just the final chapter in the history of the promise.

If apocalyptic is viewed in terms of the three basic forms of the oracle of promise, then clearly it belongs in the line of the salvation-portrayal. While, to be sure, its purpose is to announce coming events, it never stops with mere announcement but shows its very nature by transposing announcement into portrayal which broadens out into manifold details. The essential difference between apocalyptic and the preceding salvation-portrayal lies in the fact that it not only graphically places over against the present condition a future one, but it presents the transition from one to the other in a drama divided into many acts. It is this dramatic character of the transition that constitutes the very essence of apocalyptic. In this presentation of the drama of the End, it represents something completely new over against the history of the salvation-oracle.

---

[24] *Theologie des Alten Testaments,* Vol. 2 (1960), p. 131.

Within this drama of the end time, apocalyptic also contains salvation-portrayal. It is, however, precisely at this point that a clear correspondence of promise in the Old Testament and fulfillment in the New is no longer to be discerned. In the Revelation of John the decisively new element in the portrayal of the final stage of the time of salvation is only the Second Coming of Jesus Christ. All graphic delineations of this final stage have been taken from the Old Testament or at least do not contain anything basically new or different from Old Testament apocalyptic. The message proper of the Revelation of John is only that at the end of God's work with the *whole* Creation stands Jesus Christ.

Conclusion

It has only been possible to give a preliminary, rough sketch of the way of the promise through the Old Testament. The purpose has been to show that the promises or salvation-oracles in the Old Testament represent a "way"; if its entire course is to be seen, then one must sketch a history which reaches from the deliverance from Egypt—the event upon which the history of God with his people is founded—to the apocalyptic of the late Israelite period. This history, however, is not unilinear. There is no such thing as *the* promise which had only to be defined from time to time according to its content. We found three basic forms of the promise: the salvation-assurance, the salvation-announcement, and the salvation-portrayal. These three, each for itself, would have to be investigated through the whole Old Testament with reference to the three realms to which they are addressed: the people, the individual, the world; and, in addition, with reference to the manner of mediation. We have also found that the two most important points along the way of the promise through the Old Testament are, first, the Yahwist's incorporation of the blessing into the promise (Gen. 12:1–3); and second, the refraction, in the prophets' message of judgment, of the promise of salvation into the announcement of a fundamentally new saving act of God which points beyond the Old Testament.

Seen in this manner the final fulfillment of the promises of the Old Testament in the coming and the work of Christ can only be understood as a fulfillment of the *entire way* of the promise through the Old Testament, as a fulfillment of the *history* of the promises. This whole history, in its variety and multiformity, comes to final fulfillment in the event reported in the New Testament. The real, primary connection of the message of Christ with the history of the promises in the Old Testament is then not seen first of all in the quotations made in the New Testament,[25] but in the character of this message itself which is unfolded as good news of deliverance, good news of the coming of the Deliverer. This real and essential relation of the message of Christ to the promises of the Old Testament is, for example, the explicit theme of Luke's introduction (Luke 1–2). In the coming of the Deliverer the promises of the old covenant are fulfilled. In language quite akin to the Old Testament here it is told how to the waiting people of God of the old covenant, represented in the fathers and mothers, in priests and prophets, and above all in the "poor" (the shepherds), the message rings out: the one whom you have waited for, who was promised to you as the bringer of salvation, has come! Here "promise" is understood in a manner which corresponds exactly to what we found to be the essential features of the basic forms of the salvation-oracles in the Old Testament.

This understanding of the fulfillment of promises of the old covenant must have an effect upon the way fulfillment is viewed from the standpoint of the New Testament. W. Pannenberg cites

---

[25] In discussing the quotations of the Old Testament in the New, the proper place to begin is this basic relation of promise to fulfillment. Today there is widespread agreement in the field of biblical studies that we can no longer reproduce a connection between the Old and New Testaments on the basis of mere "prediction," especially when the latter is sought in sentences detached from their original context. We can no longer ignore what these sentences signified in their original context for the people to whom they were spoken. This manner of citation holds good for only a portion of the citations of the Old Testament in the New. A careful survey of the New Testament shows a variety of possibilities in drawing upon the Old Testament.

in this connection[26] the formula under which R. Bultmann and E. Fuchs comprehend this fulfillment: "Christ is the end of history. In Christ the eschaton has appeared." From the standpoint of the history of the promises in the Old Testament the question is to be raised: does this formula really take into account the variety and fullness of the history of Old Testament promises? If Jesus Christ and his work are really the fulfillment of the history of Old Testament promises, then the fulfillment must exhibit the three temporal aspects represented by the three basic forms of the promise in the Old Testament: the perfect, the future, and the present (this is meant only as an abbreviated characterization). Moreover, the fulfillment must be related clearly and unambiguously to the *three* realms with which the Old Testament promise in its complete extent has to do: the people of God, the individual, the world (= Creation). If the Christ event has reference mainly or only to the existence of the individual, then it is no longer the fulfillment of the promises of the old covenant. It is only understood as fulfillment when the event reported in the New Testament is referred first and foremost to the people of God, when it is the *new* act of God which constitutes the *new* people of God. This is the basis of the salvation which befalls the individual and which at the same time is intended for the whole world and the whole Creation. Because God's final act of deliverance in Christ has to do not only with the individual but with the three realms of the Old Testament promise, the people of God of the new covenant also has a history. It is eschatological history in so far as it extends from the departure to the return of Christ; but it is *real* history stretching out to the End. Inherent in this is also the fact that the combination of the promise with the blessing (see above) is not abrogated but is taken up into the fulfillment, as the New Testament clearly shows.[27] In the history of the end time, as in the history of the promises, the concern is for the destiny of the

---

[26] *Op. cit.*, p. 136 (Westermann, *Essays,* p. 333).
[27] See above, n. 17.

people of God as a community among other communities, for the
destiny of the individual in his bodily and spiritual existence, and
for the destiny of the world which God has created and which he
directs toward its goal.

12 The New Covenant and the Old

BERNHARD W. ANDERSON

Jeremiah's prophecy concerning the "new covenant" (Jer. 31: 31–34) provided an important motif for the Church's understanding of itself as the People of God. Although references to covenant are surprisingly few in the New Testament, there is strong reason to believe that at least in some circles the Christian community, like the Qumran sect, regarded itself as the people of the new covenant.[1] According to tradition which may go back to Jesus himself, the new covenant belongs essentially to the sacramental liturgy of the Church.[2] The covenant motif is employed significantly in both the letters of Paul and in the Epistle to the

---

[1] See G. E. Mendenhall's article on "covenant" in the *Interpreter's Dictionary of the Bible* (1962), especially pp. 721–23. Paul's understanding of himself as "minister of the new covenant" is discussed by W. C. van Unnik in "La conception paulinienne de la nouvelle alliance," *Recherches Bibliques* V ("Littérature et Théologie Pauliniennes"), by A. Descamps *et al.* (1960), pp. 109–26.

[2] In the earliest account of the institution of the Lord's Supper (I Cor. 11:23–25) Paul states that he "received from the Lord" the tradition of the "new covenant" in the blood of Jesus. The situation is not so clear in the Gospels. Mark and Matthew refer to "the blood of the covenant" (Mark 14:24; Matt. 26:28). Variant readings add "new," as also in the long variant to Luke 22:19. Bultmann believes that the conception of a new covenant, both in I Cor. 11:23–25 and in the Synoptic Gospels, does not belong to the original tradition (*Theology of the New Testament*, Vol. 1 [1957], p. 146).

225

Hebrews.[3] Eventually the custom arose of referring to the apostolic writings of Christianity as the New Covenant (Testament) and the canonical writings of Israel as the Old Covenant.

From the earliest period of Church history to the present, Christian theology has been confronted with the problem of understanding the relation between the old and the new. On the one hand the Gospel bears witness to the new and unprecedented action of God in Christ which established a deep discontinuity with all preceding historical tradition. Paul announced that "the old has passed away, behold, the new has come" (II Cor. 5:17; cf. Rev. 21:5). On the other hand, the early apostolic witness is also clear that God's action in Christ was the climax of a whole history of his dealings with his people. It was more than a feeling of blood-kinship which prompted Paul in Romans 9–11 to insist that Israel, even in the rejection of the Gospel, is beloved of God and that her survival vis-à-vis the Church is somehow—beyond human understanding—caught up in the mystery of divine election.

The Church has not provided a definitive justification for including the Old Testament in its theology and, as a matter of fact, from time to time has shown uneasiness about the presence of Israel's Scripture within the Christian Bible. This is actually not surprising, for in every generation the Church must take up its theological task anew in response to the situation in the contemporary world in which it finds itself. Older theological answers to the question of the relation between the Testaments, whether formulated in the nineteenth century, in the period of the Reformation, or in the debates between the schools of Antioch and Alexandria, can hardly be adopted outright as *our* answer, though theology today would be irresponsible if it did not rest upon an understanding of the various ways in which historically the

---

[3] In II Cor. 3 the motif of the new covenant dominates Paul's discussion and in Gal. 4:21–28 the two covenants are contrasted. Jeremiah's prophecy is quoted in Heb. 8:8–12 and partially in 10:16–17, the author's intent in these contexts being to show that the old covenant has been superseded by the new.

Church has expressed her faith. It is, therefore, important that Rudolf Bultmann has restated the question in contemporary terms and has thereby issued a challenge to the Church to face the theological task anew.

In his essay, "The Significance of the Old Testament for the Christian Faith," Bultmann has brought the accent down heavily upon the discontinuity between the old and the new. Unlike the second century Marcion, he does not say that the Old Testament is irrelevant for Christian faith. When the Bible is approached from a "genuinely historical" (*echt geschichtlich*) standpoint, it becomes apparent that there is a material (*sachlich*) connection between the Testaments. In the Old Testament a particular understanding of existence (*Daseinsverständnis*) comes to expression. For there man is concretely confronted with the divine demand, the "thou shalt," which limits him and calls him to decision as a historical being in relation to his neighbor. And further, contrary to Marcion, Bultmann wants to deal positively with the intention of the Creation faith which expresses man's self-understanding that he is limited by God and cannot exercise control over the world. This understanding of existence, which is not confined to the Old Testament but comes to its maximum clarity there, is shared with the New Testament against religions or religious philosophies which, in effect, dehistoricize man, so that he vainly tries to become himself by fleeing from his temporality and historicity into a timeless realm. *For the Christian* the Old Testament is not revelation, but is essentially related to God's revelation in Christ as hunger is to food or despair is to hope. Only he who knows himself to be limited by God's demand can receive the good news of God's forgiveness in Christ. Unlike Marcion, too, Bultmann does not want to say that the God of the Old Covenant and the God of the New Covenant are two different Gods. Israel knew that to be under the Law was to be under grace; but this grace was given to a particular people within the conditions and limitations of their history. The God who so spoke to Israel no longer speaks *to us* in the time of the new covenant. The history of

Israel is not the form in which the Christian's God-relation is brought about. The former mode of man's relation to God has been superseded by the mode of relation now in effect: the new covenant in Christ. Israel's covenant history, he says, proved to be a history of failure (*Scheitern*); only from the standpoint of the Christian revelation can this abortive history be understood as "promise" for, in retrospect, it shows negatively the impossibility of gaining access to God in history and points beyond failure to God's action in Christ which—to coin an English word—"de-worldizes" (*entweltlicht*) man and transposes him into an eschatological existence.[4]

Since the relation between the old and the new is first delineated within the Old Testament,[5] it may be helpful to turn to one of the passages which Bultmann adduces for his emphasis upon the discontinuity between the covenants. Jeremiah's prophecy in 31: 31–34, he states, bears witness to the failure of Israel's covenant history. He asks: "Is the idea of an eschatological covenant not a sign that God's covenant is in its essence an eschatological dimension which is not to be realized within the world?"[6] We shall turn attention to Jeremiah's oracle, then, though recognizing that there are other passages within the Old Testament, especially the poems of Second Isaiah, which also cast important light upon the relation between the old and the new.[7]

---

4 Bultmann, "Prophecy and Fulfillment," in *Essays Philosophical and Theological*, James C. G. Greig, trans. (1955), pp. 182–208, especially pp. 205 ff. Reprinted in *Essays on Old Testament Hermeneutics* (1963), Claus Westermann, ed., pp. 50–75.

5 James Muilenburg observes: "It is important to see that the New Testament, where the consciousness of the newness of the Messianic age is so central, is dependent upon the Old Testament for its categories of newness, and this is only natural, for the anticipation of 'the age to come' and all that accompanies it is so marked a feature of Israelite thinking, even though the expression itself is later than the Old Testament" (*The Way of Israel* [1961], p. 135).

6 *Op. cit.*, p. 194 (Westermann, *Essays*, pp. 61 f.).

7 See my essay, "Exodus Typology in Second Isaiah," in *Israel's Prophetic Heritage: Essays in Honor of James Muilenburg*, B. W. Anderson and W. Harrelson, eds. (1962), pp. 177–95.

I

The oracle concerning the new covenant constitutes a separate literary unit within the prophecies collected under the name of Jeremiah. Although some have challenged Jeremiah's authorship of the passage, there is no convincing reason for denying it to him. The conception of the covenant, the emphasis upon inwardness, and not least of all the view that only God's forgiveness can make a new historical beginning—all these are inherent in the life and message of the suffering prophet, as many scholars agree. Probably the oracle comes from the latest phase of his life and reflects many years of preoccupation with the covenant, including his reaction to the failure of the Deuteronomic reform of 621 B.C. in the earlier period of his career (see especially Jer. 11; 34:8–22).

The oracle stands out as a separate *Gattung,* with a clear beginning characteristic of eschatological oracles and a conclusion which contains the motive-clause for the new divine deed. Indeed, the particle *kî* is employed effectively to introduce the decisive moments in the movement of thought.[8]

> (31) Behold, days are coming—the oracle of Yahweh—
> > when I will conclude [*kārat*] with the house of Israel[9]
> > a new covenant;
> (32) Not like the covenant which I concluded with their fathers
> > on the day when I took them by the hand to bring them
> > out of the land of Egypt,
> > which covenant of mine [*bᵉrîtî*] they broke,
> > though I was their master[10]
> > > —the oracle of Yahweh;

---

[8] See James Muilenburg, "The Linguistic and Rhetorical Usage of the Particle *Ki* in the Old Testament," *HUCA,* Vol. 32 (1961), pp. 135 ff.

[9] The words "and the house of Judah" are undoubtedly an addition; notice their absence in vs. 33.

[10] Other witnesses (LXX, Old Latin, Syriac) presuppose the verb "loathe" (*gā'altî*); cf. Jer. 14:19. On the other hand, see 3:14 where the verb *bā'altî,* which hints at the Baal apostasy, is used.

(33) But [kî] this is the covenant I will conclude with the
house of Israel after those days

—the oracle of Yahweh:

I will put my torah in their inward being
and upon their heart I will inscribe it.
Then I will be their God
and they shall be my people.

(34) No longer will a man teach his neighbor
or a man his brother, saying, "Know Yahweh,"
because [kî] all of them will know me
from the least of them to the greatest

—the oracle of Yahweh;

for [kî] I will forgive their iniquity,
and their sin I will remember no longer.

In this oracle the particle *kî* has two main usages. The first is
adversative: it marks the transition from the description of the
new covenant by contrast ("not like") to the positive description
of its content. The second and main usage is climactic: it rounds
off and brings the oracle to a conclusion by announcing the divine
act that will establish the new relationship.[11] From beginning
to end the prophet stresses divine initiative. Hence the oracle begins with a statement of divine intention ("I will cut/conclude")
and it culminates with the verb *sālach* which uniquely expresses
divine action ("I will forgive").

Two features of this oracle deserve special attention. First, the
oracle stands in the northern Mosaic covenant tradition, not in
the southern tradition of royal covenant theology. The presupposition of this prophecy is that the covenant can be revoked by
God when, on the human side, it is "broken." Jeremiah does not
know of an "everlasting covenant" (*berît 'ôlām*) which continues
in unbroken continuity through the generations, regardless of

---

[11] At first glance the expression "the oracle of Yahweh" (*ne'um YHWH*)
seems repetitious or even awkward. Actually it appears to be used deliberately
to set forth the main structure of the unit. It is used twice in the first section,
at the beginning (vs. 31a) and the end (vs. 32b), and twice in the second section, at the beginning (vs. 33a) and the end (vs. 34b). The latter occurrence
sets off the climactic *kî* statement in vs. 34c.

man's fulfillment of the covenant stipulations. In this respect, his prophecy rests upon an entirely different theological basis from the royal covenant which finds its typical expression in Yahweh's promise to the Davidic royal house through the prophet Nathan (II Sam. 7; Ps. 89). It is true that the new covenant, according to Jeremiah, will be permanent (cf. Jer. 32:40); but this will be because Yahweh himself will work a change in the human heart, making it possible to fulfill its obligations (cf. 24:7). This, however is something different from a covenant which is valid for all ages regardless of human behavior.

A second feature is that the new covenant is eschatological, as indicated by the opening phrase, "Days are coming." The oracle points to "the new form of the God-relation in the time of salvation."[12] Like Hosea, the prophet Jeremiah sees that Israel is held so firmly in the bondage of a perverse history that only Yahweh's act of judgment can bring the history of the broken covenant to an end and make possible a new historical beginning for the people. To this extent Bultmann is right in saying that Jeremiah's prophecy moves into an eschatological dimension.

It is possible that Jeremiah's conception of the "new covenant" was influenced by the tradition of the covenant-renewal festival which was kept alive in north-Israelitic circles, as reflected in the Book of Deuteronomy. In these circles covenant renewal did not imply a return to the beginning, a restoration to a former condition, after the manner of pagan myth and ritual, but rather a reactualization (*Vergegenwärtigung*) of the covenant under the conditions of the present.[13] This is the accent in the Deuteronomic tradition: "Not with our fathers did Yahweh make this covenant, but with us, who are all of us here alive this day" (Deut. 5:3). The reform of Josiah in 621 B.C., which made a deep impression upon Jeremiah's thought, was based on a passionate attempt to re-

---

[12] Artur Weiser, *Das Buch der Propheten Jeremiah* (*ATD,* 1959), p. 294.

[13] See Brevard Childs, *Myth and Reality in the Old Testament* (1960), especially pp. 72–82, where the mythical conception of time is evaluated from the angle of Israel's faith. See p. 79 for a statement about the "qualitative difference" of the new covenant from the old.

actualize the Mosaic covenant. But Jeremiah's oracle cannot be understood as reactualization of the past sacred history. He speaks of a new covenant, not a covenant renewal, and thereby assumes a radical break with the Mosaic tradition.

Jeremiah's radical alteration in the covenant concept is seen in the fact that the covenant becomes a promise of salvation (*Heils-verheissung*). He refers to the covenant which Yahweh concluded (*kārat*) with his people "in the day when I took them by the hand to bring them out of the land of Egypt"; but in a most unusual manner he also uses this verb in the imperfect, with a futuristic sense (*'ekrōt*, vs. 33). "The real significance of the new covenant," writes Claus Westermann, "lies in the fact that here the covenant is included in the promise."[14] The oracle is addressed to Jeremiah himself and is intended as a new word from Yahweh. It is the announcement of a new divine deed which cannot be reduced to Yahweh's former actions. Through Jeremiah Yahweh *promises* a new covenant which "brings to an end the previous history of God with his people" (Westermann). Therefore the prophet says of the new covenant that it is "not like" the covenant made at the time of the Exodus from Egypt.

II

What are the essentially new features of the new covenant that are emphasized by the language "not like" (vs. 32a), "no longer" (vs. 34c)? First of all, the new covenant will be a radically inward relationship with Yahweh. It would be a false reading of the Mosaic tradition to find in it support for legalism or externalism. The covenant traditions in Exodus 19–34 clearly emphasize Yahweh's gracious dealings, which evoke from a people beholden to his benevolence a response of loyalty and a decision to be obedient: "All that Yahweh has spoken we will do and we will be obedient" (Ex. 24:7; cf. 19:3–6). The tradition that Yahweh's

---

14 Claus Westermann, "The Way of the Promise through the Old Testament," *supra*, pp. 218–19.

"words" were written in a "book" (Ex. 24:4, 7), to be deposited in a sacred place, or the tradition that these laws were inscribed upon tablets of stone (Ex. 31:18; 34:1, 28), cannot obscure the fundamentally personal relationship between God and people. The homiletical exposition of Deuteronomy, which emphasizes the unmerited mercy of Yahweh and appeals to the will of the people, is an eloquent commentary on this dimension of the Sinai covenant. It is, therefore, inaccurate to say that "the covenant originally gained its validity through sacrifice, and is constantly maintained and so renewed by the right sacrificial worship"— that is, by cultic performance.[15] It is true, however, that the Mosaic covenant did have from the first a legalistic *possibility,* as is evident in Deuteronomic circles where there was a tendency to equate covenant and commandment. One could say that Yahweh "commanded covenant" (*tsiwwāh bᵉrît,* as in Deut. 4:13; Josh. 7:11; Judg. 2:20; I Kings 11:11), or could simply identify the tables of the Law as "the covenant" (I Kings 8:21). Thus on Israel's side "keeping" the covenant could mean specifically to obey the *chuqqîm, mitswôt,* and *mishpātîm;* and, on the other side, it is said that Yahweh is the God "who keeps covenant and *chésed"* (e.g., Deut. 7:9, 12; I Kings 8:23), that is, who faithfully maintains the covenant once established at Sinai despite the people's unfaithfulness.[16]

It may be, as Wright suggests, that in the Davidic state during the period before Jeremiah and Josiah's reformation "the Sinai covenant tradition fell into the background, being virtually replaced by the Davidic covenant."[17] Jeremiah probably favored in principle the attempt to recover the old "covenant ideology" of North Israel during the reign of Josiah, but he also turned his incisive criticism against the corruptions and distortions of the covenant. He was the prophet par excellence who understood the

---

[15] Bultmann, "Prophecy and Fulfillment," pp. 192 f. (Westermann, *Essays,* p. 59).

[16] See W. Eichrodt, *Theology of the Old Testament,* J. A. Baker, trans., Vol. 1 (1961), pp. 53–56.

[17] G. Ernest Wright, "Cult and History," *INT,* Vol. 16 (1962), p. 17.

meaning of sin inwardly—a deceitful heart, a will in bondage, a misplaced loyalty. Even the holiest things could become the instruments of a sinful will, whether the covenant-sign of circumcision (Jer. 4:4), the Temple (7:1–15), or the torah (8:8). This came to expression in the so-called Deuteronomic reformation which proved to be only a surface reformation (and a short-lived one at that: Jer. 34:8 ff.). Hence over against the failure of the old covenant to effect a true relation of Israel to Yahweh he portrayed the new covenant, whose torah Yahweh would inscribe upon the heart. No longer would obligation be mere external performance; it would arise out of inner springs of faith. This, of course, was the intention of the original covenant which Yahweh had made with the fathers.

Perhaps the most radically new feature of the new covenant, according to Jeremiah, was that it would mark the end of all tradition,[18] indeed of all covenant renewal ceremonies which would have the effect of reactualizing the sacred past. One could go further: it would mark the end of all religious instruction. In Deuteronomy 6:20–25 it is said that when an Israelite "son" inquires, "What is the meaning of the testimonies, statutes, and ordinances which Yahweh our God has commanded you?" he shall be told the history in which Yahweh has made himself known to Israel, with the purpose of initiating the younger generation into the tradition which is the canonical basis of Israel's faith. But in the age of the new covenant such "instruction" will be unnecessary, whether in the home or in the community. "No longer will a man teach ($y^e lamm^e d\hat{u}$) his neighbor or a man his brother saying, 'Know Yahweh,' because all of them will know me from the least of them to the greatest." In Hosea the expression "knowledge of God" ($da'at$ $^{e}l\bar{o}h\hat{i}m$, Hos. 4:1; 6:6) apparently implies that it was the duty of the priests to instruct the people in a "theological knowledge" which included the covenant stipulations.[19]

---

[18] See Westermann, *supra*, p. 219.

[19] See H. W. Wolff, " 'Wissen um Gott' bei Hosea als Urform von Theologie," *EVT,* Vol. 12 (1953), pp. 533–51.

Jeremiah, however, insists that in the new age the relationship between Yahweh and people will be unbroken and immediate. No longer will men hear of Yahweh by the hearing of the ear, through instruction mediated by priests or through other forms of teaching, but all men in the covenant community will live in the personal knowledge that Yahweh is their Lord. Admittedly this effectively underscores the inwardness of faith, but it also marks a profound discontinuity with Israel's tradition.

And finally, the new covenant will be based upon divine forgiveness. Under the old covenant, to be sure, Israel knew that Yahweh is "merciful and gracious," as shown by the old liturgical formulation associated with the Sinai covenant (Ex. 34:6–7) and repeated in various Old Testament contexts. But, contrary to Heine's jest, God's *metier* is not to forgive. The history of the old covenant not only bears witness to Yahweh's mercy but also to his holiness, which brought his people under terrible judgment. The wonder of the new age, according to Jeremiah, is that God's people who should have been destroyed on the rock of his holiness (cf. Josh. 24:19–20) are nevertheless given a new beginning in his grace. This is indeed a miracle in that it goes contrary to what men have a right, on the basis of the covenant, to expect or claim. Hosea had previously pondered this as he portrayed the relation of "the Holy One of Israel" to his people under the metaphor of a father's relation to his son, and had affirmed that Yahweh's love transcends all logic of merit or expectation (Hos. 11). Yahweh's judgment, according to the great prophets, is salutary; it uproots in order to plant, overthrows in order to build, wounds in order to heal. Israel must go through the time of judgment if she would know, beyond the judgment, the unfathomable depths of divine mercy. Jeremiah stresses that the new age will be inaugurated by divine initiative, and that the foundation of the enduring covenant will be divine forgiveness. Israel will begin anew as the forgiven people (cf. Isa. 43:25; 44:22). Thus Jeremiah's prophecy prepares the way for Second Isaiah, who harmonizes the Exodus tradition, which had apparently been eclipsed in defeat and exile,[20] and the royal covenant tradition, which ended in failure, by announcing the inauguration of a new age for Israel and the nations in which the "everlasting covenant" will rest upon Yahweh's forgiveness (Isa. 54:6–10; 55:1–5).[21]

III

While it is appropriate to emphasize first the ways in which the new covenant is "not like" the covenant concluded in the time of Moses, Jeremiah's intention is not to draw such a sharp contrast that there is no continuity between the old and the new. It is Yahweh who is the author of the old and new covenants. He is represented as saying of the Mosaic covenant "my covenant" (vs. 32b) and the Codex Vaticanus of the LXX is right in interpreting the same language to apply to the new covenant (vs. 33a). The theological problem is how to understand the continuity which underlies, and is manifest in, the discontinuity.

Notice some elements of correlation between the old and new covenants. First, Yahweh's new covenant, like the old, includes his torah ($t\hat{o}r\bar{a}t\hat{i}$), precisely as in the covenant ceremony of Exodus 24:3–8 or in the covenant pericope as a whole (Ex. 19–34). To be sure, this torah is to be inscribed on the heart; but this does not mean that it is reduced (à la Bultmann) to a general sense of moral obligation arising out of man's relation to his neighbor. While Jeremiah does not specify the content of the torah, he probably had in mind the concrete torah of Israel's tra-

---

[20] It is noteworthy that nowhere does Second Isaiah explicitly allude to the Sinai covenant, although the sacred history which centers in the Exodus dominates the prophet's message (see my "Exodus Typology in Second Isaiah," especially pp. 182–85). The silence about the Mosaic covenant is probably explainable (as in the case of the absence of the covenant from early creedal summaries such as Deut. 26:5–9) on the basis of concentration upon the historical events that manifest God's saving action.

[21] See George E. Mendenhall, *Law and Covenant in Israel and the Ancient Near East* (1955), who draws attention to "the harmonization of the two covenant traditions" and points out the implications for the new covenant of Christianity (pp. 47–50). See also Otto Eissfeldt, "The Promises of Grace to David in Isaiah 55:1–5," in *Israel's Prophetic Heritage, op. cit.*, pp. 196–207.

dition as set forth normatively in the Decalogue (cf. Hos. 4:2) and as elaborated in the casuistic laws of the covenant tradition (Jer. 34:8–22). The prophet does not speak of a new torah but of a new covenant relationship which will enable men to obey the covenant stipulations out of inner motivation.

Secondly, the purpose of covenanting, in both instances, is the establishment of relationship between God and people. The torah is significant only in that it gives concrete expression to this relationship. Hence Jeremiah applies to the new covenant the formula which had described the basis of the old. "I will be their God and they shall be my people" (vs. 33; 7:23, 32:38; cf. Ex. 6:7, Deut. 26:16–19; Lev. 26:12). Friedrich Baumgärtel asserts that fellowship with God is the "basic promise" (*Grundverheissung*) of the Old Testament which Israel ardently hoped would be realized under the limitations of her history but which, according to the Christian Gospel, was fulfilled only in God's revelation in Jesus Christ.[22] It is doubtful whether this formula should be regarded as a promise, if the English word suggests something that is to be realized or fulfilled only eschatologically. The old covenant rested upon God's initiative to shape a people uniquely related to him and to enter into their history as the God in their midst. The words "I will be their God" are to be understood in the covenant sense that Yahweh commits or pledges himself to this people, goes with them into the future as the leader of their way, and struggles with them in all their blindness and infidelity.[23] Yahweh's pledge to identify himself with Israel is, of course, not a legal or natural bond. It is a commitment made in freedom. As Hosea stresses, Yahweh can sever the relationship on his side and declare that Israel is "not my people" and that he is "not your

---

[22] Friedrich Baumgärtel, *Verheissung: zur Frage des evangelischen Verständnisses des Alten Testaments* (1952).

[23] Walther Zimmerli rightly points out that in the history of Yahweh with his people Israel there were fulfillments of the promise, although each fulfillment became a promise of something greater yet in store. Thus the promise is not the unbroken continuity of a straight line but the movement of a history. See his article, "Promise and Fulfillment," Westermann, *Essays*, pp. 89–122.

God" (Hos. 1:9). Jeremiah is only restating in eschatological terms what was the basis of Israel's life, namely, that Yahweh *in freedom* binds himself to Israel so that he addresses them as "my people" and in faith they confess that he is "their God."

And finally the new covenant, according to Jeremiah, would be made "with the house of Israel." The addition of the phrase "and the house of Judah" in vs. 31a (note its absence in vs. 33a) brings in a national dimension which is alien to the prophecy. For although Jeremiah lived at a time when "the house of Judah" (i.e., the southern kingdom) alone was in existence, the thought of this passage rises above the concept of Israel as a national entity and embraces the whole "people of God" who shared a common memory of the crucial event of the Exodus and the making of the Sinai covenant. The covenant was made with Israel in a time before the rise of the nation under David and the subsequent division into the kingdoms of North and South Israel. It is in this sacral sense that Jeremiah uses the term here. Despite his emphasis upon the inwardness of the covenant relation, Jeremiah is no individualist. In the time of the new covenant, as in that of the old, the individual has access to God within the community of which he is a member. Bultmann suggests that Jeremiah (and Ezekiel) are "inconsistent" when they continue to conceive the eschatological covenant as "one with a future empirical people of Israel.[24] From the standpoint of Israel's faith this is absolutely consistent. The answer to the question from the standpoint of the New Testament depends upon how one understands the Christian faith: whether the Church is, as Bultmann states, "not a people as an historical entity within the world" or whether, alternatively, the Church is indeed the New Israel which has a history in the world and which reads the Old Testament as the story of its life.

IV

Thus in Jeremiah's oracle we find that the relation between the old and new covenants is characterized by both discontinuity and

---

[24] "Prophecy and Fulfillment," p. 154. (Westermann, *Essays,* p. 62).

continuity. Speaking out of his own historical situation, he high-lights the ways in which the new covenant is "not like" the old. The new covenant will not be a reactualization of the Mosaic past. Its newness will mark a deep discontinuity with Israel's history of the broken covenant. At the same time, however, Jeremiah in-dicates ways in which the new covenant will be "like" the Mosaic covenant, for it will fulfill God's purpose intended in the original covenant.

To understand how contrast and similarity are interrelated in this prophecy it is necessary to consider the theocentric basis upon which the whole covenant tradition rests. This theocentricity is expressed in the doctrine of election, to which the covenant motif is essentially related. Election is primarily an affirmation about divine grace and its corollary, Israel's vocation. To be sure, in popular thought there was a tendency to think of election statively rather than actively, i.e., to distort the doctrine nationalistically or legalistically into "the state of being elect." Vriezen points out that it is necessary to differentiate "election" (*Erwählung*) from "electness" (*Erwähltsein, Erwähltheit*); "God's election," he ob-serves, "remains but 'electness' has no place."[25] Election refers to God's action in forming a people for himself and in involving himself in the life of this people in order to accomplish his pos-sibilities for them and for the world.[26] Consistent with the election-faith, the new covenant—like the old—rests upon divine initi-ative.

Jeremiah affirms that Israel's history, the history of the broken covenant, must come to an end in order to make room for God's new possibility. The God who is Lord cannot be identified with the life of this empirical people, Israel—a people prone to idolatry and subject to every human limitation. The history of this peo-ple is not in itself a sacred history, for it shipwrecks on the rock of divine judgment. Yet more than this has to be said. Behind and

---

[25] Th. C. Vriezen, *Die Erwählung Israels nach dem Alten Testament* (1953), p. 109.

[26] See the essay by John Dillenberger, *supra*, especially pp. 161–70.

within this history is the God who in freedom commits himself to this all too human people, despite their weakness, perversity, and blindness. He pledges that he is their God and that they, in spite of everything, are his people. His election is not a guarantee of status or the promise of stability but it is rather the grace that makes them a people, holds on to them despite their infidelity, and pursues them through the brokenness and suffering of their history. Viewed theologically, the history of Israel is not only the history of the broken covenant but the history of divine grace, concretely embodied in the life of a people. Through this history Israel knows the God who with almighty grace "actualizes *his* possibilities" and whose forgiveness makes a new beginning.

Divine election implies grace which manifests itself in judgment. The God who freely links himself to his people cannot be bound by any limitation, whether the created order of the natural world (as in pagan religions) or a continuity within Israel's history (as in Israelite nationalism). His Word cannot be congealed in any formulation but ever breaks forth as new revelation. "The way of Israel in the world," observes James Muilenburg, "can never be comprehended in terms of the structures of historical existence," whether in national or cultic institutions or in "ideological structures" such as those of Deuteronomic writers, priestly historians, or apocalyptic seers.[27] For Israel the knowledge of God was mediated in a history which, from the time of the Exodus to the collapse of the nation, was marked by instability and discontinuity. To be sure, the royal covenant theology, appropriating motifs from the religions of Israel's neighbors, sought to connect God's saving purpose with the stability and continuity of a dynasty, and this type of "everlasting covenant" probably had theological antecedents in Israel's covenant tradition before David.[28] However, the promise which centered in David and the continuity

---

[27] Muilenburg, *The Way of Israel,* pp. 129–30.

[28] See Murray Newman, *The People of the Covenant: A History of Israel from Moses to the Monarchy* (1962). This discussion bears significantly upon the problem of continuity and discontinuity.

of his dynasty came to a dead end and out of this failure, as Westermann observes, arose the messianic hope for a Davidic king, quite different from David, who would combine both power and goodness.[29]

The prophets who stand in the Mosaic tradition, however, deal with failure at a much deeper level. It is in the discontinuity of history, in the divine judgment which brings Israel to an end, that Israel knows Yahweh. He shatters the old in order that he may be known anew. It is his Word alone that makes history, that "plucks up" and "breaks down," "destroys" and "overthrows," "builds" and "plants" (Jer. 1:10). There is no place for "idolatry," such as the idolatry of a historical scheme (e.g., the neat Deuteronomic view of reward and punishment), or an institutional continuity (Davidic dynasty, the Temple), or even the absolutizing of Israel as God's people. The insecurities of history are reminders that the "powers of chaos" threaten to overwhelm all patterns of continuity and structures of meaning. In a moving poem, Jeremiah envisions the return of chaos:

> I looked on the earth, and lo, it was waste and
>   void [*tōhû wā-bōhû;* cf. Gen. 1:2];
>   and to the heavens, and they had no light.
> I looked on the mountains, and lo, they were quaking,
>   and all the hills moved to and fro.
>
> I looked, and lo, there was no man,
>   and all the birds of the air had fled.
> I looked, and lo, the fruitful land was a desert,
>   and all its cities were laid in ruins
>   before Yahweh, before his fierce anger.
>
> Jer. 4:23–26

This language has a completely different meaning from the pagan mythology of the annual degeneration of time and the return to the beginning, when the primeval victory over chaos is won again

---

[29] Westermann, *supra,* pp. 215 f.

and order restored.[30] Here Jeremiah is speaking about the *wrath of Yahweh,* whose Word irrupts into history with dynamic power, tearing down the old in order to build and plant anew.

The new, however, appears within the context of God's election—his way with Israel. He commits himself to be present with this people, disciplining them, struggling with them, leading them into the future, and making their history in spite of all human failure a theophany to the world. In Jeremiah's perspective radical discontinuity discloses the continuity of God's purpose and the persistence of his grace throughout Israel's history. Thus the oracle of the new covenant is a word addressed to the prophet in the name of the God who was known in and through Israel's historical experiences: Yahweh who took his people by the hand to bring them out of the land of Egypt.

From the standpoint of the New Testament Israel's covenant history leads to the Cross and to the new covenant actualized in Jesus Christ. Here is fulfillment beyond all prophetic expectations. Yet manifest within this deepest discontinuity is the continuity of the same almighty grace which had called Israel into existence and had directed her toward the future. In various ways the Church of the New Testament seeks to express its conviction that the God who became present in the *person* Jesus Christ is the God who was present in the concrete realities of the *people* Israel. Since God is known in and through the whole history which is consummated in Jesus Christ, the Christian affirms that the God of the Old Testament is *our* God and that Israel's life-story is, in a profound sense, the story of *our* life.

---

[30] See Mircea Eliade, *Cosmos and History: The Myth of the Eternal Return* (Harper Torchbook, 1954).

13 The Significance of the Old Testament for Our Faith

EMIL BRUNNER*

Ever since the days of the heretic Marcion, Christendom has been disturbed by the question whether, for the sake of true understanding of God's redeeming work in Jesus Christ, it is advisable not only decisively to differentiate but also to dissociate the Old Testament as the Jewish Bible from the New Testament and the true Gospel. Even at that time the Old Testament was regarded as an embarrassment to the Christian faith. It was wondered whether devotional regard and the weight of tradition were sufficient to outweigh the dangers involved in full recognition of the Old Testament as divine revelation. As is well known, the early Church rejected this questioning. Through its spokesmen, Irenaeus and Tertullian, it tried to present counterevidence that behind the rejection of the Old Testament there was, not some especially sensitive Christian conscience, but on the contrary, a faith wholly irreconcilable with Christianity. Throughout the entire history of the Church the Old Testament has retained full canonicity, at least in principle. Even the Reformers, who would have had every reason to reconsider Marcion's question, owing to the use the

* This article appeared in ZZ, Vol. 8 (1930), pp. 30–48. Trans. by Bernhard W. Anderson and used here with permission.

Catholic Church had made of the Old Testament priesthood and sacrifice, devoted themselves with greater zeal and profit to understanding the Scriptures of the Old Testament. They loved them more than had been the case in the preceding centuries. In the age of the Enlightenment, however, opposition was shown toward everything not to be rationally comprehended, above all toward this portion of Holy Scripture as especially irrational, superstitious, and morally pernicious.

Old Testament chronology and historiography, but above all Old Testament stories dealing with Creation, Paradise, the Fall, and miracles, presented an inexhaustible field for rationalistic and scientific criticism. Also the Old Testament conception of God was in a special degree repugnant to the spirit of the age. Even German idealism brought about no change basically in this judgment. Of course, Herder's sensitivity to the poetic excellence of ancient Hebrew literature[1] and the newly aroused interest of romanticism in primitive folk life in some measure rehabilitated the Old Testament, at least esthetically, in the eyes of the educated. Also the concept of the spiritual development of humanity according to inner law, introduced through Herder and especially through Hegel into modern thought, was somewhat to the advantage of Israelite religion. But all of this could not enable the Old Testament to regain its earlier position as revelation valid *for us*.

Of all the leaders of that time it was only Hamann who—to put it plainly—believed in the Old Testament and pleaded and fought for his belief.[2] But the stream of development flowed past him in quite another direction. It was Schleiermacher who spoke the word which was decisive for the following century. It is characteristic of him, and likewise important for our theme, that the man whom so many regard as a reviver of the Christian faith, or

---

[1] See especially J. G. Herder, *Vom Geist der hebräischen Poesie* (1782–83). —ED.

[2] A sign of the renewed interest in this contemporary of Immanuel Kant is the book by Ronald Gregor Smith, *J. G. Hamann, 1730–1788: A Study in Christian Existence* (1960).—ED.

surely of Christian theology, put the Old Testament on a level with paganism. The decisive sentence of his dogmatics is: "Christianity does indeed stand in a special historical connection with Judaism [which for Schleiermacher meant the same as the faith of the Old Testament]; but as far as concerns its historical existence and its aim, its relations to Judaism and heathenism are the same."[3]

The interest which the theology of the following period continued to take in the Old Testament was, on the whole, essentially historical (*historisch*), corresponding to Schleiermacher's declaration that only in a historical-causal sense does Christianity have a closer relation to it than to extrabiblical religions. If this declaration is true, then it implies that the Old Testament has no significance *for our faith*. The question of historical causality is a question for scholars but not for the believing community. This is just what Schleiermacher thought; for him the Old Testament had no more weight as source and norm of his faith than any document of heathen religion. One may esteem the Old Testament ever so highly as a historical source, one may give it almost the highest place among the religious voices of mankind, one may attach unusual importance to its significance for the origin of the Christian religion, but all of this has nothing to do with the question we have posed: the significance of the Old Testament for our faith. For faith does not inquire for religious documents or historical causes, but for the Word of God.

Behind Schleiermacher's rejection of the Old Testament, which was later repeated in a similar fashion by Adolph Harnack, are arguments against its divinity other than those of a merely rationalistic kind. It is the very heart of Old Testament religion that Schleiermacher rejects, not just some particulars, not just some errors regarding cosmology or historical presentation. To him the Old Testament is the religion of legalism. There is no place in his

---

[3] Friedrich Schleiermacher, *The Christian Faith*, H. R. Mackintosh and J. S. Stewart, eds. (1928), p. 60.—ED.

dogmatics for a doctrine of the holiness of God. It is this concept of the holiness of God which also lies at the basis of Harnack's opposition. It is no accident that he dedicated his last great work to Marcion. Marcion's doubts about the God of the Old Testament are revived in him. And among us in the Christian community these doubts are much more alive and more widely spread than is commonly admitted. That is why I have chosen this particular theme. Even today there are many believers who actually find the Old Testament an embarrassment, though they would never dare to utter the demand of Marcion or Harnack; and they would be glad if they did not have to believe it as the Word of God. These doubts are not of an accidental kind but disclose a definite understanding of revelation and of faith. Today this understanding is prevalent in the Church—not just outside it—and even in the community of Bible-believing, evangelical Christians; at the same time, however, it is characteristic of modern thought in general. Therefore it is well worth while to speak of these doubts, not for their own sake but in order to clarify for ourselves the meaning of divine revelation in Scripture and the significance of Scripture itself for our faith.

I

First of all let me make a general statement and then explain it more in detail. The statement will be substantiated more precisely in the remainder of the discussion. It is this: our understanding of the Old Testament is always, and especially today, decisive for our understanding of the New Testament. By this I do not mean historical or genetic understanding. The fact that Jesus Christ arose out of the Israelite people and upon its soil is something that has significance for the historian but not for the believer. The fact that much of what is taught in the New Testament was already taught in the Old Testament and the question of how this teaching originated is a matter of scholarly learning, but not of faith. In order to understand what significance the Old Testament has for our faith we must separate in the most rigorous manner these two viewpoints, which so often are intermixed. If, in direct connection with all Protestant understanding of the Bible, I say, "Jesus Christ and the New Testament are not to be understood without the Old Testament," then I mean something quite different from the scholars with their similar-sounding statement about historical comprehension. I do not mean that the origin of the New Testament is not to be understood without the Old, but rather that the content, *the substance (Sache)*, the Word of God, *of the New Testament can be understood only in connection with that of the Old*. That holds for all times and for every individual in every time. But I hasten to add: it holds in special measure for our time. The reason is as follows.

The New Testament differs from the Old in that, as witness to the incarnation of the Word of God, it fulfills the prophecy of the prophets (I mean the prophecy that is found in the whole Old Testament); but it also differs from the Old in a manner which is seductive and dangerous for our generation. The New Testament is written in Greek. It makes use of Greek concepts to express the message of salvation in Christ. And this is no trifling superficiality; it is, rather, a fact of the greatest importance. For Greek comes alive for us not merely as the language and conceptual world of the New Testament but perhaps even more—considering the *Zeitgeist*—as Greek philosophy, Greek culture, Greek science, Greek understanding of life and the world. I call attention to only one fact: the thinking of our German classicists is more heavily determined by Hellenism than by Christianity. The Greeks are our scientific tutors. Owing to the unprecedented esteem and practical significance which science enjoys today, the Greeks are more than ever the tutors of our time. Even the thinking of the ordinary man, who knows nothing of the Greeks, is infused with Greek thought from the school, the newspaper, and daily associations.

Now it is a strange paradox of reality that the Gospel is presented to us in the language and concepts of the people whose thought constitutes today the greatest opposition to the content of the Gospel. To mention only one example, the Greek conception of spirit, and therefore of the true and the good, is a kind which equates spirit with the abstract and represents the physically concrete as its opposite, as that which ought not to be. Hence if one wants to think of the Highest, of God, he has to think of him as abstractly, as nonsensually, and—it necessarily follows—as impersonally as possible. This is precisely one reason why the Old Testament, which is replete with anthropomorphisms, is considered to be a subspiritual book. The identification of the spiritual with the abstract is one of the most fateful facts of our intellectual history. It is an inheritance from Hellenism. Yet it is in the language of this Hellenism that the New Testament is written. Certainly I do not intend to charge that here the Ruler of history has made a mistake, that he should have delivered the whole Bible to us in Hebrew or in some less dangerous language. I would even say that we can trace from afar the divine wisdom which has directed us in this fashion, and that we can understand something of the Why. However, the fact remains: for us the Greek conceptual world of the New Testament is above all a hindrance because it presents the temptation to Hellenize the content of the New Testament.

Whoever knows something of the history of theology in the last century knows, too, that I am not chasing a phantom. I wish only to remind you of the crass Hellenization in which, for instance, Fichte engaged in the exposition of the Gospel of John. By virtue of the Logos concept he read into the Gospel of John his whole mystical idealism and turned the Son of God into an eternal idea. To this day the Gospel of John has been the greatest occasion for Hellenistic misunderstanding. But also what Paul says concerning the Spirit, concerning life, concerning being in Christ, and so on, has had in part to suffer *rationalistic*-idealistic or *mystical*-idealistic reinterpretation.

Let us also not forget this: the great event of the first four centuries A.D. is the incursion of Christianity into the Greek cultural world. It is a priori self-evident and historically proven that the Gospel, in this first engagement with the Hellenic spirit, did not merely make use of its linguistic means but also appropriated much of its content. What the Catholic Church improperly assimilated from the Old Testament is minor compared with the Greek inheritance she carried along. (I call to mind only monasticism and neo-Platonic mysticism.) Today, however, owing to the Enlightenment and other powerful historical factors, and above all owing to the inner weakness of Christendom, the Church of Christ has to struggle against a rationalistic culture and a spirituality steeped completely in idealism and mysticism. In such a time it is especially imperative to know the significance of the fact that the New Testament is written in the conceptual language of the people who have transmitted to us idealism, rationalism, and mysticism.

Therefore I believe (and so my thesis is to be understood) that, for most if not all of us, the normal path to a genuine understanding of the New Testament is by way of the Old. For in the Old Testament we come upon a world completely unaffected by the whole Hellenic spirit. There we feel as does one who comes directly from the flat land of North Germany or the Netherlands to Zermatt in the Swiss Alps. Complete strangeness, a feeling of shock, above all instinctive rejection. This non-spiritual, human God who walks on earth, who is angry, who repents, who burns with passion, who crushes enemies! This terrible holiness of God, this fixed barrier between God and world, between God and man! This absence of all logical consistency and order, of all higher, finer spirituality! We sense how much closer to us are the dialogues of Plato or the mysticism of India.

But sensing this is just what is wholesome. The strangeness of the Old Testament can make us realize how strange, too, is the New Testament, when correctly understood, to our time and to our natural way of thinking. That which is peculiarly biblical, veiled in the New Testament under Greek form, appears to us in Old Testament form unveiled—yes, perhaps even enhanced, in a certain sense exaggerated. But this is what we need especially today; and this is why for us the Old Testament is necessary in a special way for understanding the New.

II

This will become evident concretely if we turn now to a second point which, it goes without saying, is more important than the first, namely, the specific reason why the Old Testament is always and for everyone essential for understanding the New Testament. Recently in missionary circles the view has been represented that for an Indian his Bhagavad-Gita, for a Chinese his Laotse or Confucius, for a Japanese his Buddhist literature could become the Old Testament. I shall attempt to show why this is a quite fatal misunderstanding. This is nothing other than what we heard from Schleiermacher: that Christianity has no closer relation to Judaism than to paganism. One can speak this way only if, in the most dubious manner, he has already smoothed away what is specifically biblical—the whole contrast between the biblical revelation and the extrabiblical, the contrast between idealism or mysticism and the Christian faith. I shall now proceed to single out and elucidate some ideas of the Old Testament which appear thus only in the Old Testament and yet without which the New Testament is not understandable. In doing this I shall illustrate at the same time what was previously said about the contrast between biblical and Greek thought.

I begin with the beginning, with the Creation and the Creator. If in the New Testament writings so little is said about this doctrine that Marcion could hit upon the idea that the Creator-God is the God of the Old Testament and not of the New, it is because the apostles simply presupposed the message concerning God the Creator. Diligent reading of the Old Testament played a very heavy part in the young churches just as soon as they were established, as we learn from the Beroeans. The teaching that God is the Creator and that we and the world are his Creation, and what that means, is enounced only infrequently and occasionally in the New Testament, and then of course with a significant deepening

of the Old Testament idea. It is, however, the basis for everything
else. The creation story of Genesis I is not only the *initium* but
also the *principium* of all that follows. But let us notice how the
Old Testament speaks of the Creator. Not in the fashion of the
theology of the Enlightenment and the songs of Gellert (for that
is the way Aristotle speaks of him); in other words, not as the
God who is to be known from nature but, rather, as the God who
reveals himself as the Lord of his people through historical deeds,
through prophetic Word. Before Israel knew God the Creator of
the world, God was known as Israel's Lord. He is also our Lord,
not because he is to be known from nature as the artificer of this
world, but because he has revealed himself to us as our Lord, as
the absolute Lord beside whom for us there is none other; and
therefore he also must be the Lord of all the world. Knowledge
of the Creator belongs not to *theologia naturalis* but to *theologia
revelata*.

And yet more is to be said. Only because he is Creator in this
biblical sense is there any revelation at all, and only for that reason is God to be known through revelation alone. When reason,
seeking to know God from nature, thinks about God, he is not
the absolute Lord of the world but the God who, so to speak,
belongs to the world, who is no more to be thought of apart from
the world than the world apart from him. Or within the realm of
human life, he is the God who can be known in the depths of
man's nature as its ultimate depth, and who as the ground of the
Ego is bound to the Ego even as the Ego is bound to him. Such a
God is not the Lord, neither my Lord nor the Lord of the world.
The Lord and Creator is rather the God whom man can know
only because and in so far as he specially reveals himself but who
outside of and apart from this revelation is the Unknown. For the
world is not as he, and he is not as the world. Therefore no image,
nor any likeness, can be made of him. This Second Commandment, which to all esthetically minded people is a special offense
in the Old Testament, is of decisive significance for the Old Testament prophets, for it is what differentiates their God from the gods

of the heathen. God and world, God and creature are to be absolutely distinct. God and world do not blend together, there is no
passage from one to the other. This is God's radically supramun-
dane character: his sovereignty over the world. The world is absolutely incomparable to him in that he is its Creator and it is his
creature, that is, it is conditioned by him, founded by him, and
dependent upon him; but he is in no way conditioned by it. He
does not need the world, but it is nothing without him.

It is important that we clarify to ourselves this content of the
word "Creation" in the Old Testament in order, on the one hand,
to differentiate this concept of Creation from what the word
elsewhere means in religion and philosophy. (The Creator as he
makes himself known in the Old Testament is known by no
philosophy or religion.) It is important, on the other hand, because only from this standpoint can we understand what it means
that this God became man and so bridged the gulf between himself and his Creation. One must move out from Isaiah in order
not to misunderstand the Gospel of John! This idea is couched in
the term, the holiness of God, a term so familiar from the Old
Testament and yet so little understood. The Holy One of Israel
is precisely this sovereign Lord whose will is the basis of all things
and whose will knows no Why. He speaks and it comes to pass;
he commands and it is so. He chooses whom he will, and he has
mercy upon whom he will.

If I said, "this God is known only through revelation, not from
the world," I could just as well say: "one has this God through
election and grace, and not nature." Israel has this God, who is
so different from the idols of others, because Israel is the chosen
people. That is not, as is so often supposed today, an expression
of national pride but just the contrary. For all other peoples the
God-relation is, so to speak, a self-evident one. They have their
God just because they are, and just as they are. Israel realizes,
however, that it has and knows its God only because it has pleased
God to show himself to this people. The basis of this relationship
is election, a special turning of God's will toward men, and not

natural necessity. The God-relation rests upon freedom and not necessity, upon God's gracious will alone and therefore not at all upon what the people itself is. Once again, this is what is meant by the expression, the Holy One of Israel. The God who is not at our disposal because we are solely at his disposal. The God whose chosen people are so completely at his disposal that he can also cast them off, just as he has accepted them. Here the natural bond which elsewhere unites God and man—not just in gross paganism but also in all philosophical and mystical teaching about God— is severed and replaced by a connection made in freedom.

But there is one more thing which needs to be said to understand this fundamental element of the Old Testament, the idea of God. We said: God gives himself to be known in special revelation. That means more exactly: in historical revelation, in historical self-disclosure. Not, however, as we say today: God in history; for in this case we again make history into a generality in which God always and everywhere discloses himself. Just the opposite is meant: in history, where elsewhere God does not reveal himself at all, he reveals himself in a special place, in a special event, in his own personal Word proclaimed through special persons. Again we should not confuse this prophetic Word of God with universal religious or moral ideas, as is commonly done today. For if that were so, then the prophets were not really prophets, heralds of God, but merely religious or moral geniuses who first discovered a truth which subsequently became common knowledge. The prophetic Word can never become common knowledge, while the word of the genius proves itself to be such precisely because it becomes common knowledge. The prophetic Word always remains bound to the person of the prophet or, rather, to his special divine mandate. The important thing is not merely what the prophet says, but that what he says is said with divine authority; or—which amounts to the same—that he says something which gains significance from the fact that no one else may say it because none other has been commissioned to—because none other may say: thus saith God himself.

Why is this distinction so important? Because precisely for this reason and in this way God can be known as the personal God. When one knows of God nothing but universal ideas, he does not know him as the personal God but as the Idea of ideas. Ideas are not personal. Ideas I can have to myself. Idea is simply that which I can have to myself alone. But a personal word, a personal encounter, absolutely requires a Thou; in this case the essential thing is that the Thou is present and confronts me. Through idea a personal relationship is never established because for the thinking of an idea one person alone is sufficient. Revelation, however, is no solitary, impersonal cogitation of God, but it is being addressed by God as my Thou. Therefore the Word of the prophets is always immediate, that is, directed to a particular situation and to particular persons. For this Word it is essential that it be a historical fact, an event. In this way God proves himself to be one who, unlike the Platonic idea of God or the God of mysticism, does not wait for men to come to him but intervenes into the midst of their history and confronts and meets them there. This is the personal God, the living God of the Old Testament.

III

Everything that we have said up to this point belongs of strict necessity together, so much so that it can be said that these are only aspects of the same thing: God the Creator, God the Lord, God who chooses, God who encounters personally. A further matter, however, pertains with equal necessity. Inherent in the fact that God personally meets men in their activity and addresses them *ad hominem*—"Thou art the man!"—is something which even the superficial critic of the Old Testament cannot help noticing as its specific element: the role of the divine Law. In speaking, God makes a claim; in choosing, he says "you belong to me." The fact that God is known as powerful will and not as world-idea signifies that he earnestly aims for my existence, and that means my will. This will he claims for himself in order to bind my existence to him. Therefore there is no philosophy in the

Old Testament. When confronted by a God who is will, philosophizing ceases. For God's call intends to be answered with life, with deed. Again we must resist a modern weakening of this idea. For instance, some say: the religion of the Old Testament belongs to the category of moral religion; the prophets put into effect the universal moral law. No, that is just what they do not do. It is precisely the prophets who know nothing of a moral law. They are unacquainted with a morality related to such a law of reason. They know only one thing: obedience to the personal God. Under some circumstances this obedience can demand the exact opposite of what a universal moral law dictates. Abraham is the paradigm of the man who obeys God but not at all of a moral man. The divine will, just because it is personal will, is not to be confined within any law of reason. Let whoever wants to acquaint himself with "moral religion" go to the Stoics; he can find it in the Old Testament only through misunderstanding. For here also the truth holds: God does not let himself be caught in any abstraction. The moral law, however, is an abstraction; and that also means it is autonomous. The moral law appears as valid in itself, detached from the will of God. Again, in the Old Testament just such autonomy is held to be the real sin. For there is nothing which in itself is morally good. The good is only and solely to do God's will, just because it is God's will. In the doctrine of the Church and also in Reformation teaching this idea unfortunately was obscured by the fatal identification of Old Testament Law with the law of reason. It is Calvin who, departing from Luther here (as elsewhere too), has comprehended the Old Testament more clearly.

Nevertheless Luther, too, put at the center of his thought a decisive idea of the Old Testament: the distinction between legalism and faith. God's address is certainly demand. But it is not demand first and most of all. Over and above its being demand stands the fact that it is the expression of divine grace. God gives before he requires. And, rightly understood, his demand consists in this, that one accepts from him what he wills to give. Indeed, the meaning of the whole Law is simply this: Ye shall be God's people. The Law of God is a moment in his making of the covenant. Rational morality knows nothing of God's concluding a covenant with his people. It can only understand the Law legalistically. The Old Testament, however, teaches us to understand the Law above all as God's gracious gift. The prophets always point out—and the later Law still points out—that God's demand for obedience issues from his election, his gracious coming to the side of the people. First the gift (*Gabe*), *then* the task (*Aufgabe*). Of course, this "then" is not chronological. Gift and task are not to be separated from each other. The act in which God comes toward his people and in which he confronts his people is the same act.

This also implies, however, that the concept of the holiness of God and that of his mercy and love, even though they must be strictly differentiated, absolutely are not to be separated from each other. Holiness is God's being who he is (*die Selbstigkeit Gottes*). It means that God cannot will other than to be himself, to do his will, and that standing outside this will and against this will spells doom. Love means, however, that God, in willing to be himself, wills us; that it is precisely his inexorable will that we should be his. He confronts his people as the Holy One—because they defect from him. But behind this confrontation, and realized in it, is his coming: for he wills nothing other than to draw the people to himself. It would not be wrong to say—if one wanted to express the difference between the Old Testament and all other teaching about God in this way—that only in the Old Testament are the holiness and the love of God conceived as one, without either weakening the other. As only the transcendent God can be truly personal, so also only the holy God can be truly loving.

Both of these become manifest, however, in the fact that God's will is directed toward a goal. God's covenant is not a stabilization or an eternalization of what is. God's covenant is prospective —as early as the covenant which he concluded with Abraham. The Old Testament is eschatological through and through. It is concerned with the divine future, with the *ad-vent*[5] in the literal sense. God wills to *come* to his people in a completely different manner than he is now present. That is what the prophets are concerned with; that is the concern of the Old Testament in general. Again, this eschatology does not imply a universal teleology of history, an idea of historical progress. The world does not move automatically, with inner necessity, toward a higher goal. It moves through struggle, rejection, and new creation. The optimistic idea of progress sees everything streaming toward one goal; evil comes to be less and less, and good more and more. The Old Testament knows nothing of this idea. For it is familiar with the idea of divine judgment, to which freedom corresponds: the freedom of God's election and the freedom of human decision. Whoever is unfaithful to God certainly has nothing good to expect; sin, or rather the sinner, is threatened with judgment. Of course, God does not will that. His real will is the will to redeem, to forgive, to deliver, to restore. This will of God, however, would not be his serious will were it not that behind the love of God is his inviolable holiness, were it not that God lets us know that he will not be mocked.

The Old Testament idea of divine judgment is the presupposition for understanding the New Testament, although in the latter, as with the idea of Creation, it appears less frequently, is perfected in content, and that means it is intensified. For how can a person be concerned about redemption and reconciliation when he does not know the anxiety of being lost?

The preacher knows by experience how easily the reader of the New Testament ignores the idea of judgment found there and holds that it is an Old Testament notion because the words about God's love and forgiveness alone are impressed upon his memory. Here is a point at which the necessity of the Old Testament becomes especially clear. Without the Old Testament there is great

---

[5] The German word for "future" (*Zukunft*) which Brunner uses here is composed of the elements *kunft* (come) and *zu* (to), that is, time that comes toward us.—ED.

danger that the Gospel of God's love will become—as it threatened to become through Marcion—a sentimentality, as is the case today far and wide.

With the word eschatology, end-hope, we have indicated what separates the world of the Bible most radically from the world of the Greeks and modern men; or, better put, the point at which the all-pervasive contrast to the latter type of thought becomes evident most clearly. The eschatology of the Old Testament is necessarily bound up with its idea of God. Because God is the holy and merciful God, he wills that all lands should become full of his glory and that, in this way, the life of man should become blessed and even holy. The Creator, who creates the world through his Word, also wills that his Word should permeate and determine this world. The Lord, who chooses for himself a people, wills that this people should be wholly his people and that through them all the peoples of the earth should be blessed. The God who is fully personal also wills to dwell fully with his people. But that which he wills is not yet realized. The holy God and unholy reality do not correspond. Measured by the holy will of God, reality appears as something not imperfect but contradictory. Measuring himself by the Law of God man knows himself to be a sinner, and remembering how God has been gracious to him he knows himself to be faithless, apostate.

When God is the object of philosophical thought this opposition is intolerable. Reason has to resolve it. It justifies the world as it is in terms of the idea of God. Since, however, the world is not in accordance with the divine will, reason concludes that the world, being finite, not being God himself, must necessarily be imperfect. By this reasoning finite, natural, concrete existence is stamped as that which really ought not to be. Accordingly, "redemption" could consist in nothing other than the dissolution of this finite world.

To all of this the thought of the Old Testament is diametrically opposed. That which ought not to be (*das Nichtseinsollende*) is not finiteness as such, for God is the Creator of this very finite

world and as his Creation it is good. Evil is not something negative, a lack of divine being, but something positive: opposition
toward God. Sensuous-natural existence and desire is not as such
evil; it only becomes evil when taken out of connection with the
Creator. Therefore evil is not something inherent in the fact of
the world as such, and to that degree something self-evident; it is
the disruption of the divine order in the world through man's rebellion against God. The idea of God in this case is not a means
for explaining and justifying the world's being as it is (*Sosein*).
On the contrary, it is the knowledge of God that gives rise to the
knowledge that the world, that mankind, is not as it ought to be,
that life as it is stands in opposition to God. Knowledge of this
opposition is found throughout the whole Old Testament. It is the
presupposition of the eschatological hope. Old Testament eschatology is understandable only against the background of this
opposition, namely, that God is Lord and Creator of the world
but that the world, through the will of man who has turned from
God, is distant from God. Therefore in drawing near to the world,
God, who is holy and determined to prevail, wills to make the unfaithful world subject to him again and to bring the distant world
back to him.

The idea that permeates Old Testament prophecy is that of
the coming God and the coming kingdom of God. The prophet is
the herald of God's advent (*Gottes-Zukunft*). His whole proclamation is to be understood only from the side of this future. For
in this future his message has its meaning, its goal, its necessity.
The prophet knows himself to be "the vanguard of God," the
fore-runner (*Vor-bote*) of coming things. The historicity of the
prophetic event of revelation is therefore not to be understood
in national-historical or world-historical but only in end-historical
terms. The thing that makes the historical moment into a moment
of decision in such an unprecedented manner is simply this eschatological reference (*End-Bezogenheit*) and hence this eschatological validation (*End-gültigkeit*) of the prophet's Word to the
present. The historical Now receives its absolute seriousness from

the viewpoint of the end of all things. Only from this angle of vision are the unprecedented imperatives of the prophetic address possible. We see from a new side how false it is to identify the prophetic ethos with a rational, moral idea. What does moral idealism know of the final judgment? What does the rational thinker understand of this simultaneous entreating and threatening, this intermingling of judgment and promise, as it is heard so movingly, for instance, in the message of Hosea? The prophet and his preaching are already an eschatological fact, a moment in God's movement toward the world.

Yes, toward the world, not away from the world! The movement away from the world, the flight out of the world of finitude into the eternity, nonworldliness, and impersonality (*Du-losigkeit*) of God is the movement of idealistic, mystical, or Greek religion: redemption from the world. This idea finds its practical expression in asceticism. Spirit stands in opposition to the earthly and natural, to the manifold, the concrete, the personal. Redemption, therefore, can be only the absorption of the individual into the universal, as God himself is to be found only in the abstraction of idea and in the vagueness of mystical feeling. The Old Testament knows nothing of this world-escaping, world-negating ascetic tendency. And that is because God is not the impassive Idea beyond existence but the Creator of the world who loves and seeks his world. Therefore the Old Testament is full of world-affirmation, indeed one could say full of worldliness. As God himself is no abstraction but is Person, with will, with love and hate, mercy and wrath, so also his relation to the world is not negative but positive through and through, even when he is the accuser and judge of all men and relationships. God is involved with the world, in spite of it! In the world, not beyond it, he wills to rule. In it his kingdom is to come.

This worldliness of prophetic eschatology is so pronounced (just compare it with the views of Indian religion or even with Plato and Plotinus!) that it appears as though the prophets were not concerned with an ultimate end, with *End-Geschichte,* but only with a historical goal. But manifestly it is this "accursed Jewish optimism" as Schopenhauer expressed it, and this very eudaemonistic worldliness, as he viewed it, that is necessary so that the New Testament idea of the kingdom of God can be secured against Schopenhauerian and other misunderstandings, according to which the New Testament idea is akin to the Buddhistic-mystical Nirvana. The whole realism of the Old Testament is necessary above all in order to teach us how rightly to appreciate the reality of the more spiritual expressions of the New Testament. That the redemption of the world in the kingdom of heaven does not mean the Platonic Beyond, the idealistic immortality of the soul, but includes the corporeal; that the world is not to be dissolved but to be brought to completion—and that this is also meant in the New Testament—all this we can understand rightly only against the background of the prophetic hope of the Old Testament.

IV

Standing in close connection with this eschatological realism is one final idea which, up to this point, we have only touched lightly. It has probably struck the reader that I have always designated the people Israel as the recipient of the divine call. Again, some have wanted to treat this as an imperfection of the Old Testament in contrast to the New, for the true spiritual religion allegedly must have to do with the individual. This misunderstanding stems from the same sources as those previously mentioned. It is idealistic-mystical individualism which is at fault. Certainly the Old Testament call to repentance and the Old Testament promise are directed to the individual. King David understood that clearly when the prophet Nathan, with his "Thou art the man!" struck him to the heart as with a sword of God. How could the prophets' call to repentance be understood otherwise than a summons to the individual? It is of the greatest significance, however, that they nevertheless always addressed the people. For God, who wills to establish his kingdom upon earth, who begins in history this eternal movement, has to do with the whole, not merely with individuals—with the people and with individuals so far as they are members of this people. In the New Testament this people is called the Church; and in the New Testament period one is still aware that *ecclesia* is only a translation of the Old Testament "People of God." From the beginning God's will is directed toward community. He regards men as bound together in solidarity, without detriment to the fact that he has to do with the individual in his conscience. He wills that they not be individuals but members of a whole. Individualism (*das Einzelsein*) is sin. The ethic of the Old Testament is social ethic throughout. Sin, in so far as its concrete expression comes into consideration, is above all sin against the fellow man, injustice to the other, denial of men's belonging together. In all mystical-idealistic religions, however, sin is above all lack of self-control, sensuousness.

In the Old Testament the latter conception plays a completely subordinate role over against sin as injustice to the brother, as denial of the Thou. In this respect, too, the Old Testament's characteristic emphasis upon personal relations comes to expression decisively. One does not sin—as the Greek, the ascetic, the mystic conceive it—against himself, but he sins against his fellow man by transgressing the divinely established bound that protects him. Thus the good is always a good related to community too: right relation to the brother, love of the neighbor, but not, however, some ascetic purity. Even the sexual ethos is not determined by the idea of purity, but by that of community.

The Old Testament is pervaded with a tremendous passion for community, with a powerful social ethos, the like of which the world has never known. But even here the idea is not that of some universal social scheme; rather, the Old Testament is governed solely by the idea of God's righteousness, God's order, and God's lordship. God wills to have a true People of God on earth. A People of God cannot result from the presence of pious individuals who by virtue of their piety also have community. Rather, piety from the outset is oriented toward community. God and the neighbor belong inseparably together. Within the community of the people God has deposited his Word; it is necessary to be an Israelite to know God. There are no private revelations. There is revelation of the living God only in living relationship with the people. God conceals his Word and his salvation behind the man whom he calls, in order that anyone who wants to find him must also find his fellow man. And the Word which he finds in this manner is one that immediately binds the recipient to the community.

Hence the astonishing fact that in Israel there are no solitary religious individuals, no mystical anchorites, hermits, monks, and the like, who in other spiritual religions are the real pinnacles. Even the prophets are not of this kind. To be sure, they bear a burden which is laid upon them alone. But it is the burden of a message to the people; it is no individualistic salvation for their own souls. They do not withdraw in order to be alone, but— difficult as it is for them—they go again and again to the people and cling to them, they run after them like the true shepherd after his strayed sheep, they carry their burden as their own and lay it as their own before God. The notion that religion is a private affair is a mystical or idealistic idea, but it is never a biblical one. The public cry of a herald is what binds God and men, not an individual Yogi-exercise or an individual philosophical way to God. Worship is public, and what God wills to do is public. But in this publicness that which is most inward is fully preserved and unmistakably called forth. For this public Word goes to the conscience of the individual.

In all this—let this be emphasized in conclusion—the Old Testament is the beginning of the New. The *beginning* of the New. The difference between the two Testaments must not be obliterated. All the ideas I have emphasized as characteristic of the Old Testament, the New Testament—the message of Jesus Christ— has brought to completion and in a certain sense spiritualized. But only "in a certain sense," and that does not mean in the modern, the Greek sense of spirit. There is, however, one God, one message, one revelation, one Word, one covenant. If it is now called the new covenant, that is not because it replaces the old but because it intends to fulfill it. The new element is that through Jesus Christ prophecy has begun to become fulfillment. Out of Advent has come Christmas, but Advent and Christmas belong together. Ideas have no beginning and no end. The revelation of God, however, is real and effective only in the totality of its occurrence. To break out of the time of Advent because we live in the time of Christ is a sign that we have not understood what the time of Christ is. Thus the understanding of the Old Testament is the criterion and the basis for understanding the New.

Selected Bibliography

AUVRAY, PAUL, et al. *L'Ancien Testament et les Chrétiens*. Paris: Les Éditions du Cerf, 1951.

BAUMGÄRTEL, FRIEDERICH. *Verheissung: Zur Frage des evangelischen Verständnisses des Alten Testaments*. Gütersloh: C. Bertelsmann, 1952.

BOISSET, J., et al. *Le Problème Biblique dans le Protestantisme*. Paris: Presses Universitaires de France, 1955.

BORNKAMM, HEINRICH. *Luther und das Alte Testament*. Tübingen: J. C. B. Mohr, 1948.

BRIGHT, JOHN. *The Kingdom of God: The Biblical Concept and Its Meaning for the Church*. New York and Nashville: Abingdon-Cokesbury, 1953.

COPPENS, J. *Vom christlichen Verständnis des Alten Testaments*. Louvain: Publications Universitaires de Louvain, 1952.

————. *Les harmonies des deux Testaments: essai sur les divers sens des Écritures et sur l'unité de la Révélation* (Cahiers de la Nouvelle Revue Théologique, vi). Tournai: Casterman, 1949.

CULLMANN, OSCAR. *Christ and Time: The Primitive Christian Conception of Time and History*. Floyd V. Filson, trans. Philadelphia: Westminster Press, 1950.

DANIÉLOU, J. *Sacramentum Futuri: Études sur les Origines de la Typologie Biblique*. Paris: Beauchesne et ses Fils, 1950.

GOPPELT, LEONARD. *Typos: Die typologische Deutung de Alten Testaments im Neuen*. Gütersloh: C. Bertelsmann, 1939.

GRANT, ROBERT M. *The Bible in the Church: A Short History of Interpretation*. New York: Macmillan, 1948.

GRELOT, PIERRE. *Sens Chrétien de l'Ancien Testament* (Bibliothèque de Théologie, Série I, Vol. 3). Tournai: Desclée & Cie, 1962.

HEBERT, A. G. *The Throne of David: A Study of the Fulfillment of the Old Testament in Jesus Christ and His Church*. London: Faber and Faber, 1941.

————. *The Authority of the Old Testament*. London: Faber and Faber, 1947.

HIRSCH, EMANUEL. *Das Alte Testament und die Predigt des Evangeliums*. Tübingen: J. C. B. Mohr, 1936.

HOFMANN, J. C. K. *Interpreting the Bible*. Minneapolis: Augsburg Publishing House, 1959. (Original German work, 1880.)

KRAELING, EMIL. *The Old Testament since the Reformation*. New York: Harper, 1955.

KRAUS, H. J. *Geschichte der historisch-kritischen Erforschung des Alten Testaments von der Reformation bis zur Gegenwart*. Verlag der Buchhandlung des Erziehungsvereins: Neukirchen Kreis Moers, 1956.

KÜMMEL, W. G. *Promise and Fulfillment*. London: S.C.M. Press, 1957.

LEVIE, JEAN. *The Bible: Word of God in Words of Men*. New York: P. J. Kenedy & Sons, 1961.

MARSH, JOHN. *The Fulness of Time*. New York: Harper, 1952.

MUILENBURG, JAMES. *The Way of Israel*. New York: Harper, 1961.

ROWLEY, H. H. *The Unity of the Bible*. Philadelphia: Westminster Press, 1953.

RULER, ARNOLD VAN. *Die christliche Kirche und das Alte Testament*. Munich: Chr. Kaiser, 1955.

SCHILDENBERGER, JOHANNES. *Vom Geheimnis des Gotteswortes*. Heidelberg: F. H. Kerle Verlag, 1950.

SMART, JAMES D. *The Interpretation of Scripture*. Philadelphia: Westminster Press, 1961.

TOOMBS, LAWRENCE E. *The Old Testament in Christian Preaching*. Philadelphia: Westminster Press, 1961.

VISCHER, WILHELM. *The Witness of the Old Testament to Christ*. London: Lutterworth, 1949.

WESTERMANN, CLAUS (ed.). *Probleme alttestamentlicher Hermeneutik: Aufsätze zum Verstehen des Alten Testaments*. Munich: Chr. Kaiser, 1960. English edition, *Essays on Old Testament Hermeneutics*, ed. by James Luther Mays. Richmond: John Knox Press, 1963.

WRIGHT, G. ERNEST. *God Who Acts*. London: S.C.M. Press, 1952.

ZIMMERLI, WALTHER. *Das Alte Testament als Anrede*. Munich: Chr. Kaiser, 1956.

See also the books on the theology of the Old Testament by Walther Eichrodt, Paul Heinisch, George A. F. Knight, Gerhard von Rad, Th. C. Vriezen, and Edmund Jacob; and the works on New Testament theology by Rudolph Bultmann, Ethelbert Stauffer, and Alan Richardson.

Index

Abraham, 30, 197, 255; Melchizedek's blessing upon, 137, 139; God as Shield of, 138–140; God's promise to, 210, 212–213, 219, 256
Adam, 84, 120, 121, 147; second, 120, 123
Advent, 257, 264
Albright, W. F., 125, 196
Allegoresis, 33, 45 f., 54, 60, 73–75, 86–88, 103
Alt, Albrecht, 138–140
Althaus, Paul, 38
Amos, 206
Anderson, B. W., 189 n.
Apocalyptic, rise of, 77–78, 175, 220–221
Apostles, 39, 74, 115, 117–122, 250
Archeology, 180 f., 185 n., 186
Aristotle, 251
Augustine, 31

Balaam, oracles of, 209
Baptism, 110, 145 n
Barth, Karl, 6, 38, 52, 61, 128, 150, 155, 185 n.
Baumgärtel, Friedrich, 128, 174 n., 201, 237
Begrich, J., 205
Being (Sein), definition of, 151 n.; see also Ontology
Benoit, Pierre, 104–105
Beracha, 131–150, 156–157; historicization of, 148–149; see also Language, religious
Bible, authority of, 58, 121; scriptural proof, 33, 73, 74, 75, 86–87, 97
Blessing, 209, 212–213; and promise, 210–211; cultic, 214; see also Abraham; Beracha; Jacob
Bonhoeffer, Dietrich, 155, 157, 158
Bornkamm, Günther, 144 n.
Brock, Werner, 151 n.
Bultmann, Rudolf, 6–7, 90–101, 145 n., 170–171, 200, 223, 225 n., 227–228,
236, 238; compared with Marcion, 7, 49–63, 227; "Das Problem der 'natürlichen Theologie,'" 67–68; demythologization, concept of, 117–120, 181 (see also Demythologization); existential hermeneutic of, 52–63; "genuinely historical," concept of, 81, 91, 179–181 (see also Hermeneutics); Geschichte und Eschatologie im Neuen Testament, 77–80; gnostic existentialism of, 64–89, 184 f.; ontology of, 66–69; Ritschl's influence on, 38–46; and Roman Catholicism, 105–107, 110–111; theological outlook of, 177–179; theology of history of, 77–86; Theology of the New Testament, 70–71, 76; Vorverständnis, concept of, 49–63, 67–68 (see also Pre-understanding); "Weissagung und Erfüllung," 51, 94–95

Calvin, John, 161, 188, 255
Canon, biblical, 1–3, 4, 5, 58, 126 n., 178, 187–188, 189 f., 225–226
Childs, Bervard, 172, 173, 231 n.
Christian art, monotestamentalism of, 62
Christianity, primitive, 8–9, 32–33, 72, 78–79, 107, 109, 119–120, 122 f., 132–134, 140–150
Christology, 9, 10, 104, 146
Church, the, 12–13, 21, 23 n., 30–31, 32, 33, 40–41, 44–45, 47, 186 f., 213, 219, 225–227, 238; early (New Testament), 4 f., 54, 57 f., 71, 103, 109, 159–160, 167, 176, 243–244, 250 (see also Apostles; Christianity, primitive); Fathers of, 31, 102–103; history of, 4–5, 47, 150, 167, 226; Roman Catholic, 106, 113, 244, 249
Community, Christian, 31, 41, 59, 78, 113, 190, 196, 213, 225, 262–263
Comte, August, 85–86
Conversion, 183

267